A FRAMEWORK FOR CULTURALLY RESPONSIVE PRACTICES

Copyright © 2021 | Myers Education Press, LLC

Published by Myers Education Press, LLC
P.O. Box 424
Gorham, ME 04038

Myers Education Press is an academic publisher specializing in books, e-books, and digital content in the field of education. All of our books are subjected to a rigorous peer review process and produced in compliance with the standards of the Council on Library and Information Resources.

LIBRARY OF CONGRESS CATALOGING-IN-PUBLICATION DATA AVAILABLE FROM LIBRARY OF CONGRESS.

13-digit ISBN 978-1-9755-0415-1 (paperback)
13-digit ISBN 978-1-9755-0414-4 (hardcover)
13-digit ISBN 978-1-9755-0416-8 (library networkable e-edition)
13-digit ISBN 978-1-9755-0417-5 (consumer e-edition)

Printed in the United States of America.

All first editions printed on acid-free paper that meets the American National Standards Institute Z39-48 standard.

Books published by Myers Education Press may be purchased at special quantity discount rates for groups, workshops, training organizations, and classroom usage. Please call our customer service department at 1-800-232-0223 for details.

Cover design by Teresa Lagrange.

Visit us on the web at **www.myersedpress.com** to browse our complete list of titles.

A Framework For Culturally Responsive Practices

Implementing the Culturally Responsive Instruction Observation Protocol (CRIOP) in K-8 Classrooms

EDITED BY

Rebecca Powell and Susan Chambers Cantrell

Myers Education Press

GORHAM, MAINE

Dedication

We dedicate this book to all the caring and committed educators with whom we have worked.

Contents

Acknowledgments

There are many individuals we need to acknowledge who have made this book possible. First and foremost, we want to thank the teachers with whom we have worked for more than a decade. To say that we have perhaps learned more from you than you have learned from us is an understatement. We are grateful for the opportunity to grow with you in our understanding of culturally responsive instruction, and your professional and practical knowledge has significantly contributed to our work as university educators. We are particularly grateful to the many teachers who agreed to write classroom scenarios for this book. Your narratives demonstrating practical applications of culturally and linguistically sustaining instruction have provided a vital contribution to this volume.

This book would not have been possible without the contributions of the various chapter authors who not only agreed to write chapters for the book but also contributed in significant ways to our grant project. We have learned from each of you and have been enriched by your professional expertise.

We also are grateful to the U.S. Department of Education, Office of English Language Acquisition for funding our work. These resources allowed us to work side by side with teachers in schools and provided the opportunity to refine the Culturally Responsive Instruction Observation Protocol instrument and model.

Finally, we wish to thank the staff at Myers Education Press. Chris Myers encouraged us to pursue this book project and gave us an outlet for our work, and Stephanie Gabaree was invaluable in responding to our multiple inquiries throughout the development of the manuscript.

Introduction

Rebecca Powell and Susan Chambers Cantrell

WHEN YOU WALK into Kim Adams's fifth-grade classroom, her students are engaged in a thought-provoking discussion of the book *Narrative of the Life of Frederick Douglass* (Douglass, 1995). It is not an easy read for them, and they stop frequently to have conversations about the text and to examine the meanings of the many difficult vocabulary words. The local park is named after this famous abolitionist, and students are reading about Douglass's life to provide a context for writing and submitting proposals to the city council to improve this historical park, which, in recent years, has fallen into disarray and become a popular spot for drug dealers.

Down the hall, students in another fifth-grade classroom are developing their debating skills. Their teacher believes that effective oral language is critical for empowerment, and she wants her students to be able to defend a position with facts and evidence. She has identified issues that are important to her students and has provided pro-and-con texts for them to annotate. Students are reading these texts, underlining arguments that would support their views, and practicing effective ways for articulating those arguments to the opposing team.

If you entered either of these classrooms at a different time during the day, however, you would find these teachers reading a script from a mandated literacy program, with their students parroting back their responses. The teachers have been told that reading real literature, engaging in meaningful writing, and learning how to present an argument can be practiced during social studies time, but reading instruction must consist of the activities presented in the scripted basal reading program adopted by the school: phonics and drills, word accuracy, and low level comprehension skills.

Classrooms are complex places, and it is naïve to believe that teachers can always be consistent in implementing culturally responsive practices given the dynamics of school and instructional decision-making. In our many years of working with teachers in classrooms, we have found that there are forces that militate against teaching in ways that are culturally and linguistically relevant, from district and school mandates to the pervasiveness of school culture (i.e., "the way we do school"). We have also found that great teachers—like the two fifth-grade teachers highlighted earlier—find ways to circumvent these barriers and teach in ways that are meaningful to themselves and their students.

That our classrooms are becoming increasingly diverse is clear. The cultural, linguistic, and socioeconomic diversity of our students is contributing to the challenges of today's teachers, in that they are often faced with a student population that takes them beyond their middle-class, English-only professional comfort zones. A recent U.S. Department of Education report documents decreases in the percentage of students who are White, decreases in the percentage of students who are U.S.-born, and challenging family income and educational outcome statistics for non-White groups of students (Musu-Gillette et al., 2017). Thus, in addition to meeting the needs of students who may be at widely varying academic levels, teachers must also consider ways for bridging the cultural and linguistic divide and for working with students and families living in severe poverty.

Our belief, however, is that increased diversity in our classrooms is a cause for celebration. Classrooms that are rich with racial, ethnic, and linguistic diversity provide greater opportunities for students to develop and learn in ways that leave them better prepared to participate in a vibrant democracy and global economy. This asset-oriented mindset is required for culturally and linguistically responsive instruction (CLRI) and is featured throughout this book, whereby teachers focus not just on meeting the academic needs of an increasingly diverse student population but also on creating socially just classroom spaces that challenge systemic inequities.

We wrote this book for current and future teachers who must navigate within today's complex classrooms. In the pages that follow, we share the experiences and voices of elementary and middle school teachers who have become exemplary teachers within culturally and linguistically diverse classrooms. We explore their journeys as well as our own, as we worked with them side by side in their classrooms serving as culturally responsive mentors and coaches. While functioning in this role for the past 5 years, we have been able to document many successful culturally and linguistically responsive practices, several of which are introduced throughout this book.

Facing the Challenge

We begin this narrative with our own story. It may be an understatement to say that when we started our collective journey as culturally responsive coaches, we really had no idea how difficult the task would be. Through a grant funded by the U.S. Department of Education, Office of English Language Acquisition, we worked in many different schools: high-poverty schools in both urban and rural districts, schools with an increasing number of emerging bilingual/ multilingual students, schools with relatively high state test scores, and several in the bottom quartile. Over the course of 8 years, we worked with hundreds of elementary and middle school educators: regular classroom teachers; special educators; science, humanities, and media specialists; and school administrators. We sat in teachers' classrooms, met with them, planned with them, co-taught, and modeled instructional practices. We also listened to their concerns and tried our best to be their advocates. On more than one occasion, it struck us how little teachers' voices mattered within the educational hierarchy and how little autonomy they had in some schools in which we have worked. Yet the teachers with whom we worked were responsible for assuring that every child learned at high levels, and the success of their work was often evaluated based upon a single test score.

The focus of this book, however, is not on teachers' limited autonomy but, rather, on how teachers might recognize and use the power they have to meet the needs of their students through CLRI. Through our work with creative and committed teachers and several years of trial and error, we have discovered ways for making CLRI work. It is not easy. It is not something you can put into a teachers' manual. There are no scripts. But we believe there are practices that we can share with readers that will make a difference in schools and classrooms.

We now look back on our initial year in schools and realize our naïveté in thinking that we could transform schools and classrooms. For several years, we had been studying the underlying research and constructing and implementing the CRIOP framework—an acronym that stands for Culturally Responsive Instruction Observation Protocol. The CRIOP provides specific elements and indicators in CRLI that teachers can reference to assist them in making their practices more culturally and linguistically appropriate for their students. Thus, we were armed with a research-based toolkit of best practices, along with a sincere desire for change and a phenomenal group of motivated teachers. With our knowledgeable assistance and the CRIOP model to guide us, the classrooms and schools in which we worked were going to become models of CLRI! As we began to "get our feet wet," however, it was clear that a commitment to CRLI often took a back seat to unreasonable district demands to raise standardized test scores quickly. The frustration we experienced and that of the teachers with whom we worked was often intense.

We also found that in some of the districts in which we worked, there was a tendency to trust the market over teachers' expertise. When one literacy program did not produce the desired results after even a single year, another one was purchased and teachers were required to create new lesson plans and learn a completely new curriculum. The math programs teachers were required to use were no better. Students who learned in more concrete ways were lost with lessons that required abstract thinking, and teachers were scrambling to find ways to supplement the curriculum. We were amazed by some of the projects teachers developed, such as leading fifth-grade students to construct small towns out of cereal boxes and measure the "buildings" to reinforce concepts about area and perimeter.

Another huge barrier teachers faced was the overwhelming magnitude of their work. We often sat in planning meetings where teachers would pull out last year's instructional plans and just go with them. We understood their tendency to do this. With all the data meetings, parent conferences, faculty meetings, accountability demands, and so on, when did they have time to plan thoughtfully, based on student needs? A typical team planning meeting lasted about 40 minutes, and the teachers we worked with somehow managed to cut out materials for projects and grade papers at the same time they talked about plans for the following week. Given this scenario, it was not unusual for us to feel a bit guilty about inserting ideas. ("Have you thought about your English learners? This worksheet will be very difficult for them." "Have you considered ways to involve your parents in this project?" "Will you be developing language targets for this activity?")

Perhaps the biggest challenge of all, however, was simply the culture of traditional schooling. We were amazed by the amount of paper used for student worksheets. We were struck by how teachers were always front and center and their students did very little talking. We were conscious of the types of questions teachers asked, and those they *didn't* ask, for example, those guess-what's-in-the-teacher's-head types of questions so prevalent in our educational institutions. We were even aware of the many ways teachers managed student behavior, such as asking them to march down hallways along certain designated lines on the floor, and just the general schedules and routines of school. While much has changed in elementary schools over the past few decades, the overall school culture has not. The culture of school is familiar to all of us who attended this institution, and for many of us, envisioning how things could be different is extremely difficult. (For discussions on barriers to implementing CRLI, see Powell, Cantrell, & Correll, 2016, 2017.)

Yet it is critical to recognize that traditional schooling is inherently structured to promote racial and ethnic inequities. Historically, school curricula have marginalized the cultural knowledge, languages, and experiences of underrepresented groups. Such marginalization has had many harmful consequences for these groups, including lower expectations for student achievement (Delpit, 2012), passivity and conformity to Eurocentric, mainstream standards (Cummins, 1986; Willis, 1995), as well as negative or conflicted identities and active resistance to schooling by students of color (Deyhle, 1995: Fernández, 2002; Fine, 1991; Katz, 2013; Valenzuela, 1999). Although some progressive changes have been made, we still find remnants of an industrial model designed to assimilate students and prepare them for their role as workers within a hegemonic social structure.

Indeed, it takes a conscious effort to deconstruct the ways in which hegemony is embedded in schooling practices. Many years ago, one of us wrote the following:

> Educated within a system that legitimated my whiteness and that endorsed my ways of seeing the world, I was committed to teaching my students to adapt to mainstream culture so that they might succeed in society. As a public

> school teacher, I basically fit into the system and was regarded by both parents
> and administrators to be a good teacher. I followed the teachers' manuals,
> managed the classroom effectively, and attempted to provide a warm and
> inviting environment for my elementary students. We assumed traditional
> roles; I taught, and my students learned. It has only been recently, however,
> that I realized that what I taught and what they learned was knowledge de-
> fined and legitimized largely by those outside of the institution and, more
> importantly, outside of their lives. (Powell, 1993, p. 3)

Similarly, we have found that teachers often are unaware of the ways in which traditional practices reinforce social and economic inequities, as their privilege allows them to
remain oblivious to the ways in which race and class define the school experiences of many
of their students. We have also found that many teachers are fearful of challenging the
systems in ways that require controversial conversations and new curricular approaches.

Despite all these hurdles, however, many teachers with whom we worked were willing to go outside of their comfort zones and become more culturally responsive educators.
Some of them had already been implementing progressive practices, while others were
more traditional. Some had already embraced culturally responsive teaching, and some
had not. There is no real defining characteristic of these teachers: They were both White
teachers and teachers of color, male and female, teachers new to the profession and those
who were veterans.

In this book, we have selected a handful of these remarkable teachers to share their
stories and practices. You will be invited into their classrooms to witness the many CRLI
practices they implement on a regular basis. You will also learn about the research base
that frames the CRIOP and the many ways that it can be realized in classrooms. We
begin, however, with an overview of the CRIOP model on which this book is based.

The Culturally Responsive Instruction Observation Protocol (CRIOP)

This book is based upon the most recent version of the Culturally Responsive Instruction Observation Protocol (CRIOP). The CRIOP instrument was originally developed
several years ago by a team of researchers in the state of Kentucky. As a research classroom
observation tool, it has undergone several iterations and has been used in numerous research studies across the nation (Malo-Juvera et al., 2013). We have used it in our own work
to document teachers' practices in the classrooms in which we have worked. Through our
research, we have found that students of teachers who are high implementers of the CRIOP
model tend to outperform those students of teachers who are low implementers (Cantrell
et al., 2013, and subsequent years; Powell et al., 2016).

The CRIOP is also a practical tool in that it can guide teachers' implementation of
CLRI. It consists of six elements—Classroom Relationships, Family Collaboration,

Assessment Practices, Instructional Practices, Discourse, and Critical Consciousness. The CRIOP instrument contains indicators that expand and clarify each element and serve as descriptors of CRLI practices.

As CRLI coaches, we frequently referenced these elements and associated indicators to assist teachers in understanding the culturally responsive model. Although no instructional model should be considered definitive, we found the CRIOP to be a useful framework in our work in classrooms, and teachers found it to be extremely helpful as they tried to address the many facets of CRLI. Here, we provide a brief description of the CRIOP model. Each element is addressed in greater depth in the chapters throughout this book.

The first two elements of the CRIOP address relationships that are necessary for implementing culturally responsive practices. *Classroom Relationships* examines interactions within classrooms, while *Family Collaboration* refers to interactions with students' families. As discussed in the first two chapters, research shows that both are essential for student learning.

To establish effective learning environments, we work with teachers on ways to create positive learning climates where students respect one another and collaborate effectively. Teachers who are culturally and linguistically responsive embrace diversity, and this quality is reflected in their interactions with students and even the messages conveyed by the physical images in their classrooms. In these classrooms, students feel safe; they feel accepted; they feel that they are an important part of a learning community. They also know that they are held to high standards and their teacher will not allow them to fall through the cracks. Students are viewed as resources for one another, and students' varied languages and cultures are not only respected but are also welcomed as providing valuable contributions to the learning of others.

Establishing culturally responsive relationships with families goes beyond parent involvement; rather, it consists of developing partnerships where parents have an integral role in the education of their children. Parents are seen as essential resources, and teachers meet them more than halfway to assure that productive relationships are established. This often means meeting parents or caregivers within their communities and assuming the role of inquirer to learn about their areas of expertise and how best to teach their child.

The last four elements of the CRIOP involve classroom learning: *Assessment Practices, Instructional Practices, Discourse,* and *Critical Consciousness.* In culturally responsive classrooms, assessment follows research-based practices. Formal assessment is kept to a minimum, and students are evaluated informally as they are actively engaged in learning. Self-assessment is also important, as students become partners in determining their learning needs and setting individualized goals.

Instruction is active, hands-on, and inquiry-based. Importantly, instruction is tied to the lives of students in that materials and learning activities are used that reflect students' linguistic and cultural knowledge. Academic language development is an important goal, and activities that boost students' academic language are as essential as expanding students' conceptual knowledge. Finally, consistent with more general effective practices that enhance student motivation, students have some choice and ownership in terms of what they learn and how they present their learning.

Discourse is an important element in culturally responsive classrooms in that it provides opportunities for students to collaborate with one another and increases student engagement. Questions and prompts are provided that intentionally elicit extended conversations, and those conversations are often scaffolded through providing students with sentence starters, phrases, and academic vocabulary. Students' native languages are viewed as strengths, and bilingualism/multilingualism is encouraged.

Last, but certainly not least, Critical Consciousness encourages students to become involved in issues that go beyond the classroom, such as human rights, climate change, and racial and ethnic inequities. Students study real-world issues and are invited to take action by becoming actively involved in solving problems at the local, state, national, and global levels. Teachers intentionally promote understanding of cultural assumptions and biases through class readings and discussions and promote dialogue that would elicit diverse perspectives.

How This Book Is Organized

In the chapters that follow, the six elements of the CRIOP are presented in greater depth, with each chapter devoted to one of the elements. In each chapter, we provide an overview of the research that supports the particular element and share numerous examples of how it has been implemented in elementary and middle school classrooms. It is important to note, however, that the various elements of the CRIOP do not stand alone but actually act in concert with one another. Thus, while the featured examples are designed to promote an understanding of a particular element, they also can serve as illustrations of other elements and how they can work together to create a culturally responsive learning environment.

Additionally, you will find teachers' voices embedded throughout each chapter. We felt it was important to include teachers' stories, as we believe teachers learn best from the experiences of other educators. Thus, in each chapter, you will read vignettes written by phenomenal teachers who have successfully implemented culturally and linguistically responsive practices.

Finally, in each chapter, we provide a comprehensive list of references. This book is specifically written for practicing educators and school leaders, yet it could also be helpful to researchers examining culturally responsive practices in school settings. Thus, in the references of each chapter is relevant literature for those interested in pursuing additional information on the various CRIOP elements.

We arrived at the six dimensions of culturally and linguistically responsive teaching after many years of study in the field, coupled with trial and error in classrooms. The

CRIOP instrument and model has been modified three times since its inception (see the book *Literacy for All Students*, Powell & Rightmyer, 2011, for an earlier version of the framework). One of our primary aims in its development was to assist teachers in realizing culturally appropriate and relevant practices that have been documented by research in many disciplines, from sociolinguistics and second-language acquisition to psychology and anthropology to educational theory and practice. The literature in CRLI is staggering in terms of its breadth and complexity, and perspectives are always evolving. Thus, we provide a caveat that the CRIOP model should not be viewed as the final word for CLRI; rather, it is designed to be used as a framework to guide teachers as they seek to learn about and implement CRLI practices.

In our work with teachers, we have found that they are sometimes a bit overwhelmed by the many facets of the CRIOP model. Therefore, we often suggest that teachers focus on one or two elements until they become comfortable with them before moving on to additional elements, particularly if they are new to CLRI. Working with other educators can provide support and encouragement when trying something new, so we believe it also would be beneficial to investigate the ideas in this book with a team, try out different strategies for a week or two, and come back together to share successes and challenges. We have found that some teachers are risk-takers while others are not, and those who are more willing to try new approaches can guide others in their collective development as culturally responsive educators.

Finally, it is also important to point out that a huge part of becoming a culturally responsive educator is a commitment to educate every student well and an understanding that all students are capable learners. Respect for students and families and for the language and cultural knowledge they bring to the classroom cannot be taught, yet it is an essential disposition for becoming an effective educator in diverse classrooms. Also, it is important that teachers reflect on and critically analyze the content and processes that permeate classroom life and the ways in which curricular and instructional practices are rooted in a Eurocentric ideology. The editors of this book are White, yet we have spent much of our lifetimes learning from those who are culturally, racially, and economically different from ourselves. We have come to understand our privilege as Whites and as professionals and to acknowledge that we will always have much to learn about the lives and perspectives of others. Indeed, one could argue that this is the heart of culturally responsive teaching; that is, we must become learners as well as teachers so that we can develop important relationships within and outside the classroom and know how best to teach our students. An examination of how teachers' race and class positions can impact classroom relationships and student learning is embedded throughout the chapters of this book.

References

Cantrell, S. C., Correll, P., & Malo-Juvera, V. (2013). *Evaluation of CRIOP professional development, 2012–2013*. U.S. Department of Education, Office of English Language Acquisition.

Cummins, J. (1986). Empowering minority students: A framework for intervention. *Harvard Educational Review, 56*(1), 18–36.

Delpit, L. (2012). *"Multiplication is for White people": Raising expectations for other people's children*. The New Press.

Deyhle, D. (1995). Navajo youth and Anglo racism: Cultural integrity and resistance. *Harvard Educational Review, 65*(3), 403–444.

Douglass, F. (1995). *Narrative of the life of Frederick Douglass*. Dover Publications.

Fernández, L. (2002). Telling stories about school: Using critical race and Latino critical theories to document Latina/Latino education and resistance. *Qualitative Inquiry, 8*(1), 45–65.

Fine, M. (1991). *Framing dropouts: Notes on the politics of an urban public high school*. SUNY Press.

Katz, S. R. (2013). Where the streets cross the classroom: A study of Latino students' perspectives on cultural identity in city schools and neighborhood gangs. *Bilingual Research Journal, 20*(3–4), 603–631.

Malo-Juvera, V., Powell, R., & Cantrell, S. (2013, April 27–May 1). *Development, validation, and factor analysis of the culturally responsive instruction observation protocol* [Roundtable presentation]. 2013 Annual Conference of the American Educational Research Association, San Francisco, CA. https://www.aera.net/Publications/Online-Paper-Repository/AERA-Online-Paper-Repository

Musu-Gillette, L., de Brey, C., McFarland, J., Hussar, W., Sonnenberg, W., & Wilkinson-Fliker, S. (2017). *Status and trends in the education of racial and ethnic groups 2017* (NCES 2017-051). U.S. Department of Education, National Center for Education Statistics. https://nces.ed.gov/pubs2017/2017051.pdf

Powell, R. (1993). *Literacy as a moral imperative: Facing the challenges of a pluralistic society*. Rowman & Littlefield.

Powell, R., Cantrell, S., & Correll, P. (2016). "How are we going to be testing that?" Challenges to implementing culturally responsive literacy instruction. In P. R. Schmidt & A. M. Lazar (Eds.), *Reconceptualizing literacy in the new age of multiculturalism and pluralism* (2nd ed., pp. 425–446). Information Age Publishing.

Powell, R., Cantrell, S. C., & Correll, P. (2017). Power and agency in a high poverty elementary school: How teachers experienced a scripted reading program. *Journal of Language and Literacy Education, 13*(1), 93–124.

Powell, R., Cantrell, S. C., Malo-Juvera, V., & Correll, P. (2016). Operationalizing culturally responsive instruction: Preliminary findings of CRIOP research. *Teachers College Record, 118*(1), ID Number 18224. http://www.tcrecord.org

Powell, R., & Rightmyer, E. (Eds.). (2011). *Literacy for all students: An instructional framework for closing the gap*. Routledge.

Valenzuela, A. (1999). *Subtractive schooling: U.S.–Mexican youth and the politics of caring*. SUNY Press.

Willis, A. I. (1995). Reading the world of school literacy: Contextualizing the experience of a young African American male. *Harvard Educational Review, 65*(1), 30–49.

CHAPTER 1

Classroom Relationships

Doris Walker-Dalhouse

TEACHERS KNOWINGLY OR unknowingly have an immeasurable influence on the lives of the students in their classrooms. They have the ability to create empowering relationships that result in positive outcomes for students (Nieto, 2010). Highly effective teachers build relationships with their students by recognizing the importance of students' knowledge and experiences and creating opportunities for personal and social dialogue (Lysaker & Furness, 2012). Teachers who support students and create environments of collegial support have been found to affect the extent of student engagement in classroom activities (Kearney et al., 2014).

Establishing and maintaining positive teacher–student relationships is important in working with all students, and they are fundamental to those who engage in culturally responsive teaching. Culturally sensitive interactions and curricula are keys to promoting success for diverse students whose backgrounds differ from those of the predominantly White teaching force (Delpit, 1996; Hamilton, 2004). The *Standards for the Preparation of Literacy Professionals 2017* by the International Literacy Association (ILA, 2018a) conveyed an expectation that teachers promote diversity in the classroom by "setting high expectations for learners and implementing instructional practices that are responsive to students' diversity" (p. 81).

This chapter focuses on research that supports the importance of teacher–student relationships in K–8 classrooms. The primary focus of this chapter is to draw connections from the research for teachers striving to establish culturally responsive classroom environments. I begin by identifying some of the challenges in establishing positive teacher–student and student-to-student relationships and then examine what has been found to be effective in the research literature.

What Does the Literature Tell Us About Classroom Relationships?

The changing demographic of students in today's classrooms has been cited as a factor in challenging teachers to create positive relationships with students. In a yearlong study investigating the relationship between a teacher and two of her second-grade students, Newberry (2013) found variations in the relationship between the students and the teacher that were attributed to differentiated teacher behaviors. The teacher's behaviors were differentiated according to her perception of students' needs, her perceived ability and necessity to address their needs, and the advantages associated with meeting the students' needs. Students who exhibit similarities in experiences, background, and personalities are generally preferred by teachers (Hamre & Pianta, 2001; Morganett, 2001). Other factors that result in differences in teacher–student relationships are cultural dissonance and deficit thinking.

Cultural Dissonance

A teacher's ability to establish community, collaboration, and connectedness with students is complicated when there is a lack of sociocultural congruity between the teacher and the students. Such was the situation in a case study involving an African American first-year teacher of the same race as her students. She was from a middle-class socioeconomic background and family structure and had school experience in a rural school setting. In contrast, her students were of a lower socioeconomic background living in an urban environment and attending an urban school. Navigating this challenge and establishing positive and culturally informed relationships with her students were important to the teacher, so she revised the curriculum, listened to students, and created safe places for student sharing (Coffey & Farinde-Wu, 2016). Through developing interpersonal relationships with her students, she learned how to teach her students in culturally responsive ways.

This example illustrates what Jacqueline Jordan Irvine (1990) identified as cultural synchronization. When there is a mismatch between the culture of the school and the students' culture, there is a loss of cultural synchronization. These cultural mismatches can be found when students' cultural ways of behaving, speaking, and dressing result in suspensions or are perceived negatively as inappropriate or threatening. Thus, cultural synchronization between teachers and students should be considered in responding to disruptive student behaviors and in developing effective classroom management plans (Monroe & Obidah, 2004).

Deficit Thinking

Deficit theories are often considered as "blaming the victim" (Ford, 1996, p. 84). Economically challenged minority children are described as being at risk for failure and disadvantaged due to multiple factors, including uninvolved families and a lack of resources (Johnson, 1994). The explanation for differences in the achievement of culturally/linguistically diverse students and majority White students is often attributed to student deficits. Instead of blaming the victim, Milner (2012) encourages teachers and researchers to move beyond seeing deficits to seeing these as opportunity gaps. Teachers and school personnel are encouraged to challenge deficit thinking fueled by tacit assumptions about the factors impacting students' academic struggles. Instead, teachers are called to focus on the untapped assets of students and teachers (Weiner, 2006).

Sociocultural Context and Racial Factors

Sociocultural context and racial factors influence teacher–student relationships and must be considered not only for historically marginalized students but also for immigrant students. Fostering a sense of belonging for immigrant students leads to higher academic engagement and school performance (DeNicolo et al., 2017; Suárez-Orozco et al., 2009). Rolón-Dow (2005) explored the intersectionality between race/ethnicity and caring. The resulting theory that she formulated was identified as "critical care praxis." Based on her work with Latino students, this theory identified the importance of the historical understanding of students' lives and its focus on individual and community levels of caring. It addresses issues such as migration, racism, and citizenship that impact the communities in which teachers teach and students are educated. She developed the theory of constructing counternarratives as a way to develop close and caring relationships by teachers with students in the Latino/a community. In applying the theory, Rolón-Dow describes the belief of middle school teachers in her study that ethnically or racially diverse "parents do not care whether their children are successful or not in school" (2005, p. 93). As a counternarrative to such negative thinking, teachers should be led to consider the impact of historical and sociocultural factors that influence the extent to which opportunities for advancement or success are available to these students. Rolón-Dow's research emphasizes the significant impact that adopting a critical-care praxis focused on race/ethnicity can have in teachers establishing caring relationships with students and their communities that ultimately influence students' educational outcomes.

In an investigation of the perspectives of adolescent Latinx students, Newcomer (2018) found that authentically caring relationships are established by teachers who demonstrate "funds of caring" for students. The resulting relationships were of utmost value in providing emotional, social, and academic resources for students. Other researchers have also found that engagement in learning and literacy is greater when immigrant students have positive relationships with teachers (Green et al., 2008; Newcomer, 2018; Stewart et al., 2017). For example, Walker (2011) conducted a study of 10 elementary teachers nominated by their principal as effective in working with predominantly African American students in a large urban school. All of the teachers noted the importance of daily interpersonal interaction with students as essential in increasing their understanding of students and student–teacher success in school achievement.

The importance of demonstrating care for students in building relationships is documented in research by Milner (2008). Working in urban schools, one of the questions guiding his examination of the narrative or lived experiences of urban teachers was, "What factors influence their interactions with students and the learning opportunities provided in their classrooms?" Milner describes the experiences of Mr. Hall, a White middle school science teacher, who demonstrated care for his students by providing them with multiple opportunities for success and by supporting their learning. Although he acknowledged challenges in getting to know some students, Mr. Hall emphasized the need for teachers to learn about aspects of students' lives outside of the classroom and subsequently using that knowledge to develop meaningful relationships in the classroom. Furthermore, not holding grudges following misunderstandings with students was essential in developing and maintaining positive teacher–student relationships. Mitchell's (1998) study of eight retired African American teachers also supports the importance of teachers being critically aware of students' in- and out-of-school experiences and the context of these experiences. This knowledge helps teachers to understand the connection between students' feelings and their behaviors.

Establishing an Ethic of Caring

Establishing caring relationships between teachers and students is an essential component of teaching and student learning. Respect is a critical element in forming and maintaining caring classroom relationships (Thompson, 2018). Furthermore, authentic caring is considered a vital component of culturally responsive teaching (Ayers, 2004; Siddle-Walker & Snarney, 2004; Thompson, 2004; Valenzuela, 1999). Authentic caring is identified as more action-centered than emotion-centered. Displaying emotions (i.e., compassion and concern) alone does not promote student learning; rather, authentic care involves actions of caring. Behaviors that promote student learning, such as demanding accountability for high-level performance from ethnically diverse students and honoring and respecting students' intellectual and life experiences, are essential for culturally responsive teaching (Gay, 2018). Culturally responsive caring is focused on "caring *for* instead of caring *about* the personal well-being and academic success of ethnically diverse students" (Gay, 2010, p. 48; emphasis in original).

Noddings (1992) emphasized that caring relationships consist of having high expectations, rigor for learning, and beliefs in students' ability to achieve (Cliatt-Wayman, 2018; Noddings, 2005). According to Noddings (2001), effective caring evolves over time and both teachers and students benefit from the relationships. The development of these relationships transforms teachers' attitudes and beliefs about students and the nature of students' learning. Teachers who are knowledgeable and caring take the lead in creating such learning environments (Nieto, 2010; Nieto & Bode, 2008). They build on the lived experiences of students, celebrate their diversity, and promote student learning through culturally conscious instruction (Baker et al., 2008; Flint et al., 2018; Gay,

2000; Noddings, 2003; Sanchez, 2007). Culturally responsive teachers recognize that trust must be at the core of their efforts to build relationships with students (Hammond & Jackson, 2015). Such trust might be manifested in scaffolding and supporting students in learning and in understanding their individual and collective needs. Patience, persistence, facilitation, validation, and empowerment are characteristics of caring interpersonal relationships that are expressed in many different ways (Gay, 2018).

Research focused on determining students' perceptions of caring teachers reveals that both middle school and urban high school students value caring as a teacher attribute (Alder & Moulton, 1998; Cothran & Ennis, 2000). The question might be asked: "What does care mean from the perspective of students?" In a yearlong investigation in which 25 middle school students were interviewed and shadowed throughout the school day to answer this question, Alder and Moulton (1998) identified the following five themes in students' responses: care as control in taking responsibility for classroom management, safety, and student behavior; care as equality in response to student differences; care as forgiveness for students' mistakes; care as concern for students as demonstrated through listening to problems, interacting, and knowledge of them; and care as good teaching which included explaining concepts, differentiating instruction, and making learning enjoyable and interesting.

In another study of middle school students in urban school classrooms, Alder (2002) sought to determine how caring relations are created and maintained between students and teachers. Information was gathered from multiple sources, including interviews and focus group sessions, and class observations. The author concluded that caring teachers have extensive knowledge of their students and demonstrate personalized leadership by providing positive guidance and clear directions to guide them in accepting responsibility for their behaviors. Students also felt that caring teachers act in ways to ensure students' understanding and hold high academic and behavioral expectations to promote student learning.

Teaching practices reflect teachers' ethics of caring in their daily interactions with all types of students in classrooms at different grade levels. Zhang-Wu's (2017) case study of a fourth-grade mainstream classroom teacher of linguistically and culturally diverse students identified caring as one of the essential elements that guided her implementation of culturally/linguistically responsive instruction. Other essential elements that were evident in her daily instruction included sensitivity to inequity in students' access to learning tools such as technology, support in enhancing students' comprehension and use of English, and development of students' voices through speaking and writing activities. Thus, a *pedagogy of caring* instructional approach incorporates activities and materials that reflect students' past and present life experiences and cultures. It also provides opportunities for student collaboration and interaction within the classroom. These practices facilitate the development of community, create communication between students and teachers, and facilitate the development of caring teacher–student relationships (Stewart et al., 2017).

Children's literature that incorporates culturally congruent themes and images has potential benefits in making connections to the lives and experiences of the diversity of students in today's schools (Zygmunt et al., 2015). To address the diversity of the school population, the ILA (2018b) included a declaration in its publication titled *The Case for Children's Rights to Read* that states, "Children should have the right to read texts that mirror their experiences and languages, provide windows into the lives of others, and open doors into our diverse world" (p. 7). In this chapter, I use the narrow definition of *multicultural literature* used by Lynch-Brown et al. (2011), which defines it as "literature by and about the groups that have been marginalized and disregarded by the dominant European-American culture in the United States" (p. 215). Different types of multicultural literature emerged in response to historical representation or absence of many cultures in the United States. Among the types of multicultural literature are African American, Asian/Pacific, Latino, Native American, religious cultures, and bilingual literature (Lynch-Brown et. al., 2011).

Multicultural literature serves as a mirror that reflects and validates students' cultural identity. It also provides students with a window for exploring a new dimension of experiences and cultures (Cox & Galda, 1990). This type of literature operates as a sliding glass door that represents different ways of seeing things (Bishop, 1990). Multicultural literature has a place in building a classroom environment that provides opportunities to change students' perceptions of others. Evans (2010) conducted a systematic study that examined the use and results of interactive read-alouds with multicultural children's books to determine their influence on children's perspectives and tolerance for others. After reading of 50 multicultural books to fourth-grade urban elementary students, followed by a discussion, the author found that the students' acceptance and respect for people different from them were heightened, that they demonstrated a greater understanding and acceptance of individuals with a shared culture and of cultural similarities and differences, and that they had a greater awareness of issues related to prejudice, bias, and tolerance.

Within the body of multicultural texts are those texts that are culturally relevant. Culturally relevant books are defined as texts "linking directly to students' particular backgrounds and experiences" (Ebe, 2012, p. 184). The knowledge that children from non-dominant sociocultural and linguistic backgrounds bring to school is often considered to be of lesser value than their counterparts from the dominant culture (Alim & Paris, 2017; González et al., 2005). However, students need to see themselves in the curriculum and have their experiences and cultures reflected if growth in learning is to occur. Teachers' perceptions of students are fundamental and must be considered as they instruct and interact with them. In a study of 13 preschool to third-grade socioculturally and linguistically diverse students in urban school classrooms, teachers' perceptions of students' reading and engagement in discussing culturally relevant texts were investigated. The experience of reading culturally relevant texts was found to be successful in promoting students' interests in reading and discussing literature. Students' reading comprehension of texts was enhanced because the texts tapped into their prior knowledge and experiences (Clark & Fleming, 2019).

The question might be asked, "What research-based instructional practices can teachers use to help connect texts to the lives of their ethnically and racially diverse students?" Thomas (2019) reports research using read-aloud or free reading to motivate African American males to develop interests in several reading series (i.e., *Miami Jackson*; *Magic Tree House*; *Horrible Harry*; *Julian's World*) that portray people of color in positive ways. Higher order thinking was encouraged through questions and deep discussions about aspects of the text to promote comprehension and students' text-to-self connections. Expressing similar concerns for engaging African American male students who are disengaged with reading or who struggle in reading, Wood and Jocius (2013) support and value being guided by a critical literacy framework that "encompasses social, political, and historical contexts and allows students to examine the influence of institutions on their everyday lives" (p. 663). The framework includes the use of culturally relevant texts, collaboration, and critical conversations to engage African American males.

Emerging bilinguals also benefit from literacy instruction and discussions using culturally relevant text. In a small-scale study investigating the reading proficiency of middle school adolescents, Ebe (2012) found that reading proficiency and comprehension was greater when reading culturally relevant texts. Jimenez (1997) found increased performance in strategic behaviors such as inferences and asking questions after the use of culturally relevant texts with middle school Latina and Latino students who struggle with reading. Improved student metacognitive awareness while reading these texts resulted in growth in reading comprehension due to the use of books that connected to their background knowledge and experiences. Similar to findings related to African American students, other researchers and educators have found increased reading engagement of English learners after reading instruction using culturally relevant texts (Ebe, 2015; Feger, 2006; Stuart & Volk, 2002). When teachers at all grade levels incorporate culturally relevant literature into their instruction, they convey respect and affirm students' cultural identities, which leads to authentic caring and higher student engagement.

High Teacher Expectations

Having high expectations for students' learning and behavior is a critical dimension of strong classroom relationships. Implications for understanding the impact of the self-fulfilling nature of teachers' expectations on students' performance can be drawn from the National Institute of Child Health and Human Development longitudinal data gathered from the Study of Early Child Care and Youth Development, which involved children from birth through age 15. Sorhagen (2013) used this data set to examine the association of first-grade teachers' over- and underestimation of students' reading, math, and language skills with their academic performance in high school. First-grade teachers' expectations were found to have a disproportionate impact on the academic performance in math and language abilities at age 15 for students from lower income families (Sorhagen, 2013). Teachers with low expectations have been found to give subgroups of diverse students less challenging work (Rosenthal & Jacobson, 1968).

Engaging teachers in targeted or direct coaching conversations to examine their underlying bias about students has been found to be effective in changing low expectations that teachers might have for students in urban settings and, we believe for teachers in all settings, in encouraging more appropriately rigorous instruction that would lead to higher student achievement (Ramkellawan & Bell, 2017). One strategy described by Ramkellawan and Bell (2017) that teachers in an urban setting can use to reflect on their practice is that of co-generative dialogue with students. With co-generative dialogue, teachers regularly seek students' feedback about lessons and co-plan individual lessons or units with students. To change teachers' mindsets about students' abilities, improvements need to be made in teachers' instructional planning. This change can be guided by another coaching strategy in which teachers respond to probing questions about what they want students to remember in the future about the class and how they connect to students' lives without devaluating their experiences and ways of communicating (Ramkellawan & Bell, 2017).

Teachers' beliefs about teaching students and their instructional practices play a key role in positioning diverse students in their academic interactions with their peers. Yoon (2007) found that teachers who were actively involved in positioning middle school English Language Learners (ELLs) as acceptable, meaning that they were considered as resourceful and intellectual and not inferior or powerless, observed increased interactions between ELLs and their mainstreamed students in literacy learning. ELLs also perceived themselves as being capable learners.

According to Delpit (2012), "high expectations and strong demands of students are not sufficient" (p. 82) in working with culturally, linguistically, and ethnically diverse students. The warm demander's approach to authority has been advocated as a culturally responsive approach for achieving a balance between demonstrating care for students and expectations for classroom discipline while communicating high expectations for learning in structured classroom communities or environments (Bondy & Ross, 2008). The type of care that is demonstrated is not only for individual African American students in high-poverty schools (Bondy et al., 2007; Ware, 2006) and racially diverse students in urban schools (Brown, 2004) but also for their community by acknowledging its cultural underpinnings.

Culturally Congruent Talk

Every aspect of the language used with students is important to establish meaningful interactions with students (Robison, 2019). Beiler (2019) states that "through these interactions, teachers inform students how much the students are (or are not) noticed and valued, and whether school is a place in which students want to stay" (p. 3). The use of direct discourse in communicating expectations for learning and behavior characterizes the caring displayed by teachers who are identified as "warm demanders." As an example, a warm demander might say to a student exhibiting off-task behavior during independent reading time, "It is independent reading time. What should you be doing? That's right. You need to sit down at the table, take out your book, and start reading like everyone else." This emphatic statement is in contrast to the teacher saying, "Your classmates and I are ready to read. Will you please take your seat and read like the rest of us?" The reason that African American students are responsive to the interactional style used by teachers who are warm demanders is because the language style is seen as reflective of the teacher's shared culture with African American students (Bondy et. al, 2007; Irvine, 2002).

However, there are differences in the success that White teachers working with African American students might experience in their attempts to be warm demanders. In a study comparing a White teacher's approach to authority with that of an African American teacher described as a warm demander, Ford and Sassi (2014) emphasized a need to reconceptualize the role of warm demander. Included in this reconceptualization is the need for White teachers to establish cross-racial legitimacy by cultivating an alliance with students to combat racism. It involves developing a greater understanding of African American students by learning about their perspectives and understanding when and how to use culturally congruent communicative practices (i.e., signifying or call-and-response) in interacting with them.

Additionally, culturally responsive teachers use familiar terms of endearment that reflect students' culture and ways of interacting. Such terms represent sincere expressions of genuine caring (Bondy et. al., 2007; Weinstein et al., 2003). These teachers use the information acquired about students' backgrounds, their cultural norms and beliefs, and parental expectations as cultural content knowledge (Weinstein et al., 2003).

Classroom questioning is also a consideration when examining effective classroom interactions. Robison (2019) cautions teachers not to ask open-ended questions that do not provide students with directions about how to respond. For example, instead of asking students, "Should we read books about homeless characters?" a teacher should provide students with guidance about how to respond by saying, "Raise your hands if you agree that we should read books about homeless characters." All these approaches and prompts reinforce the importance of teachers using language that enables students to have meaningful interactions with teachers.

Student–Student Interactions and Learning

Teachers' beliefs about teaching students and their instructional practices play a key role in positioning diverse students in their academic interactions with their peers. Yoon (2007) found that teachers who were actively involved in positioning middle school ELLs as resourceful and intelligent versus inferior or powerless observed increased interactions between ELLs and their mainstreamed students in literacy learning. ELLs also perceived themselves as being capable learners.

Cooperative learning is one way to establish equity in classroom student-to-student interactions and promote greater achievement (Boykin et al., 2004; Dill & Boykin, 2000). Access and equitable relations are elements of equity that need to be considered in implementing student learning in cooperative learning classrooms (Cohen et al., 1999). Complex Instruction is an approach used in diverse classrooms to teach higher academic-level work to students in cooperative groups. To establish equitable relationships between students and equal access to learning for low-status children in classrooms, teachers use strategies that recognize the breadth, depth, and variety of the intellectual abilities that each student brings to the classroom. Teachers broaden students' understanding of what it means to "be smart" (Cohen et al., 1999, p. 84) by publicly talking to them about the multiple abilities of students observed to have low status within the classroom prior to beginning daily group work. Once the teacher identifies the multiple abilities that these students have, the teacher relates these abilities to the expectations required for completing the task. Expectations are then set for the role that each student will fulfill in completing the group's work. The organization of the classroom encourages interdependent group tasks and increases student interactions by building on the extensive funds of knowledge that diverse or low-status students bring to the classroom (Cohen et al., 1999). The use of multiple grouping patterns for literacy learning is supported by the standards of the ILA (2018a), which challenge teachers to create physically and socially rich environments that use a variety of grouping configurations for independent and collaborative literacy learning. To accomplish this, teachers must "encourage positive interactions that allow learners to have opportunities for authentic literacy growth and to work cooperatively while developing their ability to communicate effectively with peers and adults" (ILA, 2018a, p. 81).

It is also important to establish a community of learning, where students help one another to excel. Farinde-Wu et al. (2017) conducted research to determine how award-winning teachers created culturally responsive classroom environments. The practices they used were labeled as RACCE: establishing mutual respect between themselves and their students, acting immediately as in-school and out-of-school resources, encouraging two-way communication with students, celebrating students' successes, and encouraging students. Importantly, these teachers created a familial-style classroom culture of success. This was demonstrated in two ways. First, they developed a support system in which individual student success was considered fundamental to the success of the group as a whole. Every student had the responsibility of supporting their fellow students who struggled academically or had other concerns. Second, Farinde-Wu et al. found that the award-winning teachers perceived themselves as parental figures in terms of demonstrating comparable care as parents for the academic and social aspects of their students' lives.

Classroom Relationships: From Research to Practice

Culturally responsive teaching provides teachers with the opportunity to connect with students and promote higher level thinking (Quin, 2017). To create a culturally responsive classroom environment, teachers should do the following: (1) communicate an ethic of care (e.g., equitable relationships, bonding), (2) communicate high expectations for all students, and (3) create a learning atmosphere that engenders respect for one another and toward diverse populations. Similarly, students in culturally responsive classrooms must work together productively (Powell et al., 2017). Teachers must assume the leadership role in the development of a literate classroom community (Au, 2006). At the same time, all students have resources that can benefit this community, and Au (2006) emphasizes the need for teachers to assign students to roles within the classroom that will lead them to assume responsibilities that contribute to classroom learning.

Culturally Responsive Classroom Management

Classroom management is key to establishing a productive classroom community and quality instruction. The increasingly diverse student population in today's schools makes classroom management an issue since "definitions and expectations of appropriate behavior are culturally influenced" (Weinstein et al., 2004, p. 25). Considering that there are differences between teachers' and students' cultural backgrounds, Weinstein et al. (2004) proposed a model of culturally responsive classroom management in which teacher self-knowledge and assumptions, knowledge of their students' backgrounds, and understandings of social, economic, and political issues related to diversity need to be considered before reflecting about classroom management practices. They draw on the work of Nieto (2000), who emphasized the need for teachers to monitor their behavior for equitable treatment and consider when to make accommodations based on students' culture and when to expect them to make accommodations based on classroom rules and teacher expectations.

In addressing multicultural issues in literacy, Au (2006) provides evidence that emphasizes the need for teachers to project authority or "toughness" by having high expectations for learning, being explicit in what students need to learn, and implementing appropriate consequences for inappropriate behavior. She recommends that opportunities for praise and recognition of students be applied evenly if teachers are to achieve the goal of ensuring that all students participate in learning.

This "toughness" noted by Au (2006) is consistent with a "warm demander" approach to classroom management. As noted in the research section, teachers in diverse classrooms benefit from being warm demanders who use culturally congruent discourse in communicating with students. Bondy and Ross (2008) provide an example of an exchange that might be characteristic of a warm demander:

That's enough of your nonsense, Darius. Your story does not make sense. I
told you time and time again that you must stick to the theme I gave you.
Now sit down. (Irvine & Fraser, 1998, as cited in Bondy & Ross, 2008, p. 3)

Although such exchanges may seem harsh, they are very effective with some students. We have witnessed warm demanders often in our work in diverse classrooms, and many students respond to this more direct discourse style. In essence, it communicates a sense of care. Warm demanders take on a "no excuses" philosophy. As Bondy and Ross note, "when students know that you believe in them, they will interpret even harsh-sounding comments as statements of care from someone with their best interests at heart" (2008, p. 2).

Communicating High Expectations

Warm demanders convey to students that they expect them to succeed. As noted previously, one component of culturally and linguistically responsive teaching that has been reiterated in the literature is having high expectations for all students. Such teachers insist that students meet certain expectations while providing multiple ways to support their learning. Warm demanders acknowledge that students learn in different ways, and they provide a variety of activities to help them grasp the content.

Warm demanders also believe in students' ability to improve their behavior, and they work hard to understand students' perspectives on why they may be misbehaving. In their research, Bondy and Ross (2008) note that such teachers used two main strategies to hold students to a high standard. First, they consistently reminded students of their expectations, and second, they calmly delivered consequences. These teachers spoke firmly and immediately followed through with action when warranted. That is, they clearly conveyed their expectations and assigned consequences when students failed to comply. Students tend to appreciate such disciplined classroom environments and interpret them as a sign of care.

Setting specific objectives for both content and language performance can provide concrete guidance to students in terms of what is expected. At the same time, teachers need to provide sufficient support and scaffolding so that students are able to meet those targets (see Chapters 4 and 5). Some teachers have had success by establishing specific goals for group performance. For instance, a class target for a math exam might be something like this: "As a class, our mean score on the math test will be 75%." Once this goal is reached, the goal for the next exam might be 80%. Setting group goals and displaying progress on a graph can be highly motivating for some students and can encourage students to use one another as resources in preparation for exams. At the same time, it's important to keep confidentiality in mind in terms of individual scores and to focus on celebrating group success.

Another way to show students that you have high expectations for their learning is to have them assume the teacher role. On many occasions we have seen students show great pride when they are asked to explain their thinking to the class or group, to demonstrate a math problem, or to assist a peer. Even typically low-performing students can become teachers when it's clear that they grasp a problem or concept: "You get it; now teach her." Oftentimes, the best "teachers" are those students who have struggled to understand concepts themselves.

Using Culturally Relevant Literature

An important part of being a "warm demander" is to learn about students' cultures. Culturally responsive teachers can become better acquainted with their students' lives and cultures through the use of culturally relevant and bilingual books (Sharma & Christ, 2017). Foremost in selecting books should be teachers' knowledge of the multiplicities of identities that students possess. Booklists of award-winning books include the Coretta Scott King, Pua Belpré, Tomás Rivera Mexican American, Jane Addams, and the Carter G. Woodson Awards. A list of various organizations and the focus of their awards can be found in Table 1.1 (*See page 14*).

Sharma and Christ (2017) used criteria drawn from the work of Sims-Bishop (1991; Sims, 1983), Walters (1998), and Ebe (2010) to create criteria to guide teachers in selecting culturally relevant texts:

1. The culture is represented accurately, and stereotypes are examined and dispelled.

2. The portrayal of culture depicted in the text reflects and is shared by the authors and illustrators of the text.

3. Protagonists share cultural markers (i.e., race, ethnicity, religion) with those of the reader.

4. The age and gender identity of the reader are the same as that of the main character.

5. The speech (language or dialect) of the reader is similar to that of the main character's speech.

6. The reader has experienced living in or visiting places that are represented in the book settings.

7. The reader has had similar life experiences to those described in the text.

Items 3 through 7 are drawn from the Cultural Relevance rubric developed for text selection (Ebe, 2010).

Issues that affect students' lives as determined by teachers' knowledge of their students can be explored through high-quality culturally relevant literature. Issues related to racial diversity, immigration, identity, family, and interactions with others might be among the concerns that create opportunities for increased teacher knowledge and

Table 1.1. *Organizations and Their Awards*

Focus of Award	Award
African American literature	Coretta Scott King Book Awards http://www.ala.org/rt/emiert/cskbookawards/
American Indian literature	American Indian Youth Literature Award https://ailanet.org/activities/american-indian-youth-literature-award/
Arab American literature	Arab American Book Award https://arabamericanmuseum.org/book-awards/
Asian/Pacific American literature	Asian/Pacific American Award for Literature https://www.apalaweb.org/awards/literature-awards/
Bilingual books	Lectura Books (a clearinghouse of bilingual book awards) https://www.lecturabooks.com/book-awards/
Developmental disabilities	Dolly Gray Children's Literature Award https://www.dollygrayaward.com/ Schneider Family Book Award http://www.ala.org/awardsgrants/schneider-family-book-award
Diversity (celebrates many different groups)	Carter G. Woodson Book Award https://www.socialstudies.org/awards/woodson Walter Dean Myers Award for Outstanding Children's Literature https://diversebooks.org/our-programs/walter-award/ Ezra Jack Keats Book Award https://www.ezra-jack-keats.org/section/ezra-jack-keats-book-awards/ Notable Books for a Global Society http://www.clrsig.org/notable-books-for-a-global-society-nbgs.html
Feminism	Amelia Bloomer Book List http://www.ala.org/awardsgrants/amelia-bloomer-book-list
Lesbian, gay, bisexual, transgender, and queer	Rainbow Book List https://glbtrt.ala.org/rainbowbooks/ Stonewall Book Awards http://www.ala.org/rt/rrt/award/stonewall/honored
Jewish literature	Sydney Taylor Book Award https://jewishlibraries.org/Sydney_Taylor_Book_Award
Latinx literature	Américas Award http://www.claspprograms.org/americasaward Pura Belpré Awards http://www.ala.org/alsc/awardsgrants/bookmedia/belpremedal
Mexican American literature	Tomas Rivera Mexican American Children's Book Award https://www.education.txstate.edu/ci/riverabookaward/
Peace, social justice	Jane Addams Children's Book Awards https://www.janeaddamschildrensbookaward.org/ Once Upon a World Children's Book Award http://www.wiesenthal.com/about/library-and-archives/once-upon-a-world-childrens-book-award.html

student identity and understanding. For example, Alanis (2007) describes collaborative work with teachers in using culturally relevant texts with students in a Spanish/English dual-language program. Culturally relevant texts used with students were *I Love Saturday y Domingo's* (Alda, 2004), which focuses on a young girl's weekend with her European American and Spanish American families; *In My Family/En Mi Familia* (Garza, 2000), which features the author's early life as a Mexican American in Kingsville, Texas; and *Harvesting Hope: The Story of César Chávez* (Krull, 2003), which chronicles the historical events leading to the founding of the United Farm Workers union. The author recommends reading aloud culturally relevant books to culturally and linguistically diverse students on a regular basis and providing opportunities for children to listen to stories read by Spanish speakers in English or Spanish.

Furthermore, biographies can be tools for developing students' historical-cultural understandings and provide additional opportunities for oral and written responses to a text. When combined with other culturally responsive practices, culturally relevant texts can provide possibilities for powerful learning. For instance, Feger (2006) used culturally relevant fiction and nonfiction books and poems with her bilingual–bicultural 9th- and 10th-grade students in combination with collaborative learning opportunities to promote student reading engagement. Opportunities for students to respond to culturally relevant texts in writing, art, and oral presentations can be provided to connect students and their families (Schrodt et al., 2015) and engage them in shared reading experiences (Rowe & Fain, 2013).

Morning Meetings

Within the school setting, teachers might use class meetings or morning meetings as a time to share multicultural texts and engage students in critical discussions of issues embedded in the text. These meetings also provide teachers with opportunities to become more knowledgeable about students' languages and cultures and to affirm them as individuals through the sharing of artifacts from home and teacher-initiated conversations about their lives outside of school. The following class meeting prompts can be used to help teachers make meaningful connections with students by learning about students' families and cultures and affirming their cultural and linguistic knowledge:

- Greet one another in various languages.

- Say the days of the week in other languages; count in other languages.

- Have students ask their parents about traditions they celebrated when they were their age and share during morning meeting. (This could also be a writing assignment where parents write about a tradition they remember. Teachers could pick a couple each day to read.)

- Talk about celebrations in their parents' home countries, for example, how birthdays are celebrated in _______ country.

- Have students find out something about their heritage and share (e.g., my family is from ______). You could find the places on a map.

- If students' families have visited other countries, have them bring in artifacts to share.

- Have students bring in a special item or artifact in their family and talk about why it's important.

- Have students ask their families about their dreams for their children and share them with the teacher.

- Have students ask their families about their childhoods (where they lived, what their schooling was like, songs they liked to sing; games they liked to play, etc. This could take several days with different questions each day).

- Have students bring in something that represents the work lives of their families. (For example, they could share items like rubber gloves, pens, books, hats, badges, etc. or actual items from work.)

- Ask students if they can speak another language, and ask them to share something in that language: a phrase, poem, song, and the like. English-only students could learn something in another language and share it. Emerging bilinguals could work with their parents to decide what to share.

A good resource that explains morning meetings and how they are implemented can be found at https://www.edutopia.org/blog/morning-meeting-changing-classroom-culture-lisa-dabbs. Teachers can also learn about students and their lives outside the classroom by asking questions like the following:

- What are some things you like about school? Dislike? Why?

- Share a celebration.

- Share a problem you have right now in your life.

- What is one thing you would like the class to know about you?

- What's one thing that makes you special?

- What is something that bothers you?

- What makes you happy?

- What makes you sad?

- What makes you angry?

- What are your goals for your life?

- Tell about a time you've been bullied.

All these questions and prompts have been used successfully in morning and class meetings by culturally responsive educators to develop positive relationships in the classroom.

Classroom Environment

Physical and nonphysical components must be considered to create classrooms that are conducive to learning and safe and supportive of students' academic development (ILA, 2018a). The physical aspect of the classroom should reflect the cultures of the diversity of students in the classroom. Cultural referents reflective of student diversity can promote student identity and agency. Laman and Henderson (2018) describe a teacher's use of culturally relevant photographs taken of places within students' neighborhoods and communities as an avenue to use in learning more about students and their families. We have found that photos of students' communities can be helpful in teaching phonics skills (e.g., "Bb" is for Booker T. Washington Elementary; "Dd" is for "Donato's"). These photos can also be used as prompts for writing and as a way to make curricular content more meaningful by using images related to students' experiences to support conceptual understandings (Sobel & Taylor, 2015).

Other ideas for creating culturally responsive classrooms involve creating classroom spaces (e.g., bulletin boards and displays) that represent culturally relevant events and people. We invite teachers to survey their classroom walls and bookshelves. Are there posters and pictures that represent the diversity within their classroom? Are there books in their classroom and school libraries that reflect students' lives? Are hallway signs written in the various languages represented in the school community? We often invite teachers to conduct a scavenger hunt of the classroom and school to determine if the physical spaces would be inviting for all students and families. Also, consider daily routines such as morning announcements and the Pledge of Allegiance. Are they ever conducted in students' languages? Schools that intentionally exhibit students' languages and cultures show in a very concrete way that they value students' and families' diverse cultures and histories.

Figure 1.1. *Students enjoy seeing classroom labels in their home languages.*

In addition to creating a physical space that affirms cultural diversity, culturally responsive teachers encourage an environment that is characterized by respect and care. Students develop and convey care for one another in a variety of ways, from strategies that explicitly encourage them to express care for one another to opportunities to work together productively in collaborative groups.

Classroom Scenario 1.1 shows how first-grade students were guided in displaying care and kindness toward one another. Through reading and discussing children's literature and having frequent conversations in morning meetings, students developed a chart that documented what kindness "looks like" and "sounds like" (see Figure 1.2). Throughout the study, they were rewarded with stickers for using kind words and displaying caring actions.

Figure 1.2. *Young children can benefit from explicit instruction on how to be kind to others.*

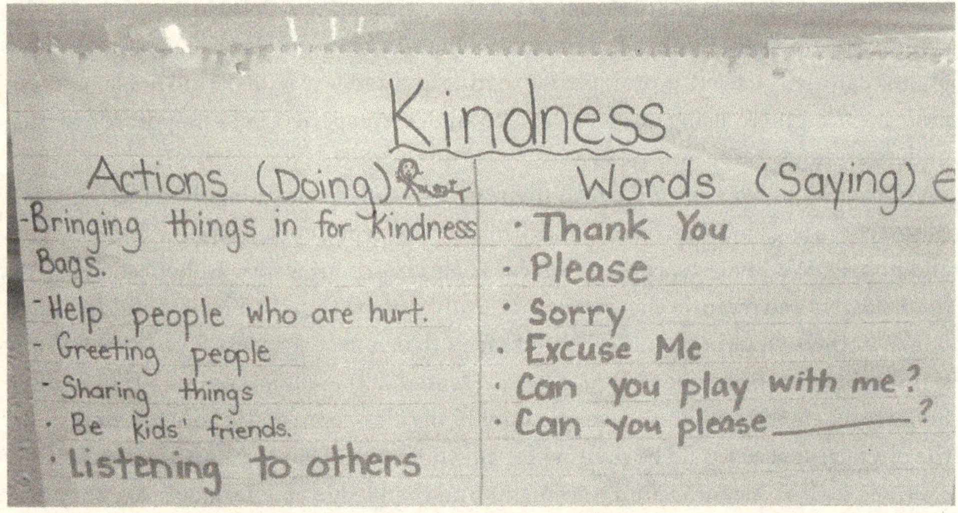

***Classroom Scenario 1.1.* Kindness Study**
Melissa Collins and Aimee Gonzalez

We teach first graders in a small rural school where the majority of our students' first language is not English. Most of our students and their families also live in poverty. Over the past 2 years, we have seen an increase in our refugee population, mostly from the Congo. We have also seen an increase in students who have experienced trauma in some form. After thinking about our student population, we decided to do a unit on kindness to promote a caring environment in our classrooms.

We began the unit by implementing class meetings. Each morning before we began instruction, we would start off the day with a class meeting. These meetings consisted of everyone sitting in a circle (teacher included). Each student would get a chance to talk. To start the unit on kindness, we asked our students to share ways that they can show kindness. We made a poster for the classroom that consisted of "What kindness looks like" and "What kindness sounds like." Students gave many examples of ways they could show kindness at school, at home, and in the community. These included helping a classmate tie their shoes, helping parents clean the house, and picking up trash in their neighborhood, as well as using manners and not saying hurtful words. These behaviors became part of our daily conversations at the beginning of each class meeting.

Students who were exhibiting these behaviors were rewarded for showing acts of kindness. When students showed kindness in the classroom or in the school, they were given a kindness sticker to wear, and the principal celebrated them as well during the morning announcements. Being able to have something tangible to show others made students excited to find new ways to show kindness.

As our unit went on, we changed topics to include things that made students happy, sad, angry, scared, and excited. Every Monday we allowed students to share something exciting or fun that they did over the weekend. Students who didn't want to share could pass, but we found that once they saw others talking, they wanted to share at the end. Within a month we saw a lot of our non-native English speakers sharing in complete sentences.

This study integrated many of the content areas. In addition to providing an opportunity for oral language development, we read books about kindness, both fictional stories and biographies about people who showed great examples of kindness. During writing, students got to write about different ways they could show kindness at school, in the home, and in the community.

To end the unit, we did a culminating project that incorporated the content areas as well. We had one student whose family had come to our community recently as refugees and we wanted to launch a project that was personally meaningful to him. Thus, we decided to partner with the Kentucky Refugee Ministries (KRM) to teach our students about the work that they do and to give students the opportunity to help this organization. We began by inviting someone from KRM to come and talk about their organization and how they help refugees living in our state. Then we asked students to bring in different hygiene items as well as gloves and hats to distribute to newcomers. Students were able to make "kindness bags" with the items they brought in as well as make cards for the families welcoming them to the community. Thus, students were able to engage in meaningful writing. We also integrated math by having the students count the different items and graph them as they came in.

Before implementing the kindness study, both of us noticed that many of our students had sharing issues and would argue with each other. We saw this mostly among our girls. As we began to focus on kindness, however, we noticed that this all changed. They were able to talk out their problems with each other with little teacher support and were looking for any way possible to show kindness toward each other. By completing the project, our classes came together and became more of a community. The kids loved our kindness unit, and once it was completed, they wanted to continue showing kindness to others throughout our classroom and school!

To promote positive peer relationships, one fourth-grade team we worked with in a high-poverty school created a message board in the hallway. Many of their students experienced trauma in their lives, and the teachers wanted to establish a mutually supportive and caring learning environment. Students used sticky notes to celebrate their peers by posting positive comments about them. They wrote statements like "Shamika helped me with my math today," and "Joey picked up my pencil for me." This same team took time out of each week to celebrate a particular student by having his or her peers give positive comments about them. Activities such as these can make every student feel special and valued as a member of the classroom community.

Another fourth-grade teacher chose a different strategy for enhancing student relationships within the classroom. To celebrate the uniqueness of each student and develop empathy, she implemented a game called "Rare Bird." See Classroom Scenario 1.2 for a description of how she implemented this game and the positive effects it had on the climate of her classroom.

Classroom Scenario 1.2. **Rare Bird**
Taylor Cain

I teach fourth grade at the largest elementary school in my small town, where we hold the highest population of elementary-aged English language learners. A large majority of the students at my school are living in poverty, but there are also students who live very comfortably. These socioeconomic disparities have sometimes resulted in conflict in my classroom.

Even with a particularly sweet group of students, I began to notice constant bickering among certain individuals. Our little classroom normally had such a positive, cheerful climate, and I so desperately wanted to have that back! Two students in particular were having difficulty getting along. I spoke with the students involved to get to the bottom of their dispute. One student said that she did not know why the other was so upset. She had just been showing her a new set of markers her parents had bought her over the weekend. The other student, obviously upset, told me that she did not understand why her friend had to show off her new things all the time. It made her upset because she loved coloring but could never have markers like those. So I had one student upset because she felt less fortunate and another student confused because she didn't know what she had said wrong to upset her friend.

This incident made me think more critically about my students' home lives and how they really don't have much insight into one another's lives outside of school. They are all coming from very different places with different opportunities and resources. I knew this . . . but they didn't. Exploring differences in socioeconomic background didn't seem like the most effective way to alleviate this issue. Rather, I felt that getting the students to understand each other on a more personal level was what would change the tone of our classroom.

I came across a little game called "Rare Bird" that I decided to include in our Afternoon Meetings. I thought this game might generate productive conversation about our personal

> *lives and help students understand one another on a deeper level. We all have rare little things about us that we don't just go around sharing with everyone we meet. I know fourth graders love sharing the "cool" stories about going to the game with friends or getting the newest iPhone, but they are a lot more apprehensive to share stories about hanging out with their little brother or making cookies with their granny during the holidays. Those are those rare things that only a few close people know about, yet those rare things are a part of us and make us who we are! We don't really know each other until we know some of those stories that really make us unique. So sharing those stories will help us better understand each other!*
>
> *I gave students an index card and asked them to write down something about them that others would not know. I told them that I would be reading the card aloud but did not want their names on the card so we could guess who had written it. I read the cards as I collected them and saw some very wholesome stories and some very intimate stories about my students' families. I realized that it may not be appropriate to guess who had written these things and decided just to read them and discuss them as a group. This way no student was singled out, but all students could share and contribute to the story being told.*
>
> *We spent 2 weeks of Afternoon Meetings discussing our "Rare Bird" stories. We talked about fun family traditions and cool places to have birthday parties. The students loved hearing about one another's personal lives and getting to relate with their classmates in different ways. They were so eager to get to our Afternoon Meetings each day! As we became more comfortable with sharing stories, we discussed some tougher topics, like dealing with a loss or a divorce. These hard-hitting topics did seem a bit overwhelming at first, but talking about these things allowed the more reserved students to speak up and, in some situations, allowed students to relate to each other on a whole new level.*
>
> *This game allowed my students to understand each other on a more personal level through simple discussions. I saw new friendships arise and more empathy from everyone. I even saw my two little friends sharing markers at recess!*

Collaborative Groups

Students can also learn to appreciate the various perspectives of others through collaboration. Interdisciplinary projects are conducive to cooperative learning strategies, which provide students with opportunities for interacting and working collaboratively with students who might have different views and experiences (Montgomery, 2001). Cooperative learning groups in culturally responsive classrooms should reflect the diversity in the classroom composition in terms of race, ethnicity, gender, social class, and ability (Gay, 2018).

When grouping students to explore the task, efforts should be made to avoid privileging high-status or -ability students whose participation is greater than that of low-status or -ability students in heterogeneous classrooms. Teachers should form cooperative groups consisting of students with multiple abilities, cultures, ethnic learning preferences, and strengths in learning modalities. Teachers and students can then discuss the abilities needed to complete the task and communicate to students that no one student is expected to demonstrate competence in completing all aspects of the task. This alters expectations that students have for themselves and each other (Cohen & Lotan, 1995), thereby positioning all students as capable learners. In Chapter 5, specific ways for promoting equitable participation in small-group settings are explored.

Figure 1.3. *In culturally responsive classrooms, students work together productively and support one another in their learning.*

In concluding this chapter, it is important to remember that meaningful interactions with students provide opportunities for teachers to learn and build on students' cultural knowledge (Moll et al., 1992; Newberry, 2013). At the core of positive relationships is trust, which is generated by caring (Hammond & Jackson, 2015). Culturally responsive teachers must use these opportunities to develop caring relationships with students. They must use the knowledge of their students to create a respectful and collaborative classroom and foster a climate that affirms students through practices, books, and images that reflect their experiences.

References

Alanis, I. (2007). Developing literacy through culturally relevant texts. *Social Studies and the Young Learner, 20*(1), 29–32.

Alda, A. F. (2004). *I love Saturday y domingos*. Altheneum Books for Young Readers.

Alder, N. (2002). Interpretations of the meaning of care: Creating caring relationships in urban middle school classrooms. *Urban Education, 37*(2), 241–266.

Alder, N., & Moulton, M. R. (1998). Caring relationships: Perspectives from middle school students. *Research in Middle Level Education Quarterly, 21*(3), 15–32.

Alim, S., & Paris, D. (2017). What is culturally sustaining pedagogy and why does it matter? In D. Paris & S. Alim (Eds.), *Culturally sustaining pedagogies: Teaching and learning for justice in a changing world* (pp. 1–24). Teachers College Press.

Au, K. (2006). *Multicultural issues and literacy achievement*. Erlbaum.

Ayers, W. (2004). *Teaching the personal and the political: Essays on hope and justice*. Teachers College Press.

Baker, J. A., Grant, S., & Morlock, L. (2008). The teacher–student relationship as a developmental context for children with internalizing or externalizing behavior problems. *School Psychology Quarterly, 23*(1), 3–15.

Bieler, D. (2019). *The power of teacher talk: Promoting equity and retention through student interactions*. Teachers College Press.

Bishop, R. S. (1990). Mirrors, windows, and sliding glass doors. *Perspectives: Choosing and Using Books for the Classroom, 6*(3), 9–12.

Bondy, E., & Ross, D. D. (2008). The teacher as a warm demander. *Educational Leadership, 66*(1), 54–58.

Bondy, E., Ross, D. D., Gallingane, C., & Hambacher, E. (2007). Creating environments of success and resilience: Culturally responsive classroom management and more. *Urban Education, 42*(4), 326–348.

Boykin, A. W., Lilja, A. J., & Tyler, K. M. (2004). The influence of communal vs. individual learning context on the academic performance in social studies of Grades 4–5 African-Americans. *Learning Environments Research, 7*(3), 227–244.

Brown, D. F. (2004). Urban teachers' professed classroom management strategies. *Urban Education, 39*(3), 266–289.

Clark, A., & Fleming, J. (2019). "They almost become the teacher": Pre-K to third grade teachers' experiences reading and discussing culturally relevant texts with their students. *Reading Horizons, 58*(3), 23–51.

Cliatt-Wayman, L. (2018). Push, don't pity, students in poverty. *ASCD Education Update, 60*(1), 3–5.

Coffey, H., & Farinde-Wu, A. (2016). Navigating the journey to culturally responsive teaching: Lessons from the success and struggles of one first-year, Black female teacher of Black students in an urban school. *Teaching and Teacher Education, 60*, 24–33.

Cohen, E. G., & Lotan, R.A. (1995). Producing equal-status interaction in the heterogeneous classroom. *American Educational Research Journal, 32*(1), 99–120.

Cohen, E. G., Lotan, R. A., Scarloss, B. A., & Arellano, A. R. (1999). Complex instruction: Equity in cooperative learning classrooms. *Theory Into Practice, 38*(2), 80–86.

Cothran, D. J., & Ennis, C. D. (2000). Building bridges to student engagement: Communicating respect and care for students in urban high schools. *Journal of Research and Development in Education, 33*(2), 106–117.

Cox, S., & Galda, L. (1990). Multicultural literacy: Mirrors and windows on a global community. *The Reading Teacher, 43*(8), 582–589.

Delpit, L. (1996). *Other people's children: Cultural conflict in the classroom.* New Press.

Delpit, L. (2012). *Multiplication is for White people: Raising expectations for other people's children.* New Press.

DeNicolo, C. P., Yu, M., Crowley, C. B., & Gabel, S. L. (2017). Reimagining critical care and problematizing sense of school belonging as a response to inequality for immigrants and children of immigrants. *Review of Research in Education, 41*(1), 500–530.

Dill, E., & Boykin, A. W. (2000). The comparative influence of individual, peer tutoring, and communal learning contexts on the text recall of African American children. *Journal of Black Psychology, 26*(1), 65–78.

Ebe, A. E. (2010). Culturally relevant texts and reading assessment for English language learners. *Reading Horizons, 50*(3), 193–210.

Ebe, A. E. (2012). Supporting the reading development of middle school English language learners through culturally relevant texts. *Reading & Writing Quarterly, 28*(2), 179–198.

Ebe, A. E. (2015). The power of culturally relevant text: What teachers learn about their emergent bilingual students. In Y. S. Freeman & D. E. Freeman (Eds.), *Research on preparing inservice teacher to work effectively with emergent bilinguals* (Advances in Teaching, Vol. 24, pp. 33–53). Emerald Group Publishing Limited.

Evans, S. (2010). The role of multicultural literature interactive read-alouds on students' perspectives toward diversity. *Journal of Research in Innovative Teaching, 3*(1), 92–104.

Farinde-Wu, A., Glover, C. P., & Williams, N. N. (2017). It's not hard work; It's heart work: Strategies of effective, award-winning culturally responsive teachers. *Urban Review, 49*(2), 279–299.

Feger, M. V. (2006). "I want to read": How culturally relevant texts increase student engagement in reading. *Multicultural Education, 13*(3), 18–19.

Flint, P., Dollar, T., & Stewart, M. A. (2018). Hurdling over language barriers: Building relationships with adolescent newcomers through literacy advancement. *Journal of Adolescent & Adult Literacy, 62*(5), 509–519.

Ford, A. C., & Sassi, K. (2014). Authority in cross-racial teaching and learning (re)considering the transferability of warm demander approaches. *Urban Education, 49*(1), 39–74.

Ford, D. Y. (1996). *Reversing underachievement among gifted Black students: Promising practices and programs.* Teachers College Press.

Garza, C. L. (2000). *In my family/En mi familia.* Children's Book Press.

Gay, G. (2000). *Culturally responsive teaching: Theory, research, and practice.* Routledge.

Gay, G. (2010). *Culturally responsive teaching: Theory, research, and practice* (2nd ed.). Teachers College Press.

Gay, G. (2018). *Culturally responsive teaching: Theory, research, and practice* (3rd ed.). Teachers College Press.

González, N., Moll, L., & Amanti, C. (2005). *Funds of knowledge: Theorizing practices in households, communities, and classrooms.* Erlbaum.

Green, G., Rhodes, J., Hirsch, A. H., Suárez-Orozco, C., & Camic, P. M. (2008). Supportive adult relationships and the academic engagement of Latin American immigrant youth. *Journal of School Psychology, 46*(4), 393–412.

Hamilton, R. (2004). School teachers and education of refugee children. In R. Hamilton & D. Moore (Eds.), *Educational interventions for refugee children: Theoretical perspectives and implementing best practices* (pp. 83–96). RoutledgeFalmer.

Hammond, Z., & Jackson, Y. (2015). *Culturally responsive teaching and the brain: Promoting authentic engagement and rigor among culturally and linguistically diverse students.* Corwin.

Hamre, B., & Pianta, R. (2001). Early teacher-child relationships and the trajectory of children's school outcomes through eighth grade. *Child Development, 72*(2), 625–638.

International Literacy Association. (2018a). *Standards for the preparation of literacy professionals 2017.*

International Literacy Association. (2018b). *The case for children's rights to read.*

Irvine, J. J. (1990). *Black students and school failure: Policies, practices, and prescriptions.* Greenwood Press.

Irvine J. J. (2002). African American teachers' culturally specific pedagogy: The collective stories. In J. J. Irvine (Ed.), *In search of wholeness: African American teachers and their culturally specific classroom practices* (pp. 33–46). Palgrave.

Jimenez, R. T. (1997). The strategic reading abilities and potential of five low-literacy Latina/o readers in middle school. *Reading Research Quarterly, 32*(2), 224–243.

Johnson, G. M. (1994). An ecological framework for conceptualizing educational risk. *Urban Education, 29*(1), 34–49.

Kearney, W. S., Smith, P. A., & Maika, S. (2014). Examining the impact of classroom relationships on student engagement. *Journal of School Public Relations, 35*(1), 80–101.

Krull, K. (2003). *Harvesting hope: The story of Cesar Chavez.* HMH Books for Young Readers.

Laman, T. T., & Henderson, J. W. (2018). Using photography in a culturally responsive curriculum: Invitations to read, write, and think. *The Reading Teacher, 72*(5), 643–647.

Lynch-Brown, C., Tomlinson, C. M., & Short, K. G. (2011). *Essentials of children's literature* (7th ed.). Pearson.

Lysaker, J. T., & Furness, S. (2012). Space for transformation: Relational, dialogic pedagogy. *Journal of Transformative Education, 9*(3), 183–197.

Milner, H. R. (2008). Disrupting deficit notions of difference: Counter-narratives of teachers and community in urban education. *Teaching and Teacher Education, 24*(6), 1573–1598.

Milner, H. R. (2012). Beyond a test score: Explaining opportunity gaps in educational practice. *Journal of Black Studies, 43*(6), 693–718.

Mitchell, A. (1998). African American teachers: Unique roles and universal lessons. *Education and Urban Society, 31*(4), 104–122.

Moll, L. C., Amanti, C., Neff, D., & Gonzalez, N. (1992). Funds of knowledge for teaching: Using a qualitative approach to connect homes and classrooms. *Theory Into Practice, 31*(2), 132–141.

Monroe, C. E., & Obidah, J. E. (2004). The influence of cultural synchronization on a teacher's perceptions of disruption. *Journal of Teacher Education, 55*(3), 256–268.

Montgomery, W. (2001). Creating culturally responsive, inclusive classrooms. *Teaching Exceptional Children, 33*(4), 4–9.

Morganett, L. (2001). Good teacher–student relationships: A key element in classroom motivation and management. *Education, 112*(2), 260–265.

Newberry, M. (2013). Reconsidering differential behaviors: Reflection and teacher judgment when forming classroom relationships. *Teacher Development, 17*(2), 195–213.

Newcomer, S. N. (2018). Investigating the power of authentically caring student–teacher relationships for Latinx students. *Journal of Latinos and Education, 17*(2), 179–193.

Nieto, S. (2000). *Affirming diversity: The sociopolitical context of multicultural education* (3rd ed.). Longman.

Nieto, S. (2010). *The light in their eyes: Creating multicultural learning communities.* Teachers College Press.

Nieto, S., & Bode, P. (2008). *Affirming diversity: The sociopolitical context of multicultural education* (5th ed.). Pearson.

Noddings, N. (1992). *The challenge to care in schools: An alternative approach to education.* Teachers College Press.

Noddings, N. (2001). The caring teacher. In V. Richardson (Ed.), *Handbook of research on teaching* (4th ed., pp. 99–107). American Educational Research Association.

Noddings, N. (2003). Is teaching a practice? *Journal of Philosophy of Education, 37*(2), 241–251.

Noddings, N. (2005). *The challenge to care in schools: An alternative approach to education* (2nd ed.). Teachers College Press.

Powell, R., Cantrell, S. C., Correll, P. K., & Malo-Juvera, V. (2017). *Culturally responsive instruction observation protocol* (4th ed.). Collaborative Center for Literacy Development.

Quin, D. (2017). Longitudinal and contextual associations between teacher-student relationships and student engagement: A systematic review. *Review of Educational Research, 87*(2), 345–387.

Ramkellawan, R., & Bell, J. (2017). Raising the bar: Using coaching conversations to address issues of low expectation for students in urban settings. *The Educational Forum, 81*(4), 377–390.

Robison, T. (2019). Improving classroom management issues through your carefully chosen approaches and prompts. *General Music Today, 32*(3), 20–22.

Rolón-Dow, R. (2005). Critical care: A color(ful) analysis of care narratives in the schooling experiences of Puerto Rican girls. *American Educational Research Journal, 42*(1), 77–111.

Rosenthal, R., & Jacobson, L. F. (1968). Teacher expectations for the disadvantaged. *Scientific American, 218*(4), 19–23.

Rowe, D. W., & Fain, J. G. (2013). The family backpack project: Responding to dual language texts through family journals. *Language Arts, 90*(6), 402–416.

Sanchez, R. M. (2007). Community as a participatory foundation in culturally conscientious classrooms. *Multicultural Education, 15*(1), 50–52.

Schrodt, K., Fain, J. G., & Hasty, M. (2015). Exploring culturally relevant texts with kindergarteners and their families. *The Reading Teacher, 68*(8), 589–598.

Sharma, S. A., & Christ, T. (2017). Five steps toward successful culturally relevant text selection and integration. *The Reading Teacher, 71*(3), 295–307.

Siddle-Walker, E. V., & Snarey, J. R. (Eds.). (2004). *Race-ing moral formation: African American perspectives on care and justice.* Teachers College Press.

Sims, R. (1983). Strong Black girls: A 10-year-old responds to fiction about Afro-Americans. *Journal of Research and Development in Education, 16*(3), 21–28.

Sims-Bishop, R. (1991). Evaluating books by and about African Americans. In M. V. Lindgren (Ed.), *The multicolored mirror: Cultural substance in literature for children and young adults* (pp. 31–34). Highsmith.

Sobel, D. M., & Taylor, S. V. (2015). Supporting novice special education teachers in delivering inclusive, culturally responsive instruction. *Journal of the Association of Special Education, 16*(1), 33–41.

Sorhagen, N. S. (2013). Early teacher expectations disproportionately affect poor children's high school performance. *Journal of Educational Psychology, 105*(2), 465–477.

Stewart, M. A., Babino, A., & Walker, K. (2017). A pedagogy of care for adolescent English learners: A formative experiment. *Tapestry, 8*(1), 1–18.

Stuart, D., & Volk, D. (2002). Collaboration in a culturally responsive literacy pedagogy: Educating teachers and Latino children. *Reading, 36*(3), 127–134.

Suárez-Orozco, C., Pimentel, A., & Martin, M, (2009). The significance of relationships: Academic engagement and achievement among newcomer immigrant youth. *Teachers College Record, 11*(3), 712–749.

Thomas, K. L. (2019). Building literacy environments to motivate African American boys to read. *The Reading Teacher, 72*(6), 761–765.

Thompson, A. (2004). Caring and colortalk: Childhood innocence in White and Black. In V. Siddle-Walker & J. R. Snarey (Eds.). *Race-ing moral formation: African American perspectives on care and justice* (pp. 23–37). Teachers College Press.

Thompson, C. S. (2018). The construct of 'respect' in teacher-student relationships: Exploring dimensions of ethics of care and sustainable development. *Journal of Leadership Education, 17*(3), 42–60.

Valenzuela, A. (1999). *Subtractive schooling: U.S.–Mexican youth and the politics of caring.* State University of New York Press.

Walters, T. S. (1998). *The language of a literate classroom: Rethinking comprehension dimensions* (ED418430). ERIC. https://files.eric.ed.gov/fulltext/ED418430.pdf

Ware, F. (2006). Warm demander pedagogy: Culturally responsive teaching that supports a culture of achievement for African American students. *Urban Education, 41*(4), 427–456.

Walker, K. L. (2011). Deficit thinking and the effective teacher. *Education and Urban Society, 43*(5), 576–597.

Weiner, L. (2006, September). Challenging deficit thinking. *Educational Leadership, 64*, 42–45.

Weinstein, C. S., Curran, M., & Tomlinson-Clarke, S. (2003). Culturally responsive classroom management: Awareness into action. *Theory Into Practice, 42*(4), 269–276.

Weinstein, C.S., Tomlinson-Clarke, S., & Curran, M. (2004). Toward a conception of culturally responsive classroom management. *Journal of Teacher Education, 55*(1), 25–38.

Wood, S., & Jocius, R. (2013). Combating "I hate this stupid book!" Black male and critical literacy. *The Reading Teacher, 66*(8), 661–669.

Yoon, V. (2007). Classroom teachers' understanding of the needs of English-language learners and the influence on the students' identities. *The New Educator, 3*(3), 221–240.

Zhang-Wu, Q. (2017). Culturally and linguistically responsive teaching in practice: A case study of a fourth-grade mainstream classroom teacher. *Journal of Education, 197*(1), 33–40.

Zygmunt, E., Clark, P., Tancock, S., Mucherah, W., & Clausen, J. (2015). Books like me: Engaging the community in the intentional selection of culturally relevant children's literature. *Childhood Education, 91*(1), 24–34.

CHAPTER 2

It Takes a Village to Teach a Child: Family Collaboration as an Essential Component of Culturally Responsive Instruction

Kristen H. Perry

WHEN I BEGAN this chapter on family collaboration, the world was several months into the COVID-19 pandemic. Teachers throughout the United States scrambled to convert the remaining months of the 2019–2020 school year into distance learning and to do their best to meet the needs of learners who were suddenly learning from home. It is now mid-July 2020, and the pandemic is still raging. School districts throughout the United States are grappling with decisions about how to begin the next school year as infection rates for the novel coronavirus skyrocket again.

The pandemic brought family collaboration into sharp focus for me, as I simultaneously coached teachers whose entire framework for teaching was unexpectedly shifted and also became the primary education provider for my own son, who was in his final months of kindergarten. While the pandemic has wrought havoc on our educational system, it also has provided an unprecedented opportunity for family collaboration. The sudden shift to distance learning has provided unique insights into students' families and their lives at home, and it has also forced teachers to think creatively about how they can use students' families and homes as resources—often the *only* resources available—for supporting learning.

What Is Family Collaboration?

Family collaboration in education has gone by many names, including *parental involvement, parent engagement,* and *family–school partnerships. Parental involvement* is not operationalized in clear and consistent ways (Fan & Chen, 2001) and "can mean countless different things to different people" (Jeynes, 2003, p. 204). In fact, parental involvement's definition is codified in law: "The participation of parents in regular, two-way, and meaningful communication, involving student learning and other school activities" (USCS 7801 (32)), but this can be broadly interpreted. Part of the challenge in defining parental involvement is that it is a complex and multifaceted construct (Hill & Tyson, 2009) that "subsumes a wide variety of parental behavioral patterns and parenting practices" (Fan & Chen, 2001, p. 3), such as providing breakfast, volunteering in the school, helping with homework, or joining the parent–teacher association. Moreover, the understanding of "parent" involvement has expanded to involve other significant caregivers, such as stepparents, grandparents, foster parents, and other important people in learners' lives (Kim et al., 2012).

Although parents are not the only ones who make significant investments in supporting education in children and youth (e.g., Anderson et al., 2010; Hannon, 1999; Perry, 2010), traditional parent involvement models place a great burden on caregivers, expecting them to behave in certain ways or carry out plans that are drawn up by educators. In other words, traditional parental involvement models tend to adopt top-down, one-way models of communication between schools, teachers, and families. In contrast, true family–school partnerships emphasize bidirectional communication and collaborative relationships between schools, families, and other stakeholders (Kim et al., 2012; Price-Mitchell, 2009). True partnerships not only emphasize the ways in which caregivers can support learners at home, but they also work to enhance relationships between schools and families (Harry, 2008). As Price-Mitchell (2009) observed, emphasizing *partnerships* instead of *involvement* highlights "the importance of parents' active power-sharing role as citizens of the education community rather than people who participate only when invited" (2009, p. 13).

How Does Family Collaboration Align With Culturally Responsive Instruction?

Family collaboration, as operationalized in the Culturally Responsive Instruction Observation Protocol (CRIOP) model, involves four elements: (1) establishing equitable partnerships with families, (2) reaching out to families in nontraditional ways, (3) encouraging family involvement, and (4) learning about and using families' funds of knowledge. Whether the term *culturally relevant pedagogy* (Ladson-Billings, 1995), *culturally responsive teaching* (Gay, 2002), or *culturally sustaining pedagogy* (Paris, 2012) is used, the concept involves using

the cultural characteristics, experiences, and perspectives of ethnically diverse students as conduits for teaching them more effectively. It is based
on the assumption that when academic knowledge and skills are situated
within the lived experiences and frames of reference of students, they are
more personally meaningful, have higher interest appeal, and are learned
more easily and thoroughly. (Gay, 2002, p. 106)

Gay noted that culturally responsive teachers engage students' cultural knowledge, experiences, and perspectives; in so doing, they also validate every student's culture while simultaneously bridging gaps between home and school (Aronson & Laughter, 2016). Such teaching requires teachers to have *cultural competence*, including the ability to help students navigate between home and school (Ladson-Billings, 1995). Building on the work of Ladson-Billings and Gay, Paris (2012) insisted that educators also need to *sustain* the linguistic and cultural competence of their communities. Family collaboration is an essential cornerstone of culturally responsive or sustaining teaching. Teachers—particularly those whose backgrounds differ from that of their students— cannot possibly use students' cultures and experiences as a foundation for learning if they do not have knowledge of those cultures and experiences.

Research consistently shows that families from a variety of backgrounds value education, yet families also "vary widely in their assumptions about schooling and the roles that they play in supporting children's school learning" (Manyak & Dantas, 2010, p. 2). Manyak and Dantas (2010) noted that these differences can, at best, be confusing to teachers and, at worst, lead to negative assumptions about families and learners that seriously impact teaching and learning. For example, culturally and linguistically diverse (CLD) parents often have traditions of deference to authority that might disempower them and over-privilege teachers' knowledge above caregivers' knowledge of learners (Harry, 2008). Similarly, Edwards and Turner (2010) argued that "when teachers and schools act out of sociocultural assumptions that devalue the contributions of poorer, less-educated families, use educational jargon that deepens the communication divide, or they ignore or disparage important economic, cultural, and language differences" (p. 139), they send a message to parents that they are not welcome. Such racist, classist, or xenophobic assumptions hinder the development of equitable partnerships with families and have real impacts on learners' academic, social, emotional, and identity development.

What Does the Literature Tell Us About Family Collaboration?

The wide body of research into parent involvement, family collaboration, and family–school partnerships can be confusing and, at times, conflicting, due to a variety of factors. As I have already noted, the construct of family collaboration is complex and multifaceted (Price-Mitchell, 2009), without clear differentiation between family collaboration, parent involvement, and similar constructs (Kim et al., 2012). Educators and researchers sometimes conflate concepts like *parental involvement, family collaboration*, or *family literacy*—constructs that assume that adults are involved in children's educational development in some way—with *programs*, which are school-sponsored initiatives designed to encourage or even compel parental/family participation in education (Anderson et al., 2010; Jeynes, 2012).

Miano (2011) observed that research and professional literature dedicated to parental involvement and family collaboration can be categorized into three general strands. The *prescriptive strand* focuses upon providing advice to teachers on working with parents and families. This strand privileges perspectives of White, middle-class, and affluent communities and reinforces deficit thinking about populations that do not align with White middle-class norms. This strand "has assumed that parents should serve schools but not necessarily vice versa" (Miano, 2011, p. 30). The *quantitative strand*, also grounded in the same normative assumptions, attempts to identify and quantify particular variables—frequently those that align with White, socioeconomically privileged behaviors—that might predict which parent behaviors or traits lead to better academic outcomes in children. Finally, the *interpretive strand*, which is grounded in qualitative perspectives, investigates parents' and families' "actual practices and perspectives" (Miano, 2011, p. 31), with a particular focus on families that represent more ethnically, socially, culturally, economically, and linguistically diverse backgrounds than does the literature in the prescriptive or quantitative strands.

The Academic Impact of Family Collaboration

Regardless of whether studies examine parents and their behaviors, beliefs, and dispositions, or focus on the effect of programs, research into the impact of parental involvement and family-school partnerships on children's learning and academic achievement tends to fall squarely into Miano's (2011) *quantitative strand*.

Quantitative studies tend to find that parental involvement has a positive impact on learners' academic achievement across K–12 grade levels, as well as across racial/ethnic and socioeconomic groups (e.g., Hill & Tyson 2009; Jeynes, 2003). For example, when looking at a variety of parental involvement components, including parents communicating with their children, checking homework, doing outside reading, and participating in school functions, Jeynes (2003) found that involvement positively impacted a variety of types of academic achievement, such as standardized test scores and grade point average (GPA). Although these effects held for all racial groups, parental involvement seemed to benefit Black and Latinx learners more than it did Asian Americans. In a follow-up study that compared general parental involvement with specific types, such as communication, homework help, parental expectations, reading to children, attendance and participation in school events, and parenting style, Jeynes (2005) found that nearly every type of involvement yielded statistically significant positive outcomes. Jeynes concluded that "parental involvement enjoys an influence that largely transcends differences in SES [socioeconomic status], race, and other issues" (2005, p. 259). Observing that middle school marks a shift in the amount and nature of parental involvement, as emergent adolescents begin to develop and assert more independence, Hill and Tyson (2009) focused specifically on parental involvement for middle school students. They found that general parental involvement supported academic achievement for middle schoolers, but this association was stronger for White families than it was for Black families.

A number of studies have found that parent involvement with learners' homework, in contrast to other behaviors and dispositions, has an inverse relationship with achievement (e.g., Hill & Tyson, 2009; Jeynes, 2005). In other words, more help with homework tends to correlate with *lower* academic achievement. This negative relationship between homework help and academic achievement might be explained by the fact that, particularly as learners get older, parents are more likely to monitor and provide support for homework only when learners struggle academically—academically successful students may need less help with homework (Hill & Tyson, 2009; Jeynes, 2005). Other researchers, however, argue that parents' attitudes about homework are often culturally driven; Lee and Bowen (2006) noted that Black and Latinx families tend to highly value homework help as a way of supporting their children's schooling, regardless of their children's actual achievement.

Researchers also analyzed programs designed specifically to encourage or require parents' involvement in children's education. Jeynes (2012), for example, conducted a meta-analysis of 51 studies of involvement programs, looking at whether they promoted parental shared reading with children, partnership with schools, homework checking, or communication. As with parental involvement in general, programs targeted at increasing parental involvement had an impact on students' academic success from prekindergarten through 12th grade, although these outcomes were stronger for standardized test scores than they were for things such as GPA. Shared reading had the strongest effect on achievement, followed by programs that emphasized partnerships and communication. However, Jeynes also noted that the majority of the studies in his meta-analysis had been at the elementary level. Whereas Jeynes argued that parental involvement programs, particularly those related to shared reading, are consistently related to higher educational achievement outcomes, Van Steensel and his colleagues' (2011) meta-analysis of involvement programs did not support this finding. They examined programs that trained parents in literacy-related activities they could carry out at home and found that these programs had very small effect sizes and made only a "modest contribution to children's literacy skills" (Van Steesel et al., 2011, p. 87).

What can we take away from such contradictory findings? It appears that parental involvement, as well as programs designed to enhance parental involvement, do have an impact on students' learning and academic achievement, particularly when we take a "big picture" view of the research. However, findings for various groups of students are less clear; some studies show that parental involvement advantages White children, while others show advantages for children of color. Others suggest that the type or nature of parental involvement may matter and that the type of involvement that matters may shift as learners grow older. Nevertheless, encouraging family involvement may produce positive outcomes for students.

Is Parent Involvement Research Culturally Responsive?

Writing specifically about family literacy programs, Anderson and his colleagues (2010) noted that, despite assumptions that parental involvement in education is a no-brainer (Sheldon, 2002), family programs are controversial because many are built on deficit discourses related to families. Indeed, such critiques have been around for more than two decades (e.g., Hannon, 1999). Price-Mitchell (2009) noted that the initial creation of parent involvement programs—really, parent *education* programs—was grounded in racism, as they were seen as "a necessary way of helping immigrant and indigent families assimilate into middle-class society, adopting the values and attitudes of the prevailing culture" (p. 11). Whitehouse and Colvin (2001) pointed out that many family literacy and parent involvement programs remain grounded in similar deficit notions of families. In an analysis of the websites of Canadian family literacy programs, Anderson and his colleagues (2008) observed that programs tended to assume that parents "need to be taught to value and promote literacy" (p. 67), despite a rich body of research evidence showing that parents, in fact, *do* value and promote literacy (e.g., Lewis, 2014; Miano, 2011; Perry, 2009; Purcell-Gates, 1996). Family literacy and other parent involvement programs have been critiqued for ignoring the rich and meaningful educational practices occurring in homes and communities and instead imposing school-based practices on CLD families (Anderson et al., 2008, 2010). Research has consistently found that "although families imported literacy practices from school, the traffic was one-way and there was very little evidence of the school taking up literacy practices from the home" (Anderson et al., 2010, p. 48).

As an illustrative example of these critiques, I share one family literacy intervention designed to support parents in children's early learning. In this study, Steiner (2014) taught techniques for building home–school partnerships to families in an urban district that served high-poverty CLD learners. Parents in the experimental group were taught about storybook reading, effective read-aloud strategies, and ways to engage children in responses to books. Books selected for the program were chosen to connect to school topics. The study's results showed that parents in the experimental group more frequently read storybooks to their children and also had "increased use of 'school-like' literacy practices, including greater use of effective storybook reading strategies, to talk about storybooks" (Steiner, 2014, p. 719). While this program was successful in increasing particular reading strategies in the home, it also clearly reflected Miano's (2011) critique of prescriptive programs that assume that parents' function is to serve the purpose of schools. This intervention also operated on deficit assumptions that CLD families in high-poverty school districts need to be explicitly taught how to read to their children properly, without consideration of ways to build on meaningful family literacy practices that may already have been occurring.

A study by O'Brien and her colleagues (2014) illustrated ways that family literacy programs could mitigate some of these pitfalls. The researchers wanted to support the English vocabulary knowledge of preK through third-grade English learners living in poverty. Like Steiner's study, O'Brien and her colleagues explicitly taught parents strategies while also supporting parents' own English development. The researchers placed emphasis on authentic literacy events that engaged children in activities already situated within families' everyday lives. Additionally, half of the time in the program was devoted to reading and writing texts of interest to the *adults* in the family; the texts were "timely and consequential, typically chosen by parents in response to interest in or questions about current events in their neighborhoods or communities, in response to their children's schools, or information about their homelands and cultural groups" (O'Brien et al., 2014, p. 392). All children in the program demonstrated substantial language and literacy growth, and the effect was particularly strong for children with the lowest pretest scores. This study shows that one way to make otherwise prescriptive family involvement programs more culturally responsive is to involve families in determining some of the program's content, as well as grounding program activities in everyday experiences rather than privileging school-based practices only.

Families' Social and Cultural Capital

For the past 20 years, educators have been exhorted to ensure that their decision-making is "data-driven" and "research-based." These educational buzzwords and their related statistics highlight the privileging of human capital approaches in education. Understanding the true impact of various family collaboration efforts requires considering social and cultural capital (St. Clair, 2008). *Human capital* approaches tend to prioritize the measurement of concrete skills; they emphasize standardized levels, test scores, and credentials such as a diploma—common components of "achievement." In contrast, *social capital* refers to social relationships and networks (Lee & Bowen, 2006; St. Clair, 2008) and "channels of com munication that help people identify the human and material resources they need, as well as share and carry information or attitudes from one setting to another" (Sheldon, 2002, p. 304). *Cultural capital* (Bourdieu & Passeron, 1990) similarly represents knowledge, behaviors, and skills that individuals can draw on to demonstrate their competence in various areas. Parents' cultural capital related to education exists in three forms: "Personal dispositions, attitudes, and knowledge gained from experience; connections to education-related objects (e.g., books, computers, academic credentials); and connections to education-related institutions (e.g., schools, universities, libraries)" (Lee & Bowen, 2006, p. 197).

St. Clair (2008) offered a fascinating example of the ways in which an over-dependence on numerical data can obscure real benefits. He reviewed the First Lady's Family Literacy

Initiative for Texas (FLFLIT) using both human capital and social capital lenses. When quantitative data were analyzed through a human capital lens, the programs appeared to be failing: Only 38% of the reviewed programs managed to meet objectives, such as increasing reading levels. However, when viewed through a social capital lens, the programs appeared to be very successful. Qualitative analyses of interviews and surveys showed that the programs built important relationships that "support the formation of learning communities, with older children, volunteers, parents, teachers, and younger children all learning from each other" (St. Clair, 2008, p. 90). In other words, focusing on relationships within family literacy programs was just as important as focusing on skills and academic achievement for fostering positive educational outcomes. Miano's (2011) qualitative study of Latina mothers supports St. Clair's conclusion. Mothers in her study communicated with school officials and each other, "essentially networking in order to grasp the lay of the land, to read the world of the U.S. educational system" and of the school their children attended (Miano, 2011, p. 36). Teachers, however, were largely oblivious to this network.

Other research has investigated aspects of social and cultural capital in family collaboration. Sheldon's (2002) survey-based study looked at parents' educational involvement at home and at school to see how their social networks might predict involvement. Families' social contexts mattered: White mothers and mothers of color had similar levels of parental involvement at home, but White parents reported significantly more involvement at school. Parents' social networks also mattered, in terms of both size and who was in the network. Parents whose networks involved mostly parents at the same school tended to be more involved at the school, while parents whose networks included others (e.g., relatives, educators, parents at *other* schools) tended to be more involved at home. "Social networks," Sheldon concluded, "may be associated with norms about becoming involved and helping the school" (2002, p. 312). Lee and Bowen (2006) looked at types of cultural capital to understand how they impacted parent involvement. School-based involvement occurred most often for parents whose culture was most similar to the school's culture—families who were White, were more affluent, and had higher parental educational attainment. Parents' awareness of racism also made it less likely that they would be involved at school but more likely that they would be involved at home. The researchers concluded that parents who were Black, Latinx, low-income, or less educated experienced cultural disadvantages that caused barriers to their being present at school. Such differences in cultural capital also might reduce parents' ability to obtain social capital from the school, even when they could be present.

Families' Funds of Knowledge

The theory of *funds of knowledge,* which originated from collaborative work between Luis Moll (an educational psychologist), Norma González (an anthropologist), and local teachers in Arizona, also represents a cornerstone of culturally responsive instruction and family collaboration. Funds of knowledge are the "historically developed and accumulated strategies (skills, abilities, ideas, practices) or bodies of knowledge that are essential to a household's functioning and well-being" (González et al., 1995, pp. 446–447). Importantly, this theory grew out of work with frequently marginalized communities—those that are often the target of deficit assumptions by educators. As the authors described,

> a critical assumption in our work is that educational institutions have stripped away the view of working-class minority students as emerging from households rich in social and intellectual resources. Rather than focusing on the knowledge these students bring to school and using it as a foundation for learning, the emphasis has been on what these students lack in terms of the forms of language and knowledge sanctioned by the schools. This emphasis on 'disadvantages' has provided justification for lowered expectations in schools and inaccurate portrayals of the children and their families. (González et al., 1995, p. 445)

They also pushed back against common and misleading notions of culture in schools that tend to center upon the "four Fs"—food, fashion, festivals, and folklore, or what González and her colleagues described as "a static grab bag of tamales, quinceaneras and cinco de mayo celebrations" (1995, p. 456). Instead, these researchers focused on the everyday lived experiences and practices of learners and their families—what families *do*—and the ways in which families' social networks facilitated the exchange of funds of knowledge.

The funds of knowledge perspective provides teachers with techniques for learning about and incorporating funds of knowledge in their teaching. Teachers involved in the initial funds of knowledge project engaged in specific practices that enabled them to learn about the funds of knowledge of students' families and connect them to the academic curriculum in deeply meaningful ways. Family visits represented one of the most important techniques. Unlike traditional home visits, in which school representatives enter homes to provide information or services, the purpose of these visits was for teachers to identify and document knowledge that existed in students' homes and communities. In other words, teachers entered families' homes as *learners* rather than as *experts*. One participating teacher noted, "Can you imagine what kind of subtle message comes across when someone comes into your home to *teach* you something?" (González et al., 1995, p. 458). This important shift in teachers' stance also altered power dynamics in important ways, supported stronger relationships between parents and teachers, and afforded parents with increased access to schools and an increased sense of themselves as "agents capable of changing their child's educational experiences" (González et al., 1995, p. 467).

Once teachers gathered information about families' funds of knowledge, they brought that knowledge into the classroom. González (2005), however, cautioned that

> the purpose of drawing on student experience with household knowledge is not merely to reproduce household knowledge in the classroom. Working-class students are not being taught construction, plumbing, or

gardening. Instead, by drawing on household knowledge, student experience is legitimated as valid, and classroom practice can build on the familiar
knowledge bases that students can manipulate to enhance learning in mathematics, social studies, language arts, and other content areas. (p. 43)

Others have also cautioned that simply recognizing and incorporating families'
knowledge, skills and resources are not enough; rather, educators need to expand on
them (Anderson et al., 2010; Rodriguez-Brown, 2004).

Drawing on other ethnographic perspectives that highlight social and cultural resources (e.g., Barton & Hamilton, 1998; Lave & Wenger, 1991; Rogoff, 2003; Scribner
& Cole, 1981), a wide body of mostly qualitative research has documented the rich and
meaningful funds of knowledge of a diverse array of families. There are too many studies
for me to elaborate here, but I will share a few. Purcell-Gates (1996) studied the home
literacy practices of 20 low-income families with young children, expecting that families would use funds of knowledge as resources for engaging their young children in
literacy. Indeed, she found that these parents engaged their children in a wide range of
everyday literacy practices, and regardless of the parents' own literacy level, they began
or increased their literacy involvement when children began formal schooling.

My own research (Perry, 2009, 2014) investigated Sudanese refugee families with
young children. Parents in these families had achieved a range of educational levels, and
while their English proficiency levels varied, all were literate in Arabic as well as various
Sudanese local languages. These families engaged their children in a wide range of literate
practices in both English and Arabic. Importantly, learning was multidirectional in these
families: Parents served as resources for their children, but children also provided a great
deal of *literacy brokering* for their families across cultural and institutional contexts.
Children were often the primary intermediaries in written exchanges between their
parents and schools, as they provided important knowledge about textual genres that
the parents may have been unfamiliar with, such as permission slips or school year-
books. The children's explanations helped their parents focus on which texts were more
important, as well as alerting them to what they were supposed to do with the text.
Indeed, while teachers tended to view the kindergarten and first-grade children as only
"emergent" readers, their parents viewed them not just as competent but also as experts
who held knowledge that the parents did not.

Lewis Ellison has documented digital literacies and technology use in Black families
with middle school students (e.g., Lewis, 2014; Lewis Ellison & Tolliver, 2018). One study
(Lewis, 2014) showed how digital technologies played an important role for a Black mother
and her son who engaged in joint blogging as a family practice. In another study, Lewis
Ellison and Tolliver (2018) documented the process as a Black middle-class family worked
together to create Christmas ball lights based on instructions found online. Each member of the family took a different role in the activity based on their expertise and interest,
and all were integral in completing the project successfully. This work purposefully

focuses on middle-class Black families as a way to counter deficit stereotypes about Black families, and Lewis (2014) also exhorts teachers to expand their notions of family support for education: "Educators too often perceive parental engagement too narrowly, and consequently might miss ways parents strive to grow their children as students" (p. 79).

In a study that focused on mathematics in families with middle school students, Goldman and Booker (2009) documented the ways in which mathematics was infused in families' daily lives and the ways in which parents informally supported the development of mathematical thinking. The researchers presented cases of three families, each focusing on a different set of events that were rich in mathematics: a mother and daughter budgeting expenses for the prom, a sports-fan family tracking game and player statistics in baseball, and another family planning the best public transportation route to a new school that would optimize both time and money. As the authors noted,

> family members set goals, plan, create budgets, and do forecasting and reconciling of budgets and expenses. They make decisions after weighing all of the variables, dabble in statistics, and optimize. They think conceptually and logically, demonstrate flexibility and adaptability, search for patterns and discrepancies, develop strategies, use approximation, estimation, and make decisions based on priorities, multiple conditions, and variables. (Goldman & Booker, 2009, p. 383)

Goldman and Booker's study shows that everyday familial activities and funds of knowledge are rich with the kinds of mathematical and scientific thinking expected in academic contexts.

Family Collaboration: From Research to Practice

In this section, I share techniques that teachers and schools can use to enhance family collaboration in two broad categories: (1) learning from and developing equitable relationships with families and (2) integrating family collaboration into the classroom and the curriculum. Broad principles across both categories can guide educators as they seek to enhance family collaboration.

First, it is important to broaden our definitions of *family*. Too often, educators' concept of family is narrowly defined based on White middle-class understandings of nuclear families—or even limited to thinking about family as individuals who live in the same household (Edwards & Turner, 2010; Perry, 2010). In their work with Black parents, Edwards and Turner (2010) showed that a wide range of caregivers were involved in a learner's education, including two-parent families, single-parent families, and grandparents. They argued that "the expanded nuclear family is a common cultural practice in many African American families, and should be viewed as a cultural tradition rather than as an indication that something is 'wrong' with the nuclear African American family" (Edwards & Turner, 2010, p. 152). The Sudanese youth and families who participated in my research (Perry, 2009, 2010, 2014) tended to define *family* even more broadly, including *fictive kin* such as "aunties," "cousins," or neighbors who were not related to the family through birth, marriage, or adoption but who nevertheless played an important role in the family's functioning, survival, and educational development (Perry, 2010). Edwards (2016) also advocated for thinking quite broadly about types of families, including unwed teenage parents, adoptive families, foster families, families with same-sex parents, single-parent families, and families in which grandparents, aunts, uncles, older siblings, cousins, or other kin act in the parental role. Similarly, she encouraged teachers to consider other factors that may impact family collaboration, such as parents who are unemployed, working multiple jobs, incarcerated, low-literate, or not yet fluent in English.

Second, it is important to be aware of and push back against generalizations of particular family structures or cultural or linguistic groups. Knowing that Black learners are more likely to have expanded nuclear families, for example, does not mean that *all* Black families have access to extended family members. As Dantas and Coleman (2010) observed, "each student is an individual independently of being Hispanic, African-American, Caucasian, and generalizations carry the risk of 'boxing' students together" (p. 173). Knowing ways in which CLD communities may differ from each other in meaningful ways is essential; it is equally essential to get to know each child and family in its own right.

Learning From and Developing Equitable Relationships With Families

Before teachers can develop equitable partnerships, and before any other elements of family collaboration can successfully be implemented, teachers must get to know and learn from the specific families with whom they work. Learning from families requires that teachers adopt a stance that often feels fairly foreign—that of a learner rather than an expert (Anderson et al., 2015; Compton-Lilly, 2009; Longwell-Grice & McIntyre, 2006; McIntyre, 2010; McIntyre et al., 2001). Especially when teachers are working with students whose families are different from theirs in meaningful ways, they must approach families with humility, based on an understanding that their current knowledge of families is likely to be quite limited and colored by unexamined stereotypes and biases. For McIntyre and her colleagues (2001), adopting this stance meant that teachers had to "erase assumptions about who we thought [families] were and how they should live" (p. 269). Edwards (2016) also advocated for thinking about *differentiated parenting*—a recognition that parents' perspectives, beliefs, practices, and abilities differ from each other, particularly with respect to school. Just as teachers differentiate instruction for learners, teachers should also ensure that tasks and activities expected of parents are also *parentally appropriate* to be compatible with their existing abilities.

A variety of practices can help teachers learn about families in authentic ways. Teachers can interview or conduct focus groups with learners, parents, or other key family members (Compton-Lilly, 2009; Edwards & Turner, 2010; González et al., 1995; Perry, 2010). Traditional home visits can be reconceptualized to be conducted in more effective ways (Compton-Lilly, 2009; Longwell-Grice & McIntyre, 2006; Manyak & Dantas, 2010; McIntyre, 2010; McIntyre et al., 2001). Teachers also can collaborate with diverse community organizations that are deeply involved with families, as well as participate in student- or parent-led tours of the local community (Allen, 2010; Compton-Lilly, 2009). Of course, not all families will respond to every opportunity; offering repeated invitations and different ways for families to interact is essential (Allen, 2010). Ensuring that opportunities are accessible to parents who may be low-literate, have limited English proficiency, or have other barriers is particularly important in efforts to build mutual and trusting relationships (Allen, 2010; Edwards, 2016; Perry, 2014).

Family Visits

Many teachers are already familiar with traditional home visits and may even conduct them, perhaps at the start of the school year as an effort to connect with families and provide important information. Getting to know families and building equitable relationships with parents, however, requires a rethinking of the traditional home visit. In line with McIntyre (2010), I recommend the term *family visit* instead of *home visit*, because many families hold negative associations with home visits since these are often conducted by social services and can have judgmental or even punitive implications. Schools typically view home visits as opportunities for teachers to provide important information and for parents to ask questions; in other words, home visits position teachers/schools as experts and parents as recipients of information. Family visits, or what González and her colleagues (1995) termed *research visits*, instead position parents and families as experts and teachers as the recipients of information (Dantas & Coleman, 2010; González, 2005; González et al., 1995; McIntyre et al., 2001; Perry, 2010). Importantly, taking a stance as a learner rather than an expert does not mean that teachers withhold information; teachers should provide information *if* it is requested (McIntyre et al., 2001), because this helps build trust and potentially empowers families within the educational system.

Because teachers are often different from students and their families in terms of race/ethnicity, family structure, culture, home language, or SES, family visits can inadvertently reinforce teachers' or parents' stereotypes or distrust of each other (Dantas & Coleman, 2010; McIntyre, 2010; McIntyre et al., 2001). Dantas and Coleman (2010) explained that *frame clashes*, or "a disruption of what one counts as the 'normal' or taken-for-granted ways to participate in social interactions" (p. 157), can occur. If not examined, these can lead to misunderstandings, stereotyping, or even potentially disastrous decisions for a student or their family. A teacher who is alert to difference, is mindful of their unconscious biases, and adopts a learning stance is more likely to turn such frame clashes into *rich points*, when "one's definition or assumptions about how things 'should' take place is challenged and thus creates the opportunity for new understanding" (2010, p. 163). Teachers should be willing to be visited by families, because it is unreasonable to expect families to be open without teachers' willingness to share the same kinds of information (McIntyre, 2001).

What does an effective family visit look like? Apart from teachers adopting a learning stance, no two approaches are exactly alike, and a variety of techniques can be effective. In their work with teachers on families' funds of knowledge, González and Moll (González et al., 1995; González et al., 2005) encouraged teachers to select two to three families in their classrooms and to visit each family at least three times. In contrast, McIntyre (2001) and the teachers she worked with attempted to visit every child in their classrooms once. Length of individual visits also can vary greatly, depending on schedules and families' comfort with welcoming outsiders into their homes. McIntyre and her colleagues (2001) suggested letting families be the guide to visit length, which may mean that teachers need to be particularly attuned to nonverbal and other contextual cues from families. Teachers should plan for a visit of about an hour, although in my experience with coaching teachers through family visits, teachers often underestimate the amount of time they will end up spending with a family—they may even find that their visit turns into an extended neighborhood picnic, as it did for one teacher I worked with! For many families, offering hospitality in the form of refreshments or a full meal is an important cultural practice, and teachers should be prepared to accept this hospitality (as far as their own dietary restrictions allow, of course). Bringing treats, small gifts, or even pizza to a family visit is a helpful way to build relationships as well as to thank families for the gift of their time.

Figure 2.1. *Family visits are an opportunity to build relationships with families and learn about their funds of knowledge.*

Family visits typically involve some kind of interviewing, and experts recommend that teachers attempt to interview both adults and children in the family. Including others in these conversations who may be meaningfully involved in the family's life on a regular basis, such as extended kin or neighbors, can provide a fuller understanding of the family (Perry, 2010). Teachers should come prepared with questions or topics for discussion (see Table 2.1 on the following page for suggestions), although these interviews tend to be more successful when they are less formal and more conversational in nature (Dantas & Coleman, 2010; González et al., 1995; McIntyre et al., 2001; Perry, 2010). To learn about funds of knowledge, González and her colleagues (1995) suggested asking about topics such as the family's history, networks, educational experiences, labor history, language use, and child-rearing ideologies. McIntyre and her colleagues (2001) recommended inquiring about children's daily routines and literacy habits, as well as what families enjoy doing recreationally, while I advocated for asking about community connections and access to resources such as faith communities, tutoring, community organizations, or social services (Perry, 2010). Conducting more than one visit with the same family will, of course, allow for exploration of a broader variety of topics, as well as greater depth into those topics. Multiple visits may not be logistically possible for most teachers, so it is important to prioritize discussion topics with a clear interview plan prior to the visit. If families are comfortable, interviews and discussions can be recorded and transcribed for later reference. McIntyre and her colleagues (2001) always provided families with a copy of the transcript: "This is always exciting and interesting to them as they then have a history of their families" (p. 270).

Teachers can also use the family visit as an opportunity to observe the home and community environment with an eye to learning about funds of knowledge and cultural capital. Using family artifacts, such as photos, pets, or special objects in the household, or asking families to create a family tree or draw a picture of who they consider to be family, can spark rich discussions (McIntyre et al., 2001; Perry, 2010). Important insights into learners can come from education-related cultural capital such as books, magazines, or other texts that adults and children might access; desktop or laptop computers, tablets, or smartphones; or educational materials, such as flashcards, workbooks, or writing or art supplies.

Alternatives to Family Visits

Families may not be comfortable having teachers visit them in their homes, for a variety of reasons (Dantas & Coleman, 2010; McIntyre et al., 2001). Families living in poverty may feel embarrassed about their living situations, while undocumented immigrants may worry that a visit could inadvertently lead to deportation. Family visits can be conducted in parks, playgrounds, community centers, public libraries, or restaurants—another advantage of referring to them as *family visits* instead of *home visits*. Offering alternative locations to families, as well as empowering families to choose the location that is most comfortable and convenient to them, is an important element in building trusting and equitable

Table 2.1. *Questions to Support Learning From Families*

Funds of knowledge (*adapted from González et al., 2005*)	• What is your family's history in this area? • What kinds of jobs have people in your family held? • What does daily life look like in your home? What activities and responsibilities do family members have? What are important routines? • What do people in your family do for fun? What interests or hobbies do you have? • What are important values and traditions for your family?
Family and community resources (*adapted from Perry, 2010*)	• Who counts as your family? Who lives in your home? • Who else plays an important role in your family's life? How are they involved in your family? • Who provides homework help? • What languages do people in your family speak? Which languages can they read and write? • What educational resources do you have access to (e.g., computer, internet, library, tutoring, etc.)?
Family experiences with education (*adapted from Edwards & Turner, 2010, and Perry, 2010*)	• What have you liked about your children's experiences in school? What do you wish could be done differently? • How have teachers treated you and your children? How do you think being _______ [Black, Latinx, an English learner, etc.] has impacted your experiences with teachers? • What would you like teachers to know about raising or teaching children who are _______? • How can teachers build a stronger relationship with you and your child?

relationships with families (Edwards & Turner, 2010). Many teachers also find it valuable to spend time in the communities they serve, perhaps attending religious services or ceremonies, students' ball games, festivals, or picnics (McIntyre, 2010; Perry, 2010). Some teachers I worked with made it a point to attend one special event for each child in their classes, allowing the child to choose what that event might be. Outside-the-home family visits offer the added benefit of interaction with extended family, friends, and neighbors who may be important in the learner's life. In Classroom Scenario 2.1, Elisabeth Darce shares the many ways she learns from the families of her students.

Classroom Scenario 2.1.:
Creating a Collaborative Relationship With Families
Elisabeth Darce

I teach kindergarten at a neighborhood school. Many of my students' parents and grandparents grew up attending this same school. Each year, however, our student population continues to grow through an influx of English learners (ELs), including refugee students and their families. I began to recognize that many of my EL students were having a hard time making connections between what they already knew while speaking their native language at home and coming to school to learn grade-level curriculum and immersion into the English language. I determined there was a need to create a culturally diverse learning environment for all students in our school.

This prompted me to gather information on how to be a culturally responsive teacher and to create a culturally diverse classroom setting. I wanted an inclusive environment where students and families could feel comfortable and equally represented. To accomplish this, I needed to learn specifics about my students, their families, and their cultures. This included families' cultural knowledge and the languages used at home. I quickly found we were lacking this valuable information regarding our students. In an effort to improve the curriculum to meet the needs of our students, we had to create a more relevant environment.

Fortunately, I had the opportunity to participate in Project PLACE (Partnerships for Learning, Achievement, and Community Engagement), a federal grant project at the University of Kentucky. Through this project, I discovered ways to make my teaching more culturally relevant. One of the most valuable ideas Project PLACE taught me was the importance of connecting with families through making home visits and attending special events, such as a student's first dance recital or a soccer tournament.

Initially, I was apprehensive. I did not want to intrude into my students' personal lives; however, Project PLACE gave me confidence and knowledge on how to initiate a meeting. I sent home a short letter to families asking them to invite me to an event that is important to their child. In the letter, I explained that this event should be very informal and can take place at home or wherever they feel comfortable. One of my most memorable invitations was to a Seder dinner. During this dinner, I learned religious and family customs, enjoyed homemade symbolic foods, learned Passover songs, and spent quality time with this family.

Throughout the meal, my student explained the rituals. His enthusiasm and pride in his heritage were evident. He enjoyed sharing this experience with me.

On another occasion, a Hispanic student invited me to his sister's Quinceañera. Although I was briefly familiar with this Mexican tradition, I immediately googled the term and read the description. I was invited to his sister's 15th birthday party. But it was not just any birthday party—we were celebrating her right of passage into womanhood. I had no idea that this would be an event I would never forget! The party was filled with deep-rooted cultural traditions from food to dancing, singing, and even traditional clothing! Most of the guests were friends and family, and it seemed that everyone spoke Spanish, except for me. Needless to say, I was uncomfortable and a bit nervous. I was out of my element. However, I was honored to be there. My student was the consummate host and was able to act as my translator and teacher, explaining traditions and introducing me to members of his family. I think he enjoyed seeing me in a different light—not in control. My student and I were able to see different sides of one another outside the classroom. I was able to see new strengths in this student. He was gracious and confident. He was able to see his teacher as a friend embracing his culture.

I end each family visit with a family photo that includes me, and it is displayed in our classroom. I also set aside time for each student to share the experience with our class. This builds excitement among my students and requests for a home visit become contagious.

I find these visits to be invaluable. I have learned how to be a listener and an observer, not just a teacher or disciplinarian. I have seen my students on a personal level and seen their interaction with family. I have seen students reading a cookbook or Bible instead of a picture book. This reading isn't any less important to the student; it is just presented in a different form. As an extended part of my students' families, I have gained insight into situations that may affect their moods and behaviors. This insight is crucial in establishing a positive environment in my classroom.

Just as important, I learned to incorporate families' interests and cultural experiences into our classroom. During home visits, families introduced me to their "funds of knowledge," that is, the talents, traditions, and skills that families possess and pass down to their children in everyday living (González, et al., 2005). As I became familiar with their culturally diverse experiences and values, I was able to integrate this knowledge into my classroom teaching. For example, if a student's parents are farmers, their funds of knowledge might include seasons, soil, head of cattle, harvest, weather changes, and agricultural factors. Farming could easily be referenced during math or social studies lessons to help students connect information relevant in their lives.

I have found that families are very willing to invite me into their world and share their lives with me. I use this insight to plan my lessons. When teaching, I incorporate words and examples that are familiar and personal to my students. I share parts of their outside lives inside the classroom. This makes a huge impact on my classroom. For instance, after visiting an Asian family, I introduced Chinese New Year traditions into our weekly centers by including themed read-alouds, creating paper lanterns, painting Chinese symbols, eating

> *dumplings, and counting lucky money packaged in red envelopes. My students attentively listen and learn to understand and appreciate important traditions that are unfamiliar. If applicable, they share additional information on the topic, some even proudly displaying their heritage. When my students can relate personally to the material I am teaching, they have a greater chance of success. Students and families are also more invested in what we are learning when we are able to connect the curriculum to their lives. Sharing cultures also becomes a learning tool for our classroom. Students are not only learners; they also become teachers. They realize there are many ways to learn and that cultural differences are to be valued.*
>
> *In addition to using families' funds of knowledge to plan curriculum and make connections to facilitate learning, I invite families into our classroom to share their expertise and funds of knowledge. This helps them gain confidence in themselves and develop pride in their cultural identities. It is easy for a student or a parent to share a talent that is familiar to them. As the class listens and excitement and participation grow, so does the confidence of the parents. This past year, I had 100% parent participation in this activity. Families were anxious to share information about their culture, holiday traditions, and diversity. We had cooking demonstrations, learned a few words in various languages, listened to multicultural fairy tales, and participated in different family traditions. These presentations allowed us to learn more about one another's lives outside the classroom.*
>
> *I genuinely appreciate getting to know the cultural diversity of my students and their families through home and classroom visits. In doing so, I am creating a collaborative relationship with families, while learning unique aspects of their personal and public lives in the community. The knowledge I gain through these visits allows me to incorporate their needs into our daily classroom activities. It gives each student a voice and an opportunity to show what makes them special and allows them to share and compare their diversities.*
>
> ### References
>
> González, N., Moll, L., & Amanti, C. (Eds.). (2005). *Funds of knowledge: Theorizing practices in households, communities, and classrooms.* Routledge.

The parent circle approach, developed by Patricia Edwards (Edwards & Turner, 2010) for use with Black families, is a method to gather information elicited through a focus group technique. Parent stories are

> the narratives gained from open-ended conversations and/or interviews between teachers and parents. . . . By using stories as a way to describe the nature of the home environment, parents can select anecdotes and personal observations from their family lives to give teachers access to complicated social, emotional, and educational information that can help teachers unravel the mystery around . . . children's home experiences and family

> routines, literacy practices, which enables them to construct classroom environments that are more congruent with their cultural knowledge and background. (Edwards & Turner, 2010, p. 141)

In contrast to techniques that focus on one family at a time, collecting group stories may help teachers avoid making assumptions or generalizations. Unlike a family interview, during which teachers may have a list of questions or topics to cover, a group interview often can generate rich information from fewer questions. During one group parent interview, Edwards and Turner (2010) asked two questions: "What do you want teachers to know about you and your children?" and "What changes do you feel need to be made at [this school] to address your concerns?" These two seemingly simple questions generated rich discussion among the participating parents, revealing four important messages that Black parents wanted teachers to know: "(1) We care about our children and their education; (2) My children have been through so much; (3) We've got to trust each other, and (4) please work with me" (2010, p. 144). Teachers gleaned that parents deeply mistrusted the schools, based on their prior experiences, but parents also recognized that trusting relationships were a two-way street and that they had to work with the school.

Learning about families' experiences and funds of knowledge is not limited to face-to-face efforts. Teachers can also gain this information through written communication, such as by sending letters home to families (Allen, 2010). Many teachers, particularly of kindergartners or other early-grade children, send letters home prior to or at the beginning of the school year. Including a personal question or two to the child—along with a self-addressed and stamped return envelope—can elicit helpful information. Indeed, my own son's kindergarten teacher used this technique as a regular part of her nontraditional literacy instruction when his school closed because of the COVID-19 pandemic (see Figure 2.2)! Teachers can also elicit similar information with a "Tell Me About Your Child" letter sent to caregivers, either at the beginning of the year or once relationships have been established. While individual letters to learners or their families may be more feasible for teachers in elementary or other self-contained classrooms who have a more limited number of students, upper grades teachers with larger numbers of students can find creative ways to learn about learners, families, and their funds of knowledge. Technology may be particularly effective to connect with older learners and their families. Teachers might post about themselves on Facebook, Instagram, or a blog and invite learners and/or their families to respond about themselves in the same way.

Enhanced Communication Techniques

Family visits, parent stories, and other similar activities often represent "big" activities that teachers might only engage with once per family. Yet developing stronger, more trusting mutual relationships takes sustained effort throughout the school year. Honestly and critically reflecting on the current state of parent–school relationships in your school and classroom is an important starting point; as Allen (2010) observed, "the face teachers

Figure 2.2. *My son's letter to his kindergarten teacher, with responses to a survey she sent.*

and principals think they show to the community may be very different from the face individual families see when they come to your school" (p. 18). Teachers must carefully consider their communication style, as well as the ways in which those styles "may serve as barriers to rather than facilitators of collaborative partnerships," particularly with CLD families (Harry, 2008, p. 383).

In my research (Perry, 2009, 2014), I found that the flurry of written communication from schools was overwhelming to refugee families—and, as a result, often ignored. While parents' levels of English proficiency were sufficient to understand the literal meaning of the texts, their unfamiliarity with U.S. cultural expectations related to schooling and with textual genres (such as permission slips) that did not exist in countries where they had lived often limited their ability to respond to the texts in appropriate or expected ways. The parents needed help navigating what schools actually expected or what they *should* do in response to that text. For example, parents knew that parent–teacher conferences were important and attendance was expected, but what about a flyer advertising a "Donuts with Dad" event or a "parent curriculum night?" Much can be done to make the information that comes home from schools more accessible and less overwhelming to parents (Perry, 2014). Teachers can create an organizational system that offers differentiated visual cues, such as particular colors of paper or special stickers or stamps for communications that require a response, those that are informational only, and those that are optional or represent opportunities outside of the school (such as sign-up forms for Little League or Scouts). Because learners themselves might be brokering these texts for parents (Perry, 2014), teachers can spend a few minutes providing an overview of the texts before sending them home. Importantly, teachers can keep in mind cultural differences in expectations for parents and schools and work to make explicit information or expectations that might be implicitly known to students from some backgrounds but hidden to others.

In my own work, I found that part of the problem with many texts that confused and overwhelmed the parents was that the communication was largely one-way—schools sent out information, and parents were expected to receive that communication and act on it accordingly. Developing stronger relationships with parents, however, requires a shift to two-way communication (Allen, 2010; Edwards, 2016; Epstein, 2001). Common forms of school communication such as newsletters, bulletin boards, report cards, school websites, or automated text, voice mail, or email messages represent traditional one-way modes of communication (Edwards, 2016). Many of these methods can be made more interactive, such as by including spaces for parent feedback on school or classroom websites or Facebook pages or by relying on phone calls or email exchanges that are not automated. Family surveys, home-to-school communication notebooks, or apps such as Remind 101, Class Dojo, or Google Classroom also represent opportunities for more authentic two-way communication between homes and schools (Edwards, 2016); the key is to ensure that these methods do not devolve into only information-providing and instead truly invite two-way communication.

Integrating Family Collaboration in Instruction

Learning about families is an important aspect of building trust and developing stronger relationships with caregivers, families, and communities. The knowledge that teachers gain from families does not stop there, however—it also should be integrated into classroom instruction. McIntyre (2010) offered an important caveat: "Contextualized teaching, or funds of knowledge teaching, is not merely a cute thing to do once in a while. It is a philosophy of teaching based on a sociocultural theory of teaching and learning" (p. 209). In other words, incorporating family knowledge is an important method that teachers can use to "help students acquire 'scientific' understandings that systematically improve literacy and mathematics skills" (McIntyre, 2010, p. 213), as well as to promote academic development in other content areas.

In the following sections, I share three ways that teachers can connect knowledge of families and funds of knowledge to instruction: within the classroom, between the classroom and the home, and to the community. Many of these techniques not only rely on knowledge of families gleaned from prior visits, interviews, and other activities, but they also provide additional opportunities to gather knowledge about families and continue developing relationships with parents, other caregivers, and community members.

Within-Classroom Strategies

As Doris Walker-Dalhouse described in the previous chapter, morning meetings are excellent for community building within classrooms. They also serve as strategic opportunities to learn about families and funds of knowledge directly from students. Students may be able to share some of their family knowledge with little preparation. For example, students could describe who counts as "family" to them, activities they do together as a family for fun, favorite food dishes, or special family celebrations. Other sharing activities might take more preparation or even research on the part of learners. For example, students might be tasked with asking parents why their name was chosen and if it has a special meaning or with bringing a special photo or family object from home and explaining its significance. Sharing during classroom meetings might also be a time that students could report on results from family- or community-related assignments, such as interviews with family members about their jobs or about elements of their culture.

Diversifying classroom libraries is a goal of many teachers who strive to better serve CLD students. Attending to the diversity of *families* represented within libraries and reading lists is also important, as Jill Robertson, a teacher featured in this chapter, discovered. Jill noticed that many students in her classroom were being raised by grandparents or other extended kin, instead of by parents, and she began to wonder if the texts in her first-grade classroom library reflected her students' family structures. Teachers can inventory their libraries and recommended-reading lists with an eye to seeing if books represent family diversity (e.g., single-parent families, stepfamilies, adoptive or foster families, extended families, etc.). Involving learners in these assessments is even more powerful. Students at all levels can evaluate the texts that exist in libraries or recommended-reading lists, conduct research to identify texts that represent missing family types, and make recommendations for purchase or further reading. Organizations like Read Brightly, Colours of Us, and Common Sense Media curate lists of books and other media, and their lists include family diversity.

Familial funds of knowledge can be used across the curriculum in many ways to support the development of academic skills, concepts, and content. In literacy and language arts, photographs of learners' families or of special events in their lives can be used to generate vocabulary for writing for emergent writers or English learners, as in the Picture Word Induction Method (Calhoun, 1999). Older, more proficient writers might use such photos as prompts to help generate topics for writing personal narratives, memoirs, descriptive vignettes, or "Where I'm From" poems, modeled after the work of former Kentucky poet laureate George Ella Lyon (1993). (See Chapter 4 for a more comprehensive discussion of these strategies.) As Table 2.2 on the following page shows, family topics can be used to introduce research-related skills. Students might conduct oral history interviews of family members in an integrated English language arts and social studies unit, or they might survey class- or schoolmates on family structures and then graph the results as part of their persuasive arguments to diversity the school library's selections. Family topics also lend themselves to science, such as when younger learners compare the different family structures and offspring care practices of various animals, or when older learners investigate genetics. Many of these ideas are extended in the following section on connecting homes to classrooms.

Connecting Classrooms to Home

Rethinking how homework is conducted is an important part of establishing strong school–family relationships and integrating family knowledge into the classroom. This is particularly true for children in early elementary grades, who often need a great deal of

Table 2.2. *Family Topics to Integrate Throughout the Curriculum*

Literacy/English Language Arts	Mathematics
<ul><li>"Where I'm From" poems (Lyon, 1993)</li><li>Family Message Journals (Wollman-Bonilla, 2001)</li><li>Family oral history projects</li><li>Photography projects (Allen, 2010)</li><li>Digital family scrapbooks</li></ul>	<ul><li>Survey classmates or school on family structure and people living in the home</li><li>Create charts/graphs to share the results</li><li>Use students' families to contextualize mathematical concepts (e.g., in word problems)</li></ul>
Science	**Social Studies**
<ul><li>Compare families in other animal species, e.g.,<ul><li>Family/group structure</li><li>How many offspring are born at one time?</li><li>How long do offspring stay with parents?</li><li>What is the role of each parent in caring for offspring?</li></ul></li><li>Genetics</li></ul>	<ul><li>Compare what families look like around the world, e.g.,<ul><li>Where is it common for multiple generations to live together?</li><li>What is the average age for marriage?</li><li>How many children do families typically have?</li></ul></li><li>Research how family names work in other cultures</li><li>Investigate what genealogists do and how they do it</li></ul>

parental support for homework. Although quite common, required reading logs are often ineffective or outright ignored by families (Allen, 2010), particularly when they may feel that "just reading" is not as important as other types of homework (Dudley-Marling, 2009). One fourth-grade teacher I worked with, Tracey Tevis, decided to revamp her reading log to be more reflective of the wide range of literacy practices (Barton & Hamilton, 1998; Perry, 2009) in which her CLD families engaged. Instead of a form to log minutes and titles, Tracey created a chart that also included items such as following a recipe to cook a family meal, playing a game together, singing karaoke, or using directions to build a model or other creation. Inspired by Tracey's work, Jill Robertson (featured in Classroom Scenario 2.2) modified Tracey's log for first graders. She included images to contextualize the activities for emergent readers and for any parents with low literacy or limited English proficiency, as well as a section for parents to offer feedback or additional ideas—effectively turning her reading log into an interactive family communication device (see Figure 2.3). Additionally, Jill had her log translated into Arabic, KiSwahili, Kinyarwanda, Nepali, and Spanish—all languages spoken by families in her classroom.

Figure 2.3. *Jill's weekly reading log, based on an idea from Tracey Tevis.*

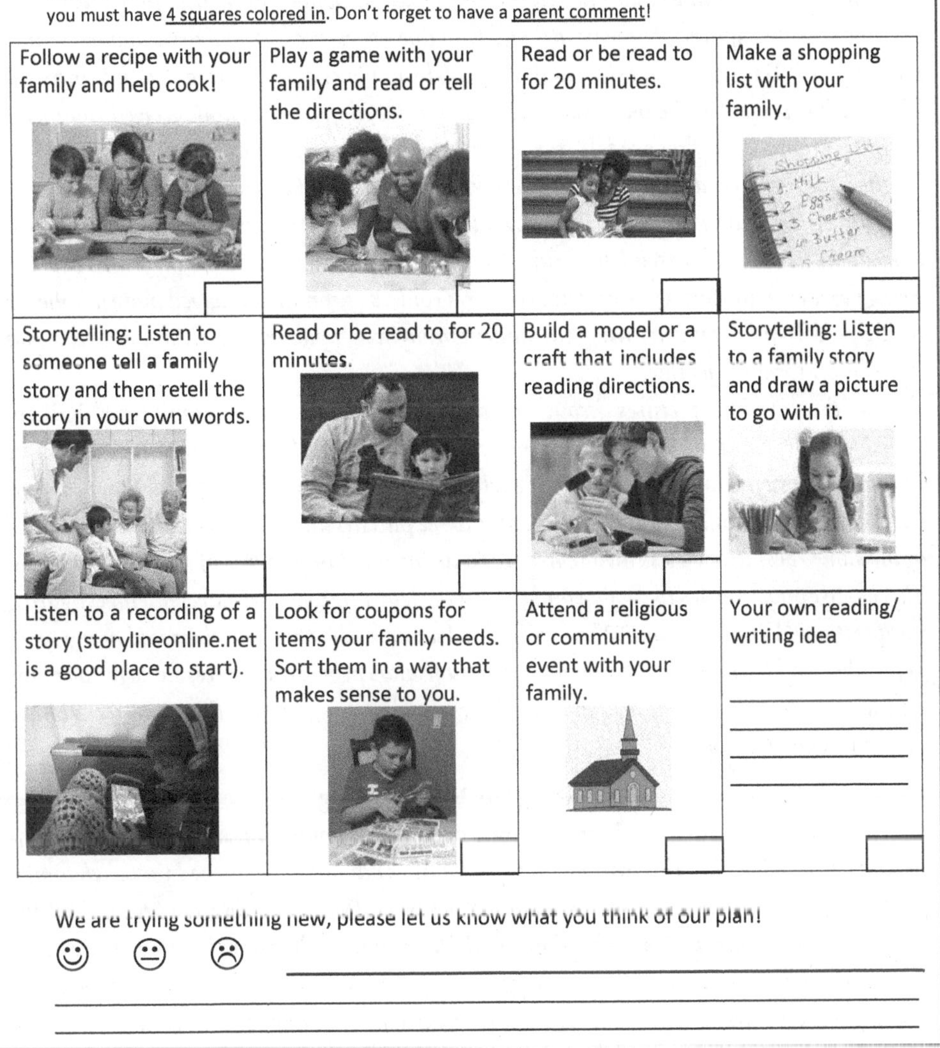

Weekly Reading Log

For first graders, we would like you to read or be read to 20 minutes each night (Monday – Thursday). This year we want to celebrate the awesome reading skills that our families practice at home. Below are different activities that students may want to do with their family and count it as reading for 20 minutes. Every week you must have 4 squares colored in. Don't forget to have a parent comment!

Follow a recipe with your family and help cook!	Play a game with your family and read or tell the directions.	Read or be read to for 20 minutes.	Make a shopping list with your family.
Storytelling: Listen to someone tell a family story and then retell the story in your own words.	Read or be read to for 20 minutes.	Build a model or a craft that includes reading directions.	Storytelling: Listen to a family story and draw a picture to go with it.
Listen to a recording of a story (storylineonline.net is a good place to start).	Look for coupons for items your family needs. Sort them in a way that makes sense to you.	Attend a religious or community event with your family.	Your own reading/ writing idea

We are trying something new, please let us know what you think of our plan!

☺   😐   ☹   _______________________________

Classroom Scenario 2.2.: Family Collaboration
Jill Robertson

I teach first grade in a Title 1 school where we have a delightfully diverse population, with more than 19 countries and 10 languages represented. Over 80% of the population is economically disadvantaged in this urban elementary school. In this vignette, I share several activities I use to get to know the families of my students.

Family Picture Wall

Each fall I commit to building relationships with students and their families, as well as help the students appreciate the varied and valuable experiences they have as a part of their own families. This past year, I started the year off by having students bring in family pictures. The students presented the pictures to the class, answered questions, and received comments from the group. With first graders, the comments were sometimes as simple as "I have two brothers too!" or "My dad has the same name as your dad!" A favorite comment was "I don't have any sisters, but I have a bearded dragon!" These conversations helped build community. Some families were able to send in a printed picture, and some sent it in digitally for me to print. Being flexible on the timetable and how pictures could be submitted allowed more families to participate. It did not matter when the student brought in a picture; we always shared it that day in our morning meeting.

We displayed the pictures throughout the school year on a large "family tree" bulletin board with the caption "We love our families." The students often would stand and browse the photos, noticing something different each time. Many students even found they had connections to other families once they were able to see parents and siblings visually. I had some of the same revelations as I saw former students included in pictures of extended families. This led to opportunities to deepen and extend the learning when we dove into investigating the question, "What is a family?" As we learned about each other, we celebrated many types of families and found that extended family and friends provide a rich resource for our kids and schools. We discovered that although our families may not look the same, we all have someone who loves us.

Revising the Reading Log

First graders at our school are encouraged to read at home and then record their readings on a log each night. This worked for some families but not all. I learned that each family participates in literacy in numerous ways. Because of this, we wanted to "count" all the wonderful things our students were doing with their families that were literacy-related that might not be the traditional act of reading a book for 20 minutes and then recording it on a reading log. Our first-grade team revised our traditional reading log in several ways. First, we included many literacy activities that families may do together. We listed these, such as playing a game as a family, or listening to someone tell a story and then drawing a picture to illustrate it, attending a worship service together, or following a recipe. We then made sure to include a picture of each activity for better understanding. We also left space for families to record other ways that they had participated in literacy activities together that week. Some families wrote grocery lists together, followed written directions on a video game, or did shared reading. Finally, we had the log translated into all the languages needed for our students. This included French, Swahili, Nepali, Spanish, Arabic, and Kinyarwanda. We found that this new reading log facilitated an increase in student and family participation. When the logs were turned in, we celebrated the successes of the students during our morning meeting. We emphasized the many and varied ways that we "do" literacy with our families and how each household has unique expertise specific to their family.

Nontraditional Instruction

When schools moved to nontraditional instruction due to COVID-19, the opportunity to get to know families grew. We shared each other's homes in a way that we could not do during our traditional in-person school. Through technology, we met siblings, parents, pets, and grandparents and toured bedrooms and living rooms. We connected in a way that we had not before, and it was sweet and valuable. While in school, we learned during our morning meetings that there were many babies in our families. On our Zoom calls, we were able to meet them! The unique setting of online learning brought challenges as well. We were all learning how to navigate this new way of school. When one of our Kinyarwanda-speaking students did not engage in online learning despite her independence in the traditional classroom, I used the language line provided by our district to find a translator so that I could speak with the mom and student to find out what she needed. Another family whose English was nearly fluent needed a bit more support for online learning, so we used our phones to FaceTime and were better able to explain and understand each other.

At the onset of each school year, I send home a parent questionnaire to find out the likes, dislikes, and favorite things of my students. Getting a brief look into the homes through Zoom provided insight into the learning of the students that I could not acquire using a parent questionnaire. Through our virtual classroom, I was privileged to get a peek into my first graders' homes. Many students live in environments with much activity, music, and conversation. It was amazing to watch them focus on listening to their peers and participating in our online school despite the goings-on around them. This gave insight into the way kids learn, and what interesting things families do. It also challenged me to provide more collaboration time among our students and with our families wherever school takes place.

Interactive writing between home and school encourages students to write to parents, as parents and learners together respond to prompts from teachers. Family message journals (Wollman-Bonilla, 2001) are an opportunity for learners to write regularly to their parents about school activities and for family members to respond in writing. Teachers can explain the importance of parents writing back to children during a school event or through other communicative means. Importantly, Wollman-Bonilla (2001) reassured her first-grade parents that they were not expected to write in "perfect" or standard English and that they were encouraged to write in languages other than English. Otherwise, she did not provide specific instructions on *how* to reply to children's writing. In fact, Wollman-Bonilla found that the parents in her classrooms frequently modeled nonschool genres, such as jokes, riddles, or other wordplays, that were important in the children's families and communities but that tended to be less reflected in the official literacy curriculum. She also found that, even without specific guidance about responding to children's writing, parents consistently provided helpful modeling and instructional-level feedback to their children in their written responses. "We may be misguided in assuming that certain families may have little to contribute instructionally," she concluded, "But, it also reveals that what families have to contribute may not always reflect the tidy, simple genre definitions teachers may embrace" (Wollman-Bonilla, 2001, p. 189).

Other types of journals also can support home connections to the curriculum in important ways. Parents and children can be encouraged to have written conversations about texts they read together at home or about other family experiences. Some teachers I have worked with send home journals with prompts that *both* learners and parents respond

Figure 2.4. *Family journals provide opportunities to connect with families on a more personal level.*

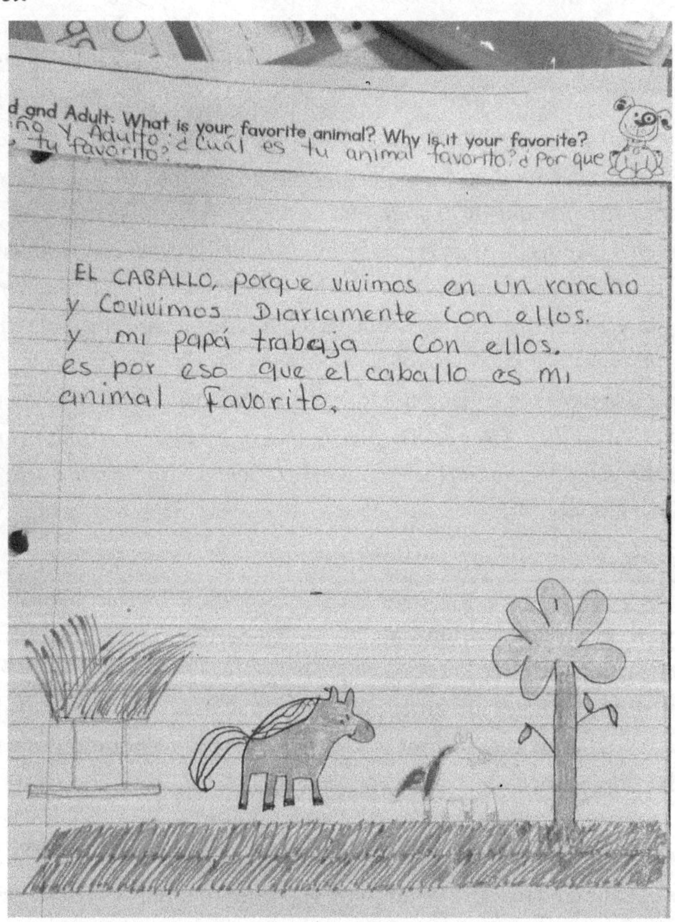

to, essentially creating a family-wide dialogue with the teacher. Sample prompts might include "What is a favorite memory of your family?" "What has someone in your family done for you that you really appreciated?" or "What is something you would like to do with your family this weekend?" The learner and another family member each take time to respond to the prompt, and family members can be encouraged to discuss the similarities and differences in their responses. I have seen such prompts used successfully with both kindergarten and fourth-grade families, showing that this technique can be successful in a wide range of classrooms. Emergent writers can respond with a picture, and families who speak languages other than English in the home can write in their preferred languages. A variety of prompts can be used that get at families' diverse backgrounds, experiences, and beliefs. When teachers take time to respond to these responses themselves, the journals can further enhance teacher–family relationships.

Family backpack projects can create curricular connections with the home, especially for families who may experience limited access to appropriate children's books in accessible languages. Rowe and Fain (2013) created backpack sets that included two books on a topic related to the science or social studies curriculum, CD recordings of the books, a CD player, a blank journal and writing implements, and an invitation letter. For learners who spoke languages other than English, everything was translated—including the books sent home. The response invitations were open-ended, "encouraging parents to create responses reflecting their family's interpretation of the book" (Rowe & Fain, 2013, p. 405). Siblings, grandparents, and aunts or uncles often collaborated with the child on their responses to the books, and families were particularly pleased to receive books in their home languages, because their children's literacy in both languages was supported. While the selected books were chosen for their alignment with curricular goals, the journals "gave families opportunities to express and display their own interests, interactions, and literacy practices" and "functioned as a way of bringing family funds of knowledge into the classroom to be used as a resource for learning" (Rowe & Fain, 2013, p. 414). Rowe and Fain's backpack project was specifically designed for young children, but their work easily could be adapted for older learners. Teachers might curate a variety of materials that are connected to curricular topics, such as magazine or newspaper articles, videos, podcasts, websites, blogs, or other media, and families might respond on a website or blog or even create a video or audio response to the materials. Creating virtual instead of physical backpacks also might allow learners to collaborate with loved ones who do not reside in the same household.

Photography projects (Allen, 2010) also can provide an important tie to the curriculum while providing teachers with insights into families' funds of knowledge. Learners can be given cameras and taught to document aspects of their homes, families, and individual lives through photos. Students might create photo essays of their own lives or the lives of a loved one, or they might document their whole family. Learners can focus on particular curricular connections, such as literacy or mathematics practices in their homes or neighborhoods; these photos often provide teachers with a great deal of insight regarding the myriad ways in which literacy and mathematics are interwoven in families' daily lives. Learners might also photograph places or objects of deep personal importance to themselves or their families. Such photos then can be incorporated into writing projects, as a spark for an essay or personal narrative or in a larger photo essay or digital scrapbook project. The ubiquity of smartphones, even in communities where families may have less access to digital technology, means that teachers may not need to supply cameras. Parents or community members with photography expertise can be invited to teach photography workshops—another excellent way to make such projects more collaborative.

Figure 2.5. Students in Annalee Peters's first-grade classroom each wrote several pages for a book about their families. On family night, parents helped their child select family pictures and publish their books.

Connecting Classrooms to the Community

Connecting with families and the broader community offers a number of benefits (Epstein, 2001), and it is mandated by programs such as Title 1. Often, teachers are familiar with community-facing events, such as back-to-school events, family literacy or math nights, or science fairs. Yet there are a variety of ways in which educators can bring community knowledge into the classroom and curriculum. The authors of *School, Family, and Community Partnerships: Your Handbook for Action* (Epstein, 2001) and *Beyond the Bake Sale: The Essential Guide to Family–School Partnerships* (Henderson et al., 2007), are respected for their expertise in this area, and these books are well worth the investment for teachers who are serious about enhancing family and community collaboration. Many collaboration programs are well intended but fail to live up to their potential. Including parent and community stakeholders in collaborative planning is essential, as is taking the time to learn about the diverse cultural roots of stakeholders (Longwell-Grice & McIntyre, 2006). It is especially important for educators to "recognize that families will support children's learning in ways that are not consistent with Western practices and perspectives" (Friedrich et al., 2014, p. 78). Parent advisory groups, such as the ones Anderson and his colleagues (2015) have been involved in designing and implementing family literacy programs targeted to immigrant and First Nations communities in Canada, are particularly effective.

Community partnerships offer additional opportunities to make family collaboration more inclusive, welcoming, and accessible. Holding school-sponsored events at libraries, parks, community centers, or other neutral locations may encourage greater attendance, particularly among families who may have had negative experiences in schools themselves. Such off-site partnerships might also encourage creativity in expanding programming to less traditional topics or audiences while still maintaining important ties to curriculum and learning. For example, in partnership with a local community center in our city, my graduate students and I designed a public family "fun and learning" night on the topic of family. We designed a variety of activities that might appeal to learners of different ages while also encouraging intergenerational interaction. Participating families could make homemade greeting cards or write letters to loved ones, create comics or superhero stories about their families, design family puppets, start a family scrapbook, record and swap family recipes, generate a collaborative family "summer bucket list," and have a family photo taken with whiteboards that prompted them to finish sentences such as "I love my family because..." or "My family is unique because..."

Teachers also can create curricular connections to families and communities in ways beyond special events. Inquiry-based learning projects might require students to survey or interview family members or community members on a topic related to the curriculum, perhaps as part of a larger unit. Parents and community members might be asked about "must-read" texts—those that are critically important to the identity and development of learners from particular communities (Allen, 2010)—to include in the official curriculum and in related experiences, such as suggested summer reading lists.

Family and community members represent an essential source for identifying these must-read texts, particularly when teachers come from different backgrounds than their students. Other learning activities can strengthen family bonds, particularly when families may be separated by divorce, military service, participation in residential addiction or mental illness programs, or incarceration. For example, Muth (2011) worked with Hope House, a family program in a Virginia prison that reconnects incarcerated men with their children. Although the fathers cannot be physically present in their children's lives, they make recordings of books to send to their children in lieu of bedtime stories and see their children for one week during a special summer camp. Educators can design experiences that can help learners connect with absent family members by incorporating activities such as letter-writing or family journal projects. Similar projects might connect learners with unrelated community members in the military, prisons, nursing homes, or residential treatment centers.

Teachers also can use families and communities as authentic audiences for the products of students' learning, particularly when that learning is tied to issues or topics important to the community. For example, Graybeal and Spickard (2018) designed the CitiZINE Project to teach students and community members about the creation of zines as a method for political engagement. Students in a wide range of grade levels can create zines to share their knowledge about a community-related topic and advocate for particular actions. Teachers might also teach students about the PhotoVoice technique, in which communities use photographs to pose meaningful questions about a community and also develop creative solutions. Through PhotoVoice, community members become both a resource and the audience for learners' work. Community-based projects such as this also represent excellent opportunities to link family collaboration with critical consciousness (see Chapter 6).

Conclusion

We have often heard that it takes a village to raise a child. I would argue that it also takes a village to *teach* a child. It takes a village to know how a child learns best, to support them in their learning, and to teach those children what they need to know and do to be competent adult members of their communities. It takes a village to ensure that children grow to be proud of their cultural and linguistic heritage—to know that they are part of a larger community that has value and worth. It takes a village to teach children that civic engagement matters and that they can make a difference in their communities. The COVID-19 pandemic has brought renewed urgency to the need to develop effective family collaborations with teachers and schools. The pandemic has connected teachers, classrooms, and families in new ways—and, perhaps, has shown that the distinction between classroom and home is not (and should not be) so distinct after all.

References

Allen, J. (2010). *Literacy in the welcoming classroom.* Teachers College Press.

Anderson, J., Anderson, A., Friedrich, N., & Kim, J. E. (2010). Taking stock of family literacy: Some contemporary perspectives. *Journal of Early Childhood Literacy, 10*(1), 33–53.

Anderson, J., Anderson, A., & Gear, A. (2015). Family literacy programs as intersubjective spaces: Insights from three decades of working in culturally, linguistically and socially diverse communities. *Language and Literacy, 17*(2), 41–58.

Anderson, J., Lenters, K., & McTavish, M. (2008). Constructing families, constructing literacy: A critical analysis of family literacy websites. *School Community Journal, 18*(1), 61–78.

Aronson, B., & Laughter, J. (2016). The theory and practice of culturally relevant education: A synthesis of research across content areas. *Review of Educational Research, 86*(1), 163–206.

Barton, D., & Hamilton, M. (1998). *Local literacies: Literacy practices in one community.* Routledge.

Bourdieu, P., & Passeron, J. C. (1990). *Reproduction in education, society and culture* (Vol. 4). Sage Publications.

Calhoun, E. F. (1999). *Teaching beginning reading and writing with the Picture Word Inductive Model.* Association for Supervision and Curriculum Development.

Compton-Lilly, C. (2009). Research directions: Listening to families over time: Seven lessons learned about literacy in families. *Language Arts, 86*(6), 449–457.

Dantas, M. L., & Coleman, M. (2010). Home visits: Learning from students and families. In M. L. Dantas & P. C. Manyak (eds.), *Home–school connections in a multicultural society* (pp. 156–176). Routledge.

Dudley-Marling, C. (2009). Home–school literacy connections: The perceptions of African American and immigrant ESL parents in two urban communities. *Teachers College Record, 111*(7), 1713–1752.

Edwards, P. A. (2016). *New ways to engage parents: Strategies and tools for teachers and leaders, K–12.* Teachers College Press.

Edwards, P. A., & Turner, J. D. (2010). Do you hear what I hear?: Using the parent story approach to listen to and learn from African American parents. In M. L. Dantas & P. C. Manyak (Eds.), *Home–school connections in a multicultural society* (pp. 137–155). Routledge.

Epstein, J. A. (2001). *School, family, and community partnerships: Your handbook for action* (3rd ed.). Sage Publications.

Fan, X., & Chen, M. (2001). Parental involvement and students' academic achievement: A meta-analysis. *Educational Psychology Review, 13*(1), 1–22.

Friedrich, N., Anderson, J., & Morrison, F. (2014). Culturally appropriate pedagogy in a bilingual family literacy programme. *Literacy, 48*(2), 72–79.

Gay, G. (2002). Preparing for culturally responsive teaching. *Journal of Teacher Education, 53*(2), 106–116.

Goldman, S., & Booker, A. (2009). Making math a definition of the situation: Families as sites for mathematical practices. *Anthropology & Education Quarterly, 40*(4), 369–387.

González, N. (2005). Beyond culture: The hybridity of funds of knowledge. In N. González, L. Moll, & C. Amanti (Eds.), *Funds of knowledge: Theorizing practices in households, communities, and classrooms* (pp. 29–46). Routledge.

González, N., Moll, L. C., Tenery, M. F., Rivera, A., Rendon, P., Gonzales, R., & Amanti, C. (1995). Funds of knowledge for teaching in Latino households. *Urban Education, 29*(4), 443–470.

Graybeal, L., & Spickard, K. (2018). The CitiZINE project: Reflections on a political engagement project. *Community Literacy Journal, 12*(2), 57–64.

Hannon, P. (1999). Rhetoric and research in family literacy. *British Educational Research Journal, 26*(1), 121–138.

Harry, B. (2008). Collaboration with culturally and linguistically diverse families: Ideal versus reality. *Exceptional Children, 74*(3), 372–388.

Henderson, A. T., Mapp, K. L., Johnson, V. R., & Davies, D. (2007). *Beyond the bake sale: The essential guide to family–school partnerships.* New Press.

Hill, N. E., & Tyson, D. F. (2009). Parental involvement in middle school: A meta-analytic assessment of the strategies that promote achievement. *Developmental Psychology, 45*(3), 740–763.

Jeynes, W. H. (2003). A meta-analysis: The effects of parental involvement on minority children's academic achievement. *Education and Urban Society, 35*(2), 202–218.

Jeynes, W. H. (2005). A meta-analysis of the relation of parental involvement to urban elementary school student academic achievement. *Urban Education, 40*(3), 237–269.

Jeynes, W. (2012). A meta-analysis of the efficacy of different types of parental involvement programs for urban students. *Urban Education, 47*(4), 706–742.

Kim, E. M., Coutts, M. J., Holmes, S. R., Sheridan, S. M., Ransom, K. A., Sjuts, T. M., & Rispoli, K. M. (2012). *Parent involvement and family–school partnerships: Examining the content, processes, and outcomes of structural versus relationship-based approaches* (CYFS Working Paper No. 2012-6). Nebraska Center for Research on Children, Youth, Families and Schools.

Ladson-Billings, G. (1995). Toward a theory of culturally relevant pedagogy. *American Educational Research Journal, 32*(3), 465–491.

Lave, J., & Wenger, E. (1991). *Situated learning: Legitimate peripheral participation.* Cambridge University Press.

Lee, J. S., & Bowen, N. K. (2006). Parent involvement, cultural capital, and the achievement gap among elementary school children. *American Educational Research Journal, 43*(2), 193–218.

Lewis, T. Y. (2014). Affinity spaces, apprenticeships, and agency: Exploring blogging engagements in family spaces. *Journal of Adolescent & Adult Literacy, 58*(1), 71–81.

Lewis Ellison, T., & Toliver, S. R. (2018). (CHAT)ting at home: A family's activity theory system. *Voices From the Middle, 25*(3), 35–40.

Longwell-Grice, H., & McIntyre, E. (2006). Addressing goals of school and community: Lessons from a family literacy program. *School Community Journal, 16*(2), 115–132.

Lyon, G. E. (1993). *Where I'm from.* http://www.georgeellalyon.com/where.html

Manyak, P. C., & Dantas, M. L. (2010). Introduction. In M. L. Dantas & P. C. Manyak (Eds.), *Home–school connections in a multicultural society* (pp. 1–16). Routledge.

McIntyre, E. (2010). Issues in funds of knowledge teaching and research: Key concepts from a study of Appalachian families and schooling. In M. L. Dantas & P. C. Manyak (Eds.), *Home–school connections in a multicultural society* (pp. 201–217). Routledge.

McIntyre, E., Kyle, D., Moore, G., Sweazy, R. A., & Greer, S. (2001). Linking home and school through family visits. *Language Arts, 78*(3), 264–272.

Miano, A. A. (2011). Schools reading parents' worlds: Mexican immigrant mothers building family literacy networks. *Multicultural Education, 18*(2), 30–38.

Muth, W. (2011). Murals as text: A social-cultural perspective on family literacy events in US prisons. *Ethnography and Education, 6*(3), 245–263.

O'Brien, L. M., Paratore, J. R., Leighton, C. M., Cassano, C. M., Krol-Sinclair, B., & Green, J. G. (2014). Examining differential effects of a family literacy program on language and literacy growth of English language learners with varying vocabularies. *Journal of Literacy Research, 46*(3), 383–415.

Paris, D. (2012). Culturally sustaining pedagogy: A needed change in stance, terminology, and practice. *Educational Researcher, 41*(3), 93–97.

Perry, K. H. (2009). Genres, contexts, and literacy practices: Literacy brokering among Sudanese refugee families. *Reading Research Quarterly, 44*(3), 256–276.

Perry, K. H. (2010). "Lost boys," cousins and aunties: Using Sudanese refugee relationships to complicate definitions of "family." In M. L. Dantas & P. C. Manyak (Eds.), *Home–school connections in a multicultural society* (pp. 19–40). Routledge.

Perry, K. H. (2014). "Mama, sign this note": Young refugee children's brokering of literacy practices. *Language Arts, 91*(5), 313–325.

Price-Mitchell, M. (2009). Boundary dynamics: Implications for building parent–school partnerships. *School Community Journal, 19*(2), 9–26.

Purcell-Gates, V. (1996). Stories, coupons, and the TV Guide: Relationships between home literacy experiences and emergent literacy knowledge. *Reading Research Quarterly, 31*(4), 406–428.

Rodriguez-Brown, F. V. (2004). Project FLAME: A parent support family literacy model. In B. H. Wasik (Ed.), *Handbook of family literacy* (pp. 213–299). Routledge.

Rogoff, B. (2003). *The cultural nature of human development.* Oxford University Press.

Rowe, D., & Fain, J. G. (2013). The family backpack project: Responding to dual-language texts through family journals. *Language Arts, 90*(6), 402–416.

Scribner, S., & Cole, M. (1981). *The psychology of literacy.* Harvard University Press.

Sheldon, S. B. (2002). Parents' social networks and beliefs as predictors of parent involvement. *The Elementary School Journal, 102*(4), 301–316.

St. Clair, R. (2008). Reading, writing, and relationships: Human and social capital in family literacy programs. *Adult Basic Education and Literacy Journal, 2*(2), 84–93.

Steiner, L. M. (2014). A family literacy intervention to support parents in children's early literacy learning. *Reading Psychology, 35*(8), 703–735.

Van Steensel, R., McElvany, N., Kurvers, J., & Herppich, S. (2011). How effective are family literacy programs? Results of a meta-analysis. *Review of Educational Research, 81*(1), 69–96.

Whitehouse, M., & Colvin, C. (2001). "Reading" families: Deficit discourse and family literacy. *Theory into Practice, 40*(3), 212–219.

Wollman-Bonilla, J. E. (2001). Family involvement in early writing instruction. *Journal of Early Childhood Literacy, 1*(2), 167–192.

CHAPTER 3

Assessment as the Bridge Between Culturally Responsive Teaching and Learning

Shannon O. Sampson and Carolyn A. Oldham

WHEN YOU THINK of assessment, what comes to mind? What does an assessment look like? What are its purposes? What are its limitations? What emotions does the word *assessment* evoke for you? What emotions might it evoke for students? For parents? For families who are not native to the U.S. educational system?

Assessment is not just an instrument or event; it should be a fundamental driver of classroom instruction that cultivates quality teaching and learning. Just as culturally responsive instruction hinges upon thoughtful self-inquiry and an exploration into students' individual contexts, how we as teachers, our students, and the community view and engage in assessment has implications for student learning. As we seek to better understand how, what, and why our students are *or are not* learning, culturally responsive teachers must engage in culturally responsive assessment. As Sally Brown and colleagues (2005) note,

> nothing that we do to, or for, our students is more important than our assessment of their work and the feedback we give them on it. The results of our assessment influence our students for the rest of their lives and careers— fine if we get it right, but unthinkable if we get it wrong. (p. xi)

A healthy approach to assessment is rooted in *evaluative thinking*. According to Patton (2018), evaluative thinking weaves together critical, creative, rigorous, and inferential thinking with democratic principles, critical consciousness, the pursuit of truth, and a focus on process use. In a classroom setting, a teacher who is an evaluative thinker will have an attitude of inquisitiveness into the multifaceted, dynamic identities of their students; check assumptions and biases regarding how teaching and learning are occurring; commit to thoughtful and collaborative inquiry with their students, school, and community members; and pursue valid evidence to drive further action (Bulkley & Henig, 2015).

In this chapter, we describe different types of assessments, drawing on what research says about their uses, strengths, and limitations. We touch on principles of measurement theory such as validity, reliability, and fairness. We provide strategies on how to identify and develop culturally responsive assessments, with examples that can be implemented immediately, and suggest ways to share results with students and their families. We hope this chapter helps you integrate assessment as a natural and low-pressure way to meaningfully interact with your students, hold them to high standards, and simultaneously hone your own craft as a teacher.

What Does the Literature Tell Us About Assessment?

The word *assessment* originates from the Latin verb *assidere,* or "to sit beside." We conceptualize assessment to be a process in which the teacher and the student together engage in critical inquiry into teaching and learning processes. Assessment at its core is about eliciting evidence of student learning to inform teaching practice with the reward being the improvement of student learning and teaching. Student learning may be measured using sophisticated methods, but the data are of no worth if findings do not impact student learning and teaching practice. To borrow the words of Xu and Brown (2016), we view assessment as "contextualized and culturally responsive practices that teachers negotiate with their students in learning communities" (p. 154). In culturally diverse contexts, educators should bring a careful and critical eye to the practice of assessment, because when used inappropriately, an assessment can have negative implications for students (we discuss many of these in this chapter). However, thoughtful assessment designed or selected by an evaluative-thinking teacher plays a vital and constructive role in a culturally responsive classroom.

Culture, Cognition, and Assessment

Neuroscience research conceptualizes culture as the software for the brain's hardware, helping us make sense of the world around us (Hammond, 2015). How we process, organize, and encode information as well as what we attend to and how, is all informed by the "cultural brain" (Park & Huang, 2010). Contemporary brain imaging provides "clear evidence that cultural values and experiences shape neurocognitive processes and influence patterns of neural activation and may even effect neural structures" (Park & Huang, 2010, p. 9). Culture's powerful impact on brain function is evidenced in the cross-cultural variability of the brain mechanisms controlling cognitive functions such as arithmetic, reading, object processing, self-representation, and attentional control (Ansari, 2012). For example, research suggests that some cultural groups' cognitive processes favor the contextual understanding of situations by focusing on the relationship between items or thoughts while others are more analytic, attending to particular objects and categories (Winerman, 2006). Modern science provides evidence of what psychologists and anthropologists have suggested for years: We experience and participate in the world around us through the lens of our culture (Spradley, 1980, p. 6). That lens is continuously reshaped by our experiences with the world around us, informing what are considered to be appropriate emotional reactions and behavioral responses, how we think, communicate care, perceive safety and belonging, and frame integrity (Kagawa-Singer, 2012; Oyserman et al., 2015).

This connection between culture and cognition has practical implications for the teaching and learning that occur within classrooms; teaching and learning are clearly cultural processes (Rogoff, 2003). Yet, although U.S. classrooms are culturally diverse, our teaching, educational goals, and assessment frameworks remain grounded in European American values (Spindler & Spindler, 2013). Trumbull and Nelson-Barber (2019) highlight that these Western values "implicitly guide approaches to every aspect of schooling, from academic content to the organization of classrooms, expected styles of speaking and interacting, instructional practices, and means of assessing student learning" (pp. 1–2). Hammond (2015) argues that by not addressing this cultural discordance and engaging students' cultures in the processes of teaching and learning, we are failing to foster independent learners who can access their brain's cognitive structures to engage in higher order thinking. We extend their argument to include this engagement in the process of assessment.

Culturally responsive assessment "refers to assessment designs, processes and adaption to individual students and classrooms as well as to assessment outcomes that are sensitive to cultural variations in ways of participating, thinking and learning" (Nortvedt et al., 2020, p. 11). What does it mean for assessment approaches and instruments to be sensitive to the experiences of diverse learners? Afflerbach et al. (1995) write:

> The design of the assessments (e.g., format, content, language), the development and application of scoring criteria (e.g., who participates in setting standards, or how the criteria may be differentially interpreted based on cultural knowledge), the integration of assessment within curriculum, and the interpretation and use of the assessment results should all reflect the commitment to equity. If these issues are not addressed, performance based measures have the potential of being one more "No, you can't do it" message to those who can least afford to hear it. (p. 442)

Culturally responsive assessment flows out of a culturally responsive pedagogy, as exemplified throughout this book. A culturally rich learning environment infused with culturally familiar assessments "provide students with an opportunity to access prior knowledge, add to existing schema, and build upon current cognitive frameworks (Bell & Clark, 1998; Rivet & Krajcik, 2008)" (Kelley et al., 2015, p. 296). According to

Montenegro and Jankowski (2017), "by being mindful of how culture affects students' meaning making processes, cognition, and demonstrations of learning, we can better understand and appreciate the learning gains that students make" (p. 13).

Assessments have come under much scrutiny regarding their validity, reliability, and fairness, particularly within contexts of cultural diversity. The scrutiny comes with good reason, as assessments can positively or negatively impact students' self-concepts, attitudes toward learning, and educational aspirations (Aronson & Laughter, 2016; Moschkovich, 2007). Criticisms of assessment are generally more focused on large-scale and high-stakes assessments, those that have "serious consequences for students or for educators" (American Educational Research Association, 2000). When schools hold up these measures as the most important indicators of success, they can narrow curricular focus. Similarly, as Stiggins (2004, p. 26) points out, over the past half century, society has trended toward "objective, third party evidence of learning"; teachers will teach and others will do the assessing. Although developers of standardized assessments may have psychometric training, they lack a teacher's deep understanding of their unique mix of students who are applying learning in a specific context. Standardized assessments play a role in painting a picture of achievement, in comparing across groups, or in diagnosing learning needs, but they should serve as one piece of evidence among an array of other measures.

Standardized Assessments: Proceed With Caution

Large-scale assessments are typically developed systematically by companies or through state efforts and reviewed for biases and data to ensure validity and reliability. However, Eurocentric referents and biases traditionally have been prevalent in standardized assessments (Spindler & Spindler, 2013). Researchers cite as faults to standardized assessments the use of inappropriate norming samples (the exclusion, or underrepresentation, of individuals from diverse backgrounds) and faulty content validity (the items on an assessment not aligning with what they seek to measure) based on test-maker biases (Noonoo, 2018; Overton, 1996). This is important because large-scale standardized assessments are often part of state accountability systems resulting from federal legislation (Emler et al., 2019). Collective lower performance on these assessments may lead to state "takeovers" for a district or school (Bulkley & Henig, 2015; Green, Bruce, & Oluwole, 2009).

Many researchers have argued that the reason culturally responsive instructional strategies are not translating into higher performance on standardized tests is that the assessments themselves are not culturally responsive (Estrin, 1993; Hood, 1998a, 1998b; Koelsch et al., 1995; Madaus, 1994). Koelsch et al. (1995) write:

> If the student's experiences in a cultural group . . . are not taken into account
> when assessment tasks are developed and scored, the evaluation process of

how well a student has learned with the school's culture will be flawed. A failing performance may indicate the degree of disconnection between the task and the student's frame of reference, rather than the degree of mastery of the knowledge and skills being assessed. (p. 21)

Assessments often contain "content that is not familiar to a subgroup in a population because that subgroup is not exposed to the necessary experiences" (Zurcher, 1998, p. 104). Kelley et al. (2015) detail their research on multicultural students at an urban middle school as it relates to *test content versus experience differential*. Specifically, they found that most errors occurred in reading comprehension questions for culturally unfamiliar reading tasks. They posit that many students revert to surface-level interpretations when faced with tasks that require interpretation and making connections with prior knowledge, which can lead to an increased number of errors for higher level thinking questions. An assessment in which the context or content impedes on accurate measurement of a construct is not fair to the learner or helpful for the teacher.

Large-scale assessments such as the ACT and the SAT, designed for college placement but often used as part of school and district evaluation measures, have been cited as problematic for these reasons. For many students, they are high stakes; they may weigh heavily into their college acceptance or the level of higher education institution they will attend. Racial and gender bias of college admissions tests remains a contentious domain within educational research, and research has shown that SAT scores are highly correlated with family income (Dixon-Roman et al., 2013; Zwick & Green, 2007). Consequently, as Emler et al. (2019) state, "children from disadvantaged families have less of a chance to attend colleges or attend colleges of high prestige, hampering their opportunity for upward social mobility and exacerbating the existing inequity and injustice disadvantaged children face" (p. 288).

On the contrary, students who engage in assessments with cultural frames of reference demonstrate higher level of achievement (Howard, 2001; Kelley et al., 2015; Ladson-Billings, 1994; Sealey-Ruiz, 2007; Ware, 2006). Similarly, Bell and Clark's research (1998) found evidence that African American children performed better on recall and comprehension assessments when readings were culturally familiar as opposed to culturally unfamiliar. Thus, teachers should use caution when drawing conclusions about student learning from assessments that are culturally unfamiliar, because the assessment itself may inhibit effective information processing.

Researchers like Wolf et al. (2008) have also called for a critical examination of how we measure the academic achievement of students who are English learners (ELs), noting that the demand large-scale assessments make on EL language proficiency and cognitive load may obscure valid insight into their grasp of the content area being assessed. ELs can take 4 to 8 years to attain English proficiency needed to be successful on academic content assessments (Collier & National Clearinghouse for Bilingual Education et al., 1995; Cummins, 1981, Hakuta et al. 2000). This is reflected in national assessment data:

in a study of the 2005 National Assessment of Educational Progress (NAEP) study, a large majority of fourth- and eighth-grade ELs (73% and 71%, respectively) scored Below Basic in reading compared to a small minority of non-ELs (34% and 27%; Perie et al., 2005). In mathematics, 46% of fourth-grade ELs and 71% of eighth-grade ELs scored Below Basic, compared to 18% and 30%, respectively, of their same-grade peers (Perie et al., 2005, p. 6). Variables such as native language and length of stay in the United States have been shown to have an impact on the assessment scores of ELs (Abedi et al., 1998). Moreover, forced-choice, forced-comparison, or true–false items have also been shown to penalize Native students and English language learners (Durán, 2011; Kachchaf et al., 2016; Macias, 1989; Trumbull & Nelson-Barber, 2019). Thus, scores from any standardized assessments should be interpreted with caution and in conjunction with other evidence, particularly if the assessment has individual-level implications, such as informing placement decisions.

For these reasons, researchers have expressed concern over disproportionately high numbers of ethnically and linguistically diverse students in special education (Artiles et al., 2005; Donovan & Cross, 2002; Dunn, 1968), because placement is generally informed by assessment results. When using universal screening tools, false positives—or mistakenly identifying students as in need of special education services—have been a concern (Speece & Walker, 2007) and have been noted as a greater possibility with ELs (Haager, 2007). Kirova and Hennig (2013) speak to the concerns of standardized assessment use in early education:

> When children come [to an educational system] with a broad range of cultural and linguistic experiences, the use of standardised measures that are not grounded in the norms and expectations of their sociocultural environment runs the risk of misrepresenting their capabilities (see, for example, Espinosa, 2005; Worthman, 2003). Any over-reliance on tools that measure children's development in relation to norms established by Western developmental psychology may lead to over-identifying children from non-Western cultural backgrounds as delayed (Heydon & Iannacci, 2008). (pp. 106–107)

Collier and Thomas (2004) recommend that ELs not be screened for special education services until 3 years after the student's arrival in an American classroom to differentiate those with disabilities from those who are struggling with learning in a second language.

This is not to say standardized assessments are inherently bad or biased; in fact, among many measures, they play a role. Diagnostic assessments such as the Measure of Academic Progress, Diagnostic Assessments of Reading, the iREADY, and STAR, often provide specific feedback to teachers around student achievement that should be considered when designing instruction and considering additional instruction, differentiated instruction, or unique instructional strategies likely to assist students in reaching high standards. In fact, standardized assessments can be constructive when used in a formative way—not to label but to reveal opportunities for growth.

However, any one assessment should not be regarded as the most important indicator, nor should any one assessment be used to attach a label to a child. Just as we use multiple strategies to teach and engage students, we should also utilize multiple methods to assess their learning. This is in line with evaluative thinking: using multiple sources of evidence, as well as multiple modalities, for demonstrating understanding. When used in this spirit, standardized and large-scale assessments can be very informative.

The Promise of Formative Assessments

Over the last few decades, education has seen a move from assessment *of* learning to assessment *for* learning (Black & Wiliam, 2009; Harlen & Deakin Crick, 2002; Wiliam, 2011), and, similarly, from an emphasis on summative assessment to one on formative assessment. Formative assessment conversation, although initiated by Bloom during the 1960s, was not widely utilized by educators and researchers until the 1980s and 1990s. Until then, assessment was conceptualized as summative, or an activity to be done at the end of an instructional sequence. Bloom (1978) was an early champion of the notion that all children can learn at high levels, when provided the opportunity. Due to Bloom's work, educators began to understand that "the normal distribution of student outcomes was not a 'natural' outcome, but caused by the failure of the instruction to recognise differences in learners" (Wiliam, 2011, p. 3). Formative assessment became a tool to help educators capture students' progress toward goals, to know where to provide extra support or different strategies.

Black and Wiliam (1998) define formative assessment as any teacher-led activity that enables students in assessing themselves and is used as evidence to adapt teaching to meet student learning needs (p. 140). Panadero et al. (2018) write that when formative assessment is done well, it assists students to

> conceptualize what it is they are trying to learn, how they will know they are
> learning, and how they will move forward with next steps. These processes
> activate students' cognitive and motivational capacities, focus students on
> their learning goals, and provide feedback and strategies they can use to help
> them reach their goals. In short, assessment can help students self-regulate
> their learning. (pp. 14–15)

Formative assessment should be embedded within the curriculum to gather data throughout the learning process. Formative assessments allow a teacher to shift direction while teaching because they give a teacher and a student feedback on whether a student understands a learning outcome or not. A formative assessment asks, "Do you understand?" in a way that provides evidence that a student *does* or *does not* understand. Formative assessment focuses on the quality of the learning process instead of on its outcomes (Stobart, 2008). These assessments are very low stakes and truly *for learning.*

As noted by Brookhart et al. (2008), "the power of formative assessment comes from the addition of student-to-teacher communication" (p. 53). Formative feedback is constructive, not punitive; it is specific, timely, and related to learning goals and provides opportunities for a student to revise and improve work products and deepen understanding. Each student shows the teacher along the way where his or her understanding is deep, shallow, or stalled. Formative assessment gives teachers the opportunity to clarify misconceptions immediately within a low-stress environment. Furthermore, as noted by Brookhart (2004), it gives students permission to think for themselves and to openly share their understandings—which frees students to become the driving force in their own learning. Formative assessment supports a culturally responsive classroom, particularly in its valuing of mutuality and equality (Bishop & Glynn, 1999; Black & Wiliam, 2006; Clark, 2011; Damon & Phelps, 1989).

Research conducted by the Organisation for Economic Co-operation and Development's (2005) Centre for Educational Research and Innovation found that formative assessment was associated with the largest achievement gains reported in educational interventions, including high gains for previously underachieving students. Additionally, attendance, retention of learning, and student quality of work all showed significant improvements with the use of formative assessment.

Formative assessment should include a number of important components that can potentially create more equitable assessment practices in multicultural classrooms, including (a) student self-assessment, (b) peer feedback, and (c) quality teacher feedback (Heritage & Wylie, 2018; O'Hara et al., 2015). With each of these practices, students become active partners who share responsibility for assessment with the teacher, prompting them to take control of their own learning (Baas et al., 2015).

Self-Assessment

McMillan and Hearn (2008) define self-assessment as a process by which students establish learning and performance strategies, monitor, and evaluate the quality of their thinking and behavior when learning, provide feedback to themselves, and identify strategies that improve their understanding and skills. At its heart, self-assessment requires that students become evaluative thinkers about their own work, using self-reflection, self-regulation, and personal accountability, all of which are associated with academic gains (Nicol & McFarland-Dick, 2006; Zimmerman & Schunk, 2011). Students are prompted to consider what constitutes quality and to appraise their own work (Tai et al., 2016).

An evidence-based strategy that helps students gauge quality is the use of instructive rubrics. The use of rubrics has been shown to increase students' perceived self-regulation, learning, and self-efficacy (Alonso-Tapia & Pandero, 2010; Panadero et al., 2012; Panadero & Jönsson, 2013). Furthermore, when students participate in the creation of rubrics, they build skills for self-regulated learning and encourage activation of learning strategies (Fraile et al., 2017). Rubrics also support a culturally responsive classroom.

According to Montenegro and Jankowski (2017), "rubrics, when they undergo a culturally conscious development process and are shared with students, can be a way to accurately assess learning for all students while allowing variation in how the learning is demonstrated" (p. 12).

Peer Feedback

Peer feedback has similarly strong evidence on its effect on student achievement. The act of engaging in evaluative processes to provide feedback to a peer exercises judgment skills that are beneficial to the peer reviewer, perhaps even more than the peer being reviewed (Nicol & McFarland-Dick, 2014). Do note that in a diverse classroom, providing peer feedback may be a culturally unfamiliar or uncomfortable way of interacting with classmates. For example, in African and Asian cultures, children are expected to listen and not to ask questions (Nerlove & Snipper, 1981); this is true of Native American students as well (Kim & Zabelina, 2015). Any student may be hesitant to critique another student's reasoning for fear of being offensive (Civil & Hunter, 2015). Because this is a helpful practice, however, it is one that likely needs to be taught and modeled in a classroom, with support and encouragement for students who are new to this way of interacting with peers.

Teacher Feedback

Teacher feedback can have a large impact as well, but only when provided properly (Brookhart et al., 2008). Constructive formative feedback on a task (as opposed to praise, reward, or punishment as "feedback"), is "the most powerful single moderator that enhances achievement" (Hattie, 1999, p. 9). Hammond (2015) communicates why feedback is critical, stating,

> too often, culturally and linguistically diverse students who struggle have developed a set of learning moves that aren't effective and they aren't sure what's going wrong or what to do about it. They cannot do higher order thinking or complex work if they cannot learn to adjust their learning moves, acquire new ones, or strategize about how to tackle a task. (p. 101)

Studies have shown that feedback in the form of written comments is often more effective at driving student performance improvement than grades (Black & Wiliam, 1998; Butler, 1988; Cardelle & Corno, 1981; Crooks, 1988; Elawar & Corno, 1985; McLaughlin, 1974). Culturally responsive and sustaining feedback treats language accuracy and linguistic appropriateness separately from content knowledge (e.g., Abedi, 2003; Carjuzaa & Ruff, 2010; Noble et al., 2014; Trumbull et al., 2016; Trumbull & Nelson-Barber, 2019; Wolf et al., 2008), but constructive feedback should include linguistic factors. The culturally responsive teacher will look for opportunities to provide feedback that honors students' cultural knowledge, points out strengths, and highlights specific ways to grow.

Culminating Activities to Drive Instruction

As indicated in the research, formative assessment has strong evidence of increasing student achievement. However, it is critically important to attend to what frames the formative assessment, to ensure we are working toward meaningful outcomes. In an NPR spot of *All Things Considered*, Robert Krulwich (2011) notes an interesting human phenomenon: "If you blindfold someone, put them in a large field, and tell them to walk forward in a straight line, within minutes and without fail, they will walk in a circle" (1:59-2:07).

Without a frame of reference or external focal point like a mountaintop or the sun, humans tend to wander aimlessly. Formative assessment alone will not necessarily move all students toward high standards. A vision of what students should know and be able to do—one that is complex, supports critical thinking and real-life application, is accompanied by an assessment that allows students to demonstrate their learning around this vision—provides a road map for implementing formative assessment practices. A performance assessment that serves as a culminating event can be this sort of focal point (Wiggins & McTighe, 2005).

Assessments that are designed with end goals in mind bring intentionality to the teaching and learning process. These assessments are most culturally responsive when they are authentic, or meaningful, to students and allow them to make connections between school and the world outside of the classroom in relevant ways (Baker & O'Neil, 1994; Gall et al., 1996; Koelsch et al., 1995; Litchfield & Dempsey, 2015; Wiggins, 1998). Students should have options about context, content, and tasks that prompt them to draw on their funds of knowledge, a critical piece of culturally responsive instruction (Baker & O'Neil, 1994; Linn, 1994). Students should also have options of modalities (Montenegro & Jankowski, 2017) to be able to demonstrate learning in a variety of ways. And assessment tasks should be culturally familiar or related to students' frames of reference in a way that enables them to demonstrate their mastery or competence (Bell & Clark, 1998; Koelsch et al., 1995; Rivet & Krajcik, 2008).

Concluding Thoughts on Assessment Research

Concluding the overview of research, there are a variety of forms and purposes for assessment, and all have strengths, particularly when they are used in formative ways. However, there is also the potential for enormous misuse within culturally and linguistically diverse classes. Educators should be particularly wary of any assessment that is highly consequential for an individual student. If an assessment will lead to the assignment of a label such as "special needs," "failing," "Limited English Proficient," "novice," or affects placement in a leveled reading or math program, assessments should be selected and results should be reviewed critically using measurement principles (we talk about those next) and in conjunction with multiple measures. The Assessment for Learning Project (2019) effectively summarizes keys to quality assessment: relevant, rigorous instructional tasks situated within community definitions of success and assessed using a variety of modalities; clear, actionable feedback that prompts student reflection and is culturally inclusive; student-centered systems; supportive of positive mindsets and diverse identities; and active student participation with structured reflection. We encourage teachers to embrace assessments that drive instruction and support learning in ways that honor and empower individuals and to resist—and even speak out against—punitive or inappropriate uses of assessments.

Measuring Learning of Culturally Diverse Students Through Assessment

Many of the issues identified in the literature relate to principles of sound assessment practices, considerations of validity, reliability, and fairness. Standardized tests and published instruments have typically been vetted for psychometric quality, but this does not mean they are better than other tests in specific contexts. As Stiggins (2004) writes,

> the typical teacher will spend one-quarter to one-third of his or her professional time involved in assessment-related activities. If teachers assess accurately and use the results effectively, then students prosper. If they do it poorly, then student learning suffers. And it has. Therefore, the new belief must be that, without question, teachers need to know and understand the principles of sound assessment. (p. 26)

When teachers do not consider principles of sound assessment, they run the risk of forming false beliefs or misunderstandings about their students based on inaccurate or incomplete data.

Validity

According to the *Standards for Educational and Psychological Testing*, validity is "the degree to which evidence and theory support the interpretations of test scores for proposed uses of test scores" (American Educational Research Association et al., 2014, p. 11). Naturally, an instrument should measure the knowledge, skills, abilities, traits, interests, processes, competencies, or characteristics it is *supposed* to measure. A number of factors can threaten the validity of interpretations, such as drawing conclusions based on personal impressions or evaluating students' abilities based on unrelated factors such as how they dress, their accent, or how their siblings performed (Airasian, 2001). As evaluative thinkers, teachers must take steps to uncover and address our assumptions. Just because an assessment has been designed by content experts and assessed for bias does not make it inherently "good" or useful in a teacher's context. In turn, just because a teacher-made assessment has not been created by experts and vetted through a validity process does not yield it "invalid." Generally, questions that address validity would include the following:

- To what extent is the assessment task representative and relevant to content and skill outcomes of interest?

- Is language or language variety familiar to students (Solano-Flores & Trumbull, 2008)?

- Are assessment questions phrased clearly, avoiding unnecessarily complex grammar and unfamiliar vocabulary that is not germane to the content (e.g., Abedi, 2003; Noble et al., 2014; Trumbull et al., 2016)?

- Do the assessment practices align with students' culturally based ways of participating (Cumming & Van der Kleij, 2016), such as a student's preference not to be asked for a personal response or to critique another student's reasoning for fear of being offensive (Civil & Hunter, 2015)?

- Are the assessment results consistent with what I know about the students or how they have performed on other assessments?

Additional considerations should include whether the assessment mode or modality works well with the identities of the students in a classroom. Language is "one of the greatest keys to cultural validity in assessment" as "assessment depends on language in some way, and language differences among students are associated with differences in the ways they construe the language of an assessment question or task" (Solano-Flores & Trumbull, 2003, 2011 as cited in Trumbull & Nelson-Barber, 2019, p. 3).

To ensure validity, a teacher must consider whether language or content is the construct being assessed. Even in the case of native English-speaking students, content knowledge can be confounded with academic English language proficiency; thus, all teachers must reflect on whether an assessment is appropriate in its linguistic complexity. When considering the linguistic complexity of an assessment, teachers should consider if the language used is one that is most often used in instruction and with which students are familiar; every attempt should be made to avoid complex grammar and usage (e.g., Abedi, 2003; Noble et al., 2014; Trumbull et al., 2016; Trumbull & Nelson-Barber, 2019).

Reliability

Whereas validity relates to the appropriateness and accuracy of a measure, reliability relates to its consistency. Reliability should always be secondary to validity; reliability is irrelevant apart from validity. However, validity is affected by reliability. For example, if scores are not consistent across replications of a testing procedure, if different forms of a test produce different results for the same students, or (in the case of observers assigning scores) if raters assign very different scores to the same task for the same student, these threats to reliability also limit the test's validity. In a classroom setting, reliability is particularly relevant in the grading of student work, particularly with projects or open-ended work. Reliability-related questions for a classroom assessment might be the following:

- In assigning grades to student work, is the first person in the stack evaluated consistently with the last? In other words, if the ordering were changed, would students still get the same score and feedback?

- If one were to evaluate the quality of work at another time when less tired or more engaged, would students' scores be the same?

- If someone else were to evaluate this work, would the scores be the same?

A well-constructed rubric can help with the reliability of grading classroom work because it provides a clear definition of quality that the teacher can apply consistently. It also helps students understand what quality looks like. We detail how to develop rubrics later in the chapter.

Fairness

Fairness relates to the validity of test score interpretations for the intended use(s) for individuals from all relevant subgroups. In a culturally diverse context, the test user should look for "construct irrelevance" present in assessment. This refers to the "degree to which test scores are affected by processes that are extraneous to the test's intended purpose" (American Educational Research Association et al., 2014, p. 12). For example, on a test designed to measure a mathematics skill, the inclusion of items that require reading comprehension might introduce construct irrelevance for ELs.

To mitigate bias, a teacher can use accommodations, that is, adjustments that do not alter the assessed construct and are applied to test presentation, environment, content, or format (including response format) for particular test takers. An example of an accommodation would be eyeglasses. Eyeglasses allow access to visual material but provide no unfair advantages to processing that material (unless one is assessing vision quality!). Just as it would be unfair to deny glasses to someone with poor vision, teachers should provide students assistance that removes barriers to access and process.

To evaluate the fairness of a classroom assessment, a teacher might ask the following:

- Would any of my students likely have performed better if this same assessment were in their native language or offered with a different modality?

- Is any vocabulary or contextual information likely to distract or confuse the student on knowledge or skills I am trying to measure through this assessment?

- Are any of the contexts included in my test unfamiliar to my students?

- What are the consequences of low or high scores, and are they fair and reasonable?

The higher the stakes of the assessment, the more emphasis is needed on measurement principles. For example, if a test simply guides instruction, validity is certainly relevant but less critical. In the assignment of a grade, validity becomes more important.

If the results impact placement in a course or identification for services like special education, validity, reliability, and fairness should be held in high regard. In consequential situations, the validity claim articulated by a test developer should be reiterated by the test user within the specific context; the test user is ultimately responsible for determining if an assessment is appropriate for use in a particular setting. However, as Stiggins (2004) stresses, any teacher designing or using any assessment should be thoughtful about measurement principles.

Culturally Responsive Assessment: From Research to Practice

We offer a framework for how an assessment cycle might look for an evaluative thinker in a culturally and linguistically diverse classroom, with many practical examples. The assessment cycle has measurement principles in the center with culturally responsive considerations around the outer edges, driven by an evaluative thinking cycle: identify learning objectives or target questions, identify or develop assessments for evidence, grade and give feedback, and analyze and use results. Communication with stakeholders is present around the figure because it is important at every stage of the cycle. "Stakeholders" refer to anyone with a vested interest in students, including the students themselves. These might include students, parents, cultural informants, school decision-makers, and the like. Communication flows in multiple directions; the teacher has the responsibility to listen to students and parents in the identification of goals, in the choice of assessments, throughout the feedback process, in analyzing results, and in ensuring parents and students understand what results mean and how they are being used. The cycle is displayed in Figure 3.1; we explain each step and provide suggestions and resources in the remainder of this chapter.

Figure 3.1. *Assessment cycle.*

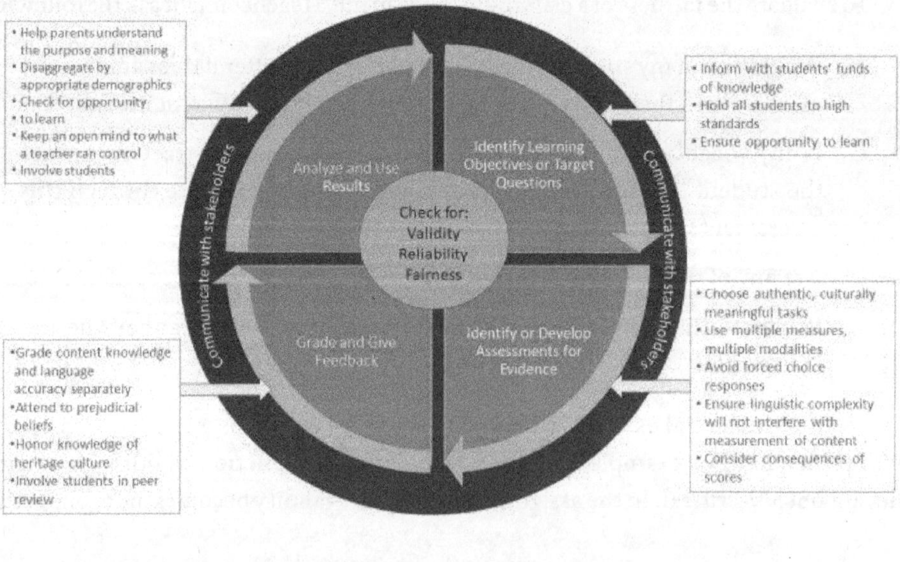

The Cycle

Step 1: Identify Learning Objectives or Target Questions

A critical step in an assessment system is considering goals for student learning; assessment should align with these goals. Specifically, teachers must ask what process, application skill(s), or content knowledge students should know and be able to do. Chapter 4 details how teachers can plan instruction toward specific outcomes. As illustrated in that chapter, the outcomes should hold students to high standards but not be so rigid as to suggest that knowledge is a fixed body of facts; outcomes should account for multiple perspectives and convey to learners how knowledge is developed from the vantage point of the knower. They should also include language objectives in classrooms with ELs.

Teacher mindset is critical here. In selecting objectives and asking questions, teachers must believe that all children can learn at high levels. This belief will be reflected in high standards for all students. In turn, the teacher should commit to using assessment to identify student strengths and promote student growth rather than to deny students access to learning opportunities. To increase equity and guard against making erroneous assumptions, teachers should ensure the learning targets are high for all students and that all students will have instructional opportunities to learn the material (Baker & O'Neil, 1994). To increase the cultural responsiveness of the learning objectives, teachers can consider whether they are informed by students' and families' cultural knowledge, and they can consider what language objectives should be incorporated in the lesson. (See Chapters 4 and 5.)

Student/Teacher Pacts. A tool for identifying learning objectives or target questions is using what Hammond (2015) calls student/teacher "pacts." With pacts, the teacher serves as an ally and warm demander, and students become the drivers of their own learning (Hammond, 2015, p. 94). To foster this alliance, Hammond recommends that teachers talk with students in a way that creates space for them to share their thoughts and empowers them to engage in dialogue and the learning process. Specifically, Hammond advises teachers to do the following:

- Ask the student to identify barriers to achieving a particular learning goal.

- Select with the student a learning goal that is targeted, small, and impactful, along with a deadline for mastery.

- Engage the student in conversation regarding learning moves and cognitive strategies.

- Create check-in points to meet with the student and redirect if necessary.

- Discuss with the student that the teacher's role is a supportive ally in the learning process.

- Clearly and authentically communicate the student's strengths and that they can achieve the learning goal.

- Advise that the pursuit of learning goals may give rise to discomfort but that the teacher is there to provide support. Provide opportunities for the student to discuss these challenges; validate their feelings.

- Ask the student about the plan to achieve the learning goal. Offer additional insight into what could be added to the plan. Give suggestions about how to track and record progress.

- Create a ritual with which to positively mark these conversations. Hammond recommends as examples, "A handshake, fist bump or high five. A pencil with an inspirational slogan on it. It is important to cue the brain so that the experience is infused with emotion so the brain remembers" (2005, p. 96).

- Write down key agreements after meeting with the student.

- Provide the student with regular opportunities to reflect on progress and new learning goals.

Preassessments. With standards and essential questions in mind, teachers can also conduct diagnostic assessments to gauge where students are starting. Drawing on work with mastery learning by Ben Bloom, Guskey (2007) suggests administering brief formative assessments based on the unit's learning goals. These assessments are designed to give students and teachers feedback about prior knowledge to focus student work throughout the unit. A preassessment might be a pencil-and-paper test that asks students questions about certain academic content. It might involve having students develop "concept maps" as a brainstorm around a topic or be an informal discussion in which teachers ask students about their past experiences. It might be a simple "thumbs-up/thumbs-down" survey in which students indicate whether they know foundational content before beginning a new unit of study. Teachers can then select specific activities to provide needed foundational knowledge or address learning difficulties with the feedback they have received (Guskey, 2018). Walqui (2006) recommends anticipatory guides, in which a teacher asks the class to collaboratively fill out a two-column graphic organizer, with one column for what students know about a topic and the other for questions about the topic that they are interested in answering. Teachers can also use what they have learned about students' experiences with a topic and their interests about the topic in shaping the culminating assessment.

Step 2: Identify or Develop Assessments for Evidence of Student Learning

Following the identification of learning goals, teachers should consider what assessments might allow students to demonstrate what they know. The assessments should be focused on outcomes but allow for students to have choice and creativity within the task. Once teachers have identified a culminating assessment, they can use a "backward mapping" approach (Wiggins & McTighe, 2005) to teach the skills and processes needed for every student to succeed. The hope is that the assessment is cognitively challenging enough that engaging and authentic instruction will be *necessary* to prepare students to be successful.

Performance Assessments. An effective culminating assessment is a performance assessment, a real-life application of skills and knowledge. These assessments are usually open-ended, engage higher order thinking, and relate to complex problems that require considerable student engagement. For example, in a second-grade classroom that had been studying insects, children each selected their own insect of study. They crafted an accurate and detailed version of their insect and presented it to their parents with facts learned during an open house in which all figures were on display (see Figure 3.2). Teachers then, during teacher conferences, provided students and parents written feedback on their figures.

Figure 3.2. *A second grader displays her work to friends and family.*

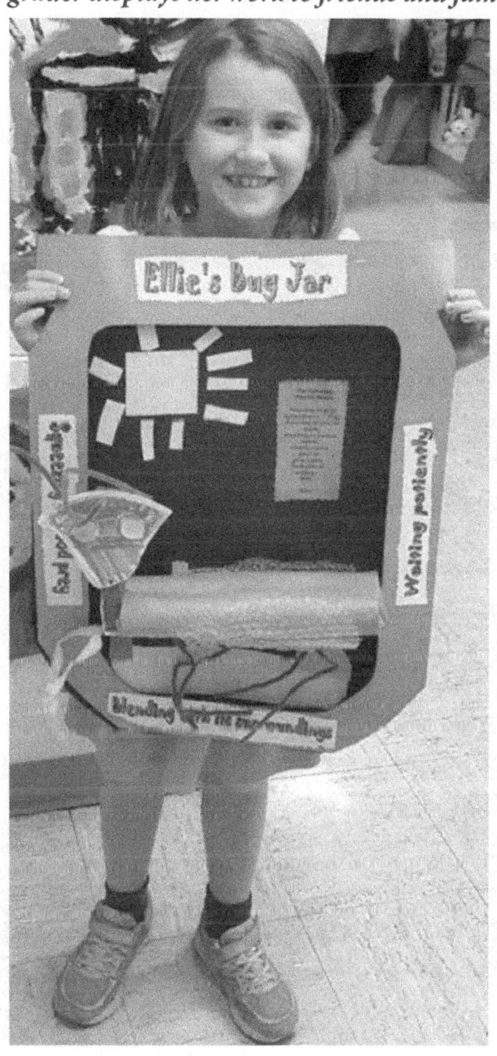

In another early elementary example, students studied American settlers by interviewing their parents about their family's immigration to America and comparing family stories to those they had read about. Students then crafted maps and paper dolls representative of the countries their family emigrated from. Students were assessed according to map accuracy and how their country was represented in their paper dolls' details.

These assessments may be conducted individually or in a group and can involve a significant degree of student choice (Baker et al., 1993, p. 1211). For example, in a unit on slavery, students could choose between mapping out the Underground Railroad, presenting on historical texts, creating chalk illustrations of and poems about abolitionists, acting out the speeches of anti-segregationists, analyzing spirituals, fashioning spiritual quilts, or engaging in unit-long reflective journals (see Figure 3.3).

Figure 3.3. *A student assessment that incorporated choice in topic and modality and included a presentation to classmates and families.*

In group performance assessments, we recommend the careful construction of groups, mindful of language proficiency, culture, and funds of knowledge, so that students can build off one another's strengths and learn from one another. Teachers can assess products as well as processes such as teamwork. As such, performance assessment may accommodate both individually and collectively oriented students. Wiggins and McTighe (2005) point to performance assessment as an effective way to bridge classroom learning to real life, positing that realistically contextualized problems provide evidence of "genuine understanding" (p. 153). Performance assessment has the potential to draw on critical consciousness (see Chapter 6). When using performance assessments, teachers will want to help students come up with a specific goal for the performance task, which may be a challenge to address or an application of a learning outcome. Teachers can invite students to brainstorm situations for performance assessments, encouraging them to incorporate their strengths and cultural knowledge to the framing of the task. Teachers will also want to help students think about their roles in completing the task, the specific audience for their work (e.g., other students, school staff, parents, the community), as well as the product they will be creating (such as a speech, letter to the editor, or poster). Finally, it is important to provide specific success criteria so that students understand how they will be assessed.

In other words, when developing performance assessments, teachers should consider the "what" (the competence, process, or product to be assessed), the "why" (the purpose for the assessment), and the "how" (the methods to be used; Andrade, 2019). In linguistically diverse classrooms, teachers can incorporate opportunities to target aspects of English-language proficiency, although it is helpful to think of language accuracy as separate from the content when grading and providing feedback. We recommend that EL instructors focus on comprehension of topical content or organization of thoughts first and then, as students progress in their language acquisition, grade, and provide feedback on grammar and word choice. When selecting or modifying an assessment, we encourage teachers to consider students' language proficiency and cultural backgrounds. Although students of some backgrounds may be comfortable with oral presentations, others may best convey their knowledge in written form or through a diagram and illustration. Similarly, teachers can provide modifications for ELs, such as templates, word banks, and models of quality work. They can also allow students to do the work in their native language, perhaps contextualizing the performance assessment within their own culture. Students could accompany their native language-based work with a diagram or illustration or partner with another student who shares the native language and has a more advanced English proficiency to share the work in English with the class. Bridging presentations with small-group presentations or teacher–student presentations might be a good way to encourage student confidence and linguistic and presentation skills, particularly at the beginning of an academic year when trust is being built between teacher and classmates.

Many ideas for culturally responsive performance assessments are available at https://www.cce.org/work/quality-performance-assessment/performance-assessment-examples. The sample assessments can be modified to engage ELs in deep thinking and build English proficiency. For example, an assessment gauged for Grades 6 through 12 has students address the essential questions around how social media affects social movements and how the benefits of social media outweigh the potential costs. (See https://www.cce. org/uploads/files/Social-Media-Assessment-Blueprint.pdf.) Students work in groups to research movements in which social media has played a role and then collectively create a 5- to 8-minute podcast to address the question of costs and benefits. ELs could conduct the research about their home country and in their native language and still participate in the English podcast by summarizing what they learned through their 1-minute speech in English. This allows students to dive deeply into the content in the language that is most accessible and to work with peers and the teacher to prepare and rehearse a statement in English about what they have learned. Teachers could use models of speeches and templates for how to communicate a response. This activity would allow ELs to participate in a complex activity and give them the opportunity to practice English communication.

Ways for Scaffolding Student Performance. Students can benefit from various supports that can be embedded in assessment tasks. Kang et al. (2014) provide several suggestions for scaffolds that can assist students as they complete an assessment. These scaffolds can be particularly beneficial for English learners. They include "(a) allowing students to draw in combination with writing, (b) contextualizing the explanation within a focal phenomenon or event, (c) providing checklists, (d) using rubrics, and (e) providing sentence frames" (2014, p. 682). Here, we highlight Kang et al.'s checklists and sentence frames. Later, we will discuss rubrics.

Checklists and Sentence Frames. Kang et al. (2014) describe a few types of checklists that may be employed for scaffolding: a "simple checklist" like a word bank and an "explanation checklist" that prompts students to explain multiple points about a topic as well as "some relationships among ideas, observations, and key patterns" (p. 685). Sentence frames provide students with "linguistic lead-ins" (2014, p. 686), prompting them to fill in blanks to explain, define, give examples or make connections between phenomena. Examples of frames based on Kang et al.'s suggestions:

"What I saw was________________."

"I know this because ______________."

"Evidence for ________ comes from the [activity or reading] because____.
(2014, p. 686)

An example that applies Kang et al.'s (2014) insights is provided in Figure 3.4. This example lends itself to peer checks with language-rich follow-up. After individually completing this assessment question, students could work with a partner to talk about the order of the animals. They could be provided prompts such as "I said the ______ sleeps the ______ most/ least (second, third, fourth, fifth, sixth) and, "I disagree with ______ because ______." This would allow them to talk about their processes.

Figure 3.4. *This math assessment provides prompts and invites students to consider further investigation.*

Sleep varies greatly from animal to animal, but all animals need at least a little sleep! Here is a chart that shows average sleep time for many animals. Study the chart, then answer the questions below.

Animal	Fraction of the day spent sleeping
Cat	15/24
Rat	5/6
Elephant	1/12
Sheep	1/4
Horse	5/24
Giraffe	1/6
Python	3/4

Show your work here:

1. In this table, list the animals by how much they sleep each day.

Order		Animal
Least	1	Elephant
	2	Giraffe
	3	Horse
	4	Sheep
	5	Cat
	6	Python
Most	7	Rat

2. How did you do your work? Use these phrases: First, I _______.   Then, I _______.   Finally, I _______.

First, I made equivalent fractions. Then, I looked at the numerator to see what animal slept the least. Finally, I made the list.

3. What do you notice about the animals as their sleep time increases?

The biggest animals sleep the least and the smallest slept the most.

4. Now, write down approximately how many hours *you* sleep each night. Write this as a number and a fraction.

5. The average recommended hours of sleep for a child is equivalent to 5/12 of the day. Do you sleep more or less than the recommended number? How much more or less?

I sleep 1 more hour than the recommended number of hours.

6. What questions does this raise that you would like to explore further?

How do giraffes sleep?   How long do dogs (pugs) sleep?

Do fish sleep?

Similar to scaffolding, students can prepare for an assessment by answering questions such as "Why am I taking this test? Who will use the results? How? What is it testing? How do I think I will do? What do I need to study? With whom might I work?" (Stiggins & Chappuis, 2005, p. 16). Students can reflect on this in writing or discuss it with peers. This is an excellent way for students to articulate their understanding and to identify material they may need to review.

Rubrics. A rubric provides a clear way to describe standards for quality work. It can be either holistic, providing students with one overall score, or analytic, articulating to students how they performed on various criteria. We recommend analytic rubrics because they clearly communicate expectations on a task and offer students insight with which to evaluate their work, thereby improving their performance (Arcuria & Chaaban, 2019). As such, analytic rubrics "represent not only scoring tools but also, more important, instructional illuminators" (Popham, 1997, p. 75).

Arcuria and Chaaban's colleague van Leusen (2013) provides the following questions to guide the construction of a rubric:

- What you would like your students to achieve?

- What are the criteria that show that students have achieved this goal? (evaluation criteria)

- Can these criteria be broken down into individual traits? (levels of competencies)

- How does one differentiate between quality levels of traits? (description and values)

Rubrics can help students grow in their ability to evaluate their own work. Many teachers involve their students in the development of rubrics, encouraging conversation around what high-quality work looks like, perhaps gauging this by looking at sample work or a "mentor text" as a model for what they expect as a student outcome. Students dissect the mentor text to determine success criteria. For example, they might say that the author used good transitions, used academic language, included a lot of relevant information, and had a good introduction and conclusion. All of this would be included in the rubric, which students could then use as reminders of what they should include to produce high-quality work. This information can all go into a rubric. The teacher can then guide students to apply rubrics to their own work or that of their peers and identify improvement strategies.

Stiggins and Chappuis (2005) recommend having students review weak work samples in addition to strong ones, to help students determine attributes of a good performance or product. He also recommends having students practice using criteria to evaluate anonymous strong and weak work and then having students review their evaluation in pairs. This practice may help mitigate some of the cultural discomfort in reviewing the work of peers. For example, in Tabetha Housekeeper's fourth-grade classroom, students were creating brochures on endangered animals to distribute to various locations in the community. They began their study by reading a mediocre flyer followed by a proficient flyer on saving the vaquita and determining which flyer was better. Through carefully examining each mentor text and a great deal of conversation, students generated the success criteria for their own flyers: good lead (introduction), voice (talking directly to the reader), good word choice (like the word *culprit*), use of headings, pictures that support the text, good conclusion, using complex sentences, and lots of details. Tabetha then worked with her students to develop a "kid-friendly" rubric that was used to guide peer evaluation and individual self-assessment.

Continuous, Informal Assessment. While standardized assessments, a published assessment that comes as a textbook resource, or a traditional test constructed by the teacher can provide evidence of learning, teachers also can gather evidence systematically during instruction using methods such as anecdotal notes and targeted observations. For example, as teachers observe students at work, they can attend to and record an individual student's or group's approach to problem-solving along with their understanding of the concept(s) being assessed (see Figure 3.5). In fact, informal, targeted observation and feedback can be a highly effective form of assessment. Teachers can record notes for future reference using a journal, computer, iPad, or sticky notes for later interpretation. Notes can be taken "in the moment," during a break, or at the end of the day, or teachers can videotape a class or small group and take notes at a later time.

Figure 3.5. *Third-grade teacher Kelsey Davis carefully observes students as they solve various math problems with partners on the whiteboard.*

As a way to determine student understanding while working independently, teachers can provide students with cards they can display to signal when they need assistance (see Figure 3.6). Alternately, some teachers we have worked with have provided different colored paper cups that students can use to flag their confusion. These cards (or cups) provide a system for feedback to the teacher such that they can quickly gauge whether a class reteach would be helpful or individual attention would be most productive.

Figure 3.6. *Feedback systems such as this one can help teachers discern who needs assistance as they work independently or in partners or small groups.*

One of the simplest and most powerful ways to elicit evidence of student learning is through teacher questioning. Once a question is asked, the teacher should provide 3 seconds of wait time and then should provide for as many students to answer as feasible. This can be accomplished through the use of hand gestures, through the use of whiteboards, or through a Think–Pair–Share with follow-up from the teacher. Teachers should pay close attention to student responses and use the activity as an opportunity to inform the next steps of instruction.

Divergent responses and reasoning should be encouraged, and students should be invited to justify their responses or share the processes they used to arrive at an answer. When students have limited English proficiency, they can show their conceptual learning through other forms of representation such as drawing or completing graphic organizers.

Questions do not have to be limited to content. Questions that elicit students' processing or self-concept can also be very useful, such as "What would you like to do better as a writer?" or "What do you do when you are reading and you come to a word you don't know?"

Retelling Assessments. An effective way to gather evidence of a student's understandings of a text is a retelling assessment. Appreciative of oral language traditions and grounded in language-based learning theory (Halliday, 1977; Vygostsky, 1978), retelling assessments are culturally responsive in that they provide insight into students' understandings and connections with texts. Piazza (2012) explains:

> According to Brown and Cambourne (1990), retelling a story or experience is a natural linguistic behavior and an authentic way to assess. The documentation of oral language traditions (Delpit, 1995; Smitherman, 2000) in many African-based, and Aboriginal or Native American cultures supports the use of oral communication as a valid way to assess understandings of text. (p. 136)

To keep students on track and teach them how to produce comprehensive retellings, we have used simple retelling frames that can be displayed on a wall chart. Initially, students use these frames to support an oral retelling of a story. As students become proficient in their retellings, the chart can be removed. See Figure 3.7.

Figure 3.7. *Story Retelling Frame.*

Story Retelling Frame

The title of this story is ______________.

The setting is ______________.

The characters of the story are ______________.

The problem in the story is that ______________.

Here is what happened.

First, ______________.

Then, ______________.

Next, ______________.

Finally, ______________.

Although retellings are typically associated with narrative texts, oral or written re-counting of a text or procedure can also be applied to other subject areas. For instance, in some classrooms in which we have worked, teachers ask their students to describe the procedures they use to solve math problems using whiteboards (see Figure 3.8). This task requires a sophisticated knowledge of math language and a deep understanding of the process and can serve as an effective formative assessment both of students' use of academic language and understanding of math concepts. At the same time, we have found that this task requires modeling and language supports (such as sentence frames) as students begin the process.

Figure 3.8. *An example of a student unpacking their thinking through writing.*

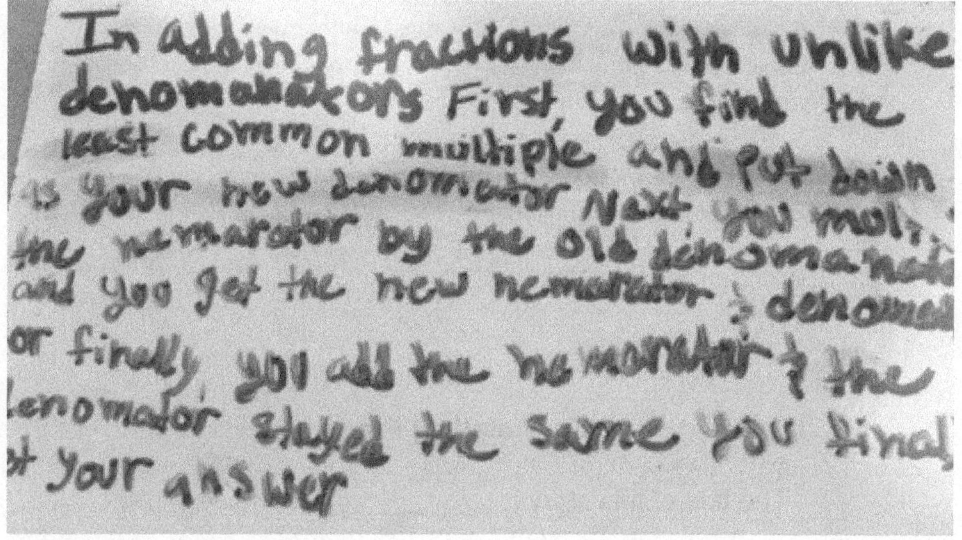

We have had teachers create impressive hallway displays that illustrate students' abilities to comprehend and recall content. For example, third-grade teacher Kelsey Davis asked her students to show how they solved math problems using various strategies. The students wrote out and explained the process they used, then read their texts orally, and recorded them using QR codes. Parents and visitors were able to use their cell phones to listen to students' explanations for solving math problems using strategies that were unfamiliar to them. In another example, Jennifer Caudill, a fifth-grade special education teacher who is featured in Classroom Scenario 3.1, created a similar display with QR codes illustrating her students' abilities in recalling important information in their content-area reading. Both of these examples (shown in Figure 3.9) illustrate how assessment can be integrated with instruction in ways that are meaningful to students.

Any student vocalization of understanding, a thought process, or a new perspective can serve as an opportunity for formative assessment. When the teacher attends to these statements in ways that confirm learning or inform the next steps of instruction, they are excellent assessment tools.

Figure 3.9. *Hallway displays with QR codes can demonstrate student learning in various content areas and are highly motivating for students.*

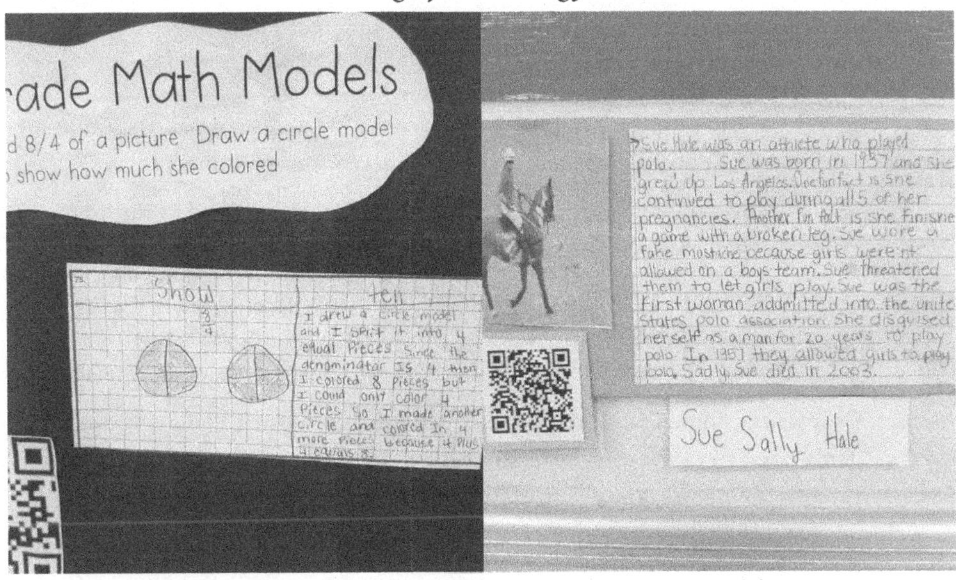

It is important to recognize that instructional tasks (such as completing graphic organizers) are also assessments, and a skillful teacher will use these tasks to determine who needs assistance, whether reteaching is needed, and the next steps for instruction. These tasks can be modified for ELs. For example, T-charts or Venn diagrams can be used to compare/contrast two texts, and ELs can write single words, short phrases, or even draw their responses. For a character map that asks students to label a character's physical, mental, or emotional features, ELs can use words from a word bank that include illustrations (e.g., *angry* with an angry face emoji). Talk frames similar to the literature retelling frame shown above can be provided for students as they discuss procedures for solving a math problem: First, _______, next, _______, then, _______, and last _______. The use of talk frames is discussed in more detail in Chapter 5. As with all learning tasks, ELs can discuss and retell texts in their native languages.

Step 3: Give Feedback.

Students should walk away from an assessment activity with insight into how to improve performance or how to adjust their learning, and a sense of confidence that they *can*. This comes with giving feedback, which can take many forms, from providing in-the-moment guidance to interacting meaningfully with a student text. The most useful form of feedback is that which is instructional and encourages student self-regulated learning. Findings cited by Black et al. (2004) reiterate that written feedback is the most effective means of grading student work. In fact, assigning a grade can have a negative effect on learning in that, when given a grade, students may ignore constructive comments (Butler, 1987). Furthermore, Butler (1988) found that when assigned grades, students see themselves in relation to others, whereas when given only comments, students see themselves in relation to the task; in Butler's study, the latter group outperformed the former. Guskey (2019, p. 6) offers a succinct list of suggestions based on a review of research on feedback:

1. Always begin with the positive. Comments to students should first point out what students did well and recognize their accomplishments.

2. Identify what specific aspects of students' performance need to improve. Students need to know precisely where to focus their improvement efforts.

3. Offer specific guidance and direction for making improvements. Students need to know what steps to take to make their product, performance, or demonstration better and more in line with established learning criteria.

4. Express confidence in students' ability to achieve at the highest level. Students need to know their teachers believe in them, are on their side, see value in their work, and are confident they can achieve the specified learning goals.

The delivery of targeted, timely, and actionable feedback, as opposed to a mere presentation of assessment results, encourages students to develop metacognitive awareness.

For feedback to advance student learning, it must address three major questions for the student: "Where am I going? (What are the goals?), How am I going? (What progress is being made toward the goal?) and Where to next? (What activities need to be undertaken to make better progress?)" (Hattie & Timperley, 2007, p. 86). Teachers are an obvious provider of feedback, but peer feedback is a powerful classroom tool as well. In culturally responsive classrooms, we have seen teachers embed peer feedback within partner work. For instance, students might use whiteboards to solve a math problem individually, and then work with a partner to compare their answers and explain their thinking. Using accountable talk, students discuss their answers (e.g., "I agree/disagree with your answer because . . ."). As students unpack their answers, teachers circulate, listening for math language as well as problem-solving processes, offering targeted feedback as appropriate. This then allows for teacher feedback to enhance peer feedback.

An important component of feedback is the expectation that students will integrate it to improve their understanding and their work. This draws on self-assessment, as it puts the responsibility on the student to have a good sense of goals for learning and a motivation to strive toward a goal. Students should be given opportunities to revise and improve tasks or performance (Goodrich, 1996, as cited in Andrade & Valtcheva, 2009, p. 13) and should be encouraged to re-engage with concepts that they did not previously understand. Figures 3.10a and 3.10b are examples of student self-reflection forms.

In line with Muñoz and Guskey's (2015) suggestions on meaningfully grading student work, we suggest that a student's grade reflect current understanding and performance in relation to a standard instead of an average that includes lower grades from

Figure 3.10. *Examples of self-reflection templates.*

Self-Reflection

Date: _______________________________   Topic: _______________________________

I understood these topics, but I missed these items because of a simple mistake:

Item	Topic	What I can do next time to get this correct

I am still learning these topics:

Item	Topic	What is still confusing?

These words or phrases were new or difficult for me:

Item	Word/Phrase	Meaning?

I can get this! What I will do now to learn the material:

- ☐ Meet with my teacher
- ☐ Look back at the textbook
- ☐ Watch an instructional video online
- ☐ Work with a family member or a friend
- ☐ Other ____

	My feelings	Comments for my teacher
I was able to **understand** our class discussion.	😎 🙂 ☹️	
I was able to **share my thoughts** with the class.	😎 🙂 ☹️	
I was able to **use new lesson vocabulary** when sharing my thoughts with the class.	😎 🙂 ☹️	
I was able to **listen** to my friends' comments.	😎 🙂 ☹️	
I feel confident that I could **explain** what we discussed to my parents or friends.	😎 🙂 ☹️	
I **asked** questions.	😎 🙂 ☹️	
I helped my classmates answer questions.	😎 🙂 ☹️	
I could **connect** our discussion to a real-life problem or situation.	😎 🙂 ☹️	
I saw different perspectives from my classmates.	😎 🙂 ☹️	

earlier work around the same target. Muñoz and Guskey posit that grades are more meaningful when separated into categories such as product (in relation to student performance on a standard), process (student effort), and progress (student growth). Breaking grades into categories can be helpful with ELs who might also have limited education in their home country. Their efforts and growth can be recognized and celebrated as they navigate a steep linguistic and academic learning curve, without ignoring the fact that they have not yet met standards.

Dialogue Journals. A strategy we have seen used in culturally responsive classrooms is dialogue journals. Staton et al. (1988) define a dialogue journal as writing employed for "the purpose of carrying out a written conversation between two persons, in this case a student and a teacher, on a regular continuous basis" (p. 4). Although used mostly in writing classrooms, dialogue journals have been employed across the disciplines. The dialogic endeavor begins first with the student's response to a teacher- or student-directed prompt and followed with the teacher responding to the student's content and questions. This provides students the opportunity to use their voice and demonstrate knowledge and teachers the opportunity to provide instruction through modeling correct grammar and usage through writing or prompting further clarification of the student's understanding of the topic being informally assessed. Usually in the form of an online or bound notebook, dialogue journals minimize the power differential between teacher and student, generating trust and building rapport while also providing space for individualized assessment and instruction. A dialogue journal is a purposeful activity that provides an opportunity for a teacher to assess written language proficiency, discover students' cultural knowledge, gauge metacognitive awareness and scaffolding processes, and provide targeted feedback.

Student-Led Conferences. A student-led conference (Bailey & Guskey, 2001) is a strategy for placing ownership of learning in students' hands. In student-led conferences, students lead conversations about their work with their family, and the teacher acts as a facilitator in identifying student work and a guide in what the student might discuss with the family. Portfolios are an excellent tool for a student-led conference, not to mention an effective strategy on their own, to deepen students' educational experiences by encouraging them to make connections among conceptual issues, theoretical knowledge, and real-world experiences (Singer-Freeman & Bastone, 2016). Kuh et al. (2018) mention a few of the advantages that portfolios have for assessment, including advancing student success, catalyzing change, and making learning more visible for students. Student-led conferences give students the opportunity to talk about their successes and places they would like to grow.

Student-led conferences are easily scaffolded; teachers can provide graphic organizers for students to describe their portfolios. Stiggins and Chappuis (2005) suggest sentence frames students can use in reflecting on their portfolios; for example, "I have become a better _______ this quarter. I used to _______, but now I _______." Or, "Here is what I learned: _______; Here is what I need to work on: _______" (p. 16). Student-led conferences are also opportunities for ELs to describe their work to their families in their native languages. Finally, a student-led conference can serve as an opportunity for a teacher to collect feedback about what the student sees as success, what they see as important next steps in their own learning, and hear from families in terms of their hopes for their child. Classroom Scenario 3.1 describes the implementation of student-led conferences in a special education classroom.

Classroom Scenario 3.1.:
New Learning Experiences, From Instructional Practices to Assessment
Jennifer Caudill

As a special education teacher, I have a passion for providing students with opportunities to learn at high levels while allowing them to take ownership of their learning. Over the past year, I have had a drastic mindset change in the way I plan and deliver instruction to my students. This, in turn, has sparked a change in the manner that I assess my students' learning. The training and guidance that I received through Project PLACE (Partnerships for Learning, Achievement, and Community Engagement, a Culturally Responsive Instruction Observation Protocol–based professional development project), coupled with the atmosphere and mission of my school, has allowed me to grow as an educator.

I serve as the special education teacher for fifth-grade students at a Title 1 elementary school. This school houses approximately 450 students, ranging in grades from kindergarten to fifth. Twelve percent of our school population is comprised of English-language learners. Our school mission states that "through collaboration, celebration, and communication we will ensure confidence in student learners." As a special educator, I strive to ensure that as I provide specially designed instruction to students with autism, specific learning disabilities, attention-deficit/hyperactivity disorder, seizure disorders, and emotional-behavior disabilities, I encompass the beliefs of the school mission.

This past year, my students spent the majority of their school day in the general education classroom setting with their peers. They were "pulled out" into my resource room for approximately 30 to 90 minutes per day based on the needs specified in their individual education plan (IEP) so that they could receive supplemental instruction on their level to address their deficits. I worked very closely with my fifth-grade teammates and created lessons that tied into and correlated with skills and themes being taught in the general education classrooms. The fifth-grade teachers were using the English Learner Education Language Arts curriculum that served as a comprehensive, research-informed, core language arts program that engaged teachers and students through compelling, real-world content. It was created by teachers for teachers and is based on college and career readiness standards. Four units of study were taught, each unit lasting 9 weeks. Students explored the issues of human rights, biodiversity in the rainforest, athletes of social change, and the impact of natural disasters. To ensure that my students had cohesive learning opportunities as they traveled back and forth between the resource classroom and general education classroom, I used these themes as I developed reading materials on my students' reading levels that encompassed the research-based strategies that allow students with disabilities to grasp reading decoding, comprehension, and fluency skills.

Rather than using premade or purchased assessment probes that matched my students' IEP objectives, I developed my own assessments. These assessments allowed me to monitor my students' IEP goals (which I am obligated by law to do) while providing my students with the opportunity to continue their growth in critical consciousness skills through the exploration of the units of study. For example, one of John's reading IEP objectives stated, "When given 10 words consisting of 5–9 letters that contain r-controlled vowels, John will read the words with 80% accuracy for 3/5 sessions." Instead of choosing random words and presenting these words to John in isolation, I collected assessment data related to this skill while John was reading from a snippet of Iggie's House, a moving novel by Judy Blume that tackles racism and neighborhood prejudice. Our units of study provoked incredible discussions, debates, and conversations within our classroom. The material we read in the resource room connected with real-life situations—they were not fictional stories with contrived vocabulary based on phonetic rules that led to a dead-end discussion.

The students loved writing about their learning, summarizing what they read, and displaying their work in the hallway. These, too, served as authentic assessments of my students' reading and writing proficiency. In addition to displaying their work in the hallway for others to see, my students took pride in learning how to record their oral reading so that they could share their knowledge with others through the use of a QR code. They practiced reading their work multiple times to ensure appropriate accuracy and speed before they recorded their reading on a QR code that was then displayed next to their written products in the hallway. Using this strategy of repetitive reading in an authentic manner allowed my students' reading fluency skills to improve. After leaving my resource room, my students were able to reenter their general education classroom with an understanding of the concepts taught when they were not present. They loved sharing with their peers what they learned in the resource room.

I believe there is power in building student ownership, and because of this, I strived to create opportunities for my students to be partners in their learning journey and reflect on their needs as well as their accomplishments. One such opportunity that I explored was having student-led Admissions and Release Committee (ARC) meetings. My students actively participated and shared their progress on their IEP goals during their annual review ARC meeting. Typically, annual review meetings are led by the special education teacher and include parents, the regular education teacher, any related service personnel, and the principal, but these meetings were different from any other special education meeting held in my county. My students were in charge of their meeting! They led the meeting and shared their progress with the committee through varying methods. Some students developed PowerPoint presentations, while others made cue cards with words or pictures to help them remember key points to share with the committee. Students chose how they wanted to present their learning based upon what they felt would be most

> *helpful to them. Watching my students take ownership of their learning and discuss all that they had accomplished made my heart swell. Every one of my students' families attended these ARC meetings so that they could hear their child share about their progress. (There were even several meetings where grandparents and other relatives flooded the conference room, and additional chairs were needed!)*
>
> *Because of the results that I witnessed from my students, I am devoted to diving deeper into units of study that explore critical consciousness. My instructional strategies and practices will be wrapped around this model because opportunities to assess my students' skills can naturally occur in all areas. I learned that I no longer needed to create a separate, stand-alone probe to monitor and assess my students' reading decoding, comprehension, or fluency skills. Not only was this time-consuming on my part, but my students also did not have buy-in and student engagement/choice were not present, which, in turn, negatively impacted my students' ability to demonstrate their knowledge. My students will continue to take ownership of their learning by serving as co-pilots through the process and will be given multiple opportunities to reflect on their learning. I truly believe that the changes that I made to my instructional practices and assessments led my students with disabilities to learn at higher levels than ever before with an increased level of engagement. My classroom did not resemble the typical special education classroom setting, and I am so thankful that I stepped out of my comfort zone so that this could happen. All students deserve this opportunity.*

Exhibitions. Similarly, exhibitions can be used to display student work. Exhibitions are public demonstrations of mastery that occur at culminating moments (e.g., the end of a unit of study or graduation). Their purpose is to support sustained, personalized learning while assuring commitment, engagement, and high-level intellectual achievement aligned with established standards (Andrade et al., 2012, p. 11). An exhibition would be an excellent way to display performance-based assessments. The preparation of an exhibition provides an opportunity to provide teacher and peer feedback; the exhibition provides an additional opportunity for community feedback. Because the audience for exhibitions typically includes practicing experts, they provide an authentic space to share work, which can be very motivating to students (Andrade et al., 2012). Exhibitions provide information about student learning to students, teachers, parents, administrators, and community members. Like a student-led conference, teachers can provide scaffolding to help the student prepare to present their work.

Assessment without feedback is not productive for teaching or learning. In designing assessments, teachers should consider ways to incorporate constructive feedback to students and ways to provide meaningful feedback to families that honors student work and points to opportunities for growth. Also important is student and family feedback to the teacher. Assessment results should serve as feedback to a teacher in planning instruction for the class and for individuals. In step four, we highlight ways that teachers can use results to teach more effectively.

Step 4: Analyze and Use the Results

Evaluative thinkers are evidence-informed decision-makers (Mandinach & Gummer, 2016; Xu & Brown, 2016). Using evidence to make instructional decisions, teachers test assumptions and avoid drawing erroneous conclusions. An evaluative thinking teacher will not limit the use of assessments to assign students a grade but will view assessment as a constant opportunity to get and give feedback that supports learning and improves instruction. Working with assessment evidence for a whole class provides a teacher insight into how to move forward and adjust instruction at a class level. In looking at data across a class, Boudett et al. (2013) encourage teachers to ask themselves, either individually or in professional learning communities: "What do I see?" "What do I make of it?" and "What will I do about it?" Students can also be involved in this conversation. The teacher should adjust instructional strategies when students are not learning, reteaching with new approaches when current approaches are not working. Teachers can also prepare a test analysis chart for students to fill out, with three columns: My Strengths (learning targets they mastered), Quick Review (simple mistakes or miskeys), and Further Study (wrong answers that represent concepts that are still unclear; Stiggins & Chappuis, 2005).

In reviewing results, whether these results are from a graded work or simply student answers to in-the-moment formative assessments like whiteboard responses, teachers can consider what questions students missed consistently and what skills most students lack. Consider new ways to reteach content to students who did not meet expectations, so all students master all core concepts. Avoid excuses for why certain students do not reach goals, and instead, look for factors teachers can control. Similarly, instead of blaming students or external causes for failure, look for barriers to learning. Look for ways to involve students and parents in analyzing their own data and setting new goals.

Stiggins (2007) offers a compelling thought about the use of assessment results, writing,

> We must abandon the limiting belief that adults represent the most important assessment consumers or data-based decision makers in schools. Students' thoughts and actions regarding assessment results are at least as important as those of adults. The students' emotional reaction to results will determine what they do in response. Whether their score is high or low, students respond productively when they say, "I understand. I know what to do next. I can handle this. I choose to keep trying." From here on, the result will be more learning. The counterproductive response is, "I don't know what this means. I have no idea what to do next. I'm probably too dumb to learn this anyway. I give up." Here, the learning stops. (p. 26)

In this vein, the teacher serves as a mediator between students and assessments. An assessment *should* provide information that is productive for moving learning forward; it should never be allowed to influence a student's identity. Recognizing the potential for assessment results to stifle students' motivation, teachers should continually encourage students toward the former response. Part of that encouragement comes with the teacher's role as a partner in helping students understand, identifying what to do next, encouraging them to keep trying, and finding creative ways to help them move forward in learning.

Conclusion

Culturally responsive assessment is hard work and takes time to develop. Like Adie (2013) and Lukin et al. (2004), we encourage teachers to network with colleagues and collaborate on the development of culturally responsive assessments and rubrics, and on data interpretation. Assessment may have a reputation—and history—of being culturally insensitive. Without a thoughtful approach, it still has the potential to exclude, to overidentify, and "fail" culturally and linguistically diverse students. However, we hope this chapter sheds a hopeful light on the value of assessment. We encourage teachers to harness the potential of assessments by cautiously interpreting standardized results as one piece of evidence, using multiple instruction-embedded measures to test assumptions about learning and guide instruction, and employing a range of classroom assessments that emphasize consistent constructive feedback and student ownership. In accord with Shepard (2000), assessment form and function should "create a learning culture where students and teachers . . . have a shared expectation that finding out what makes sense and what doesn't is a joint and worthwhile project, essential to asking the next steps in learning" (p. 10). When used within an evaluative thinking framework, assessment can be a useful and even a culturally empowering tool.

References

Abedi, J. (2003). Testing of English language learner students. In K. F. Geisinger, B. A. Bracken, & J. F. Carlson (Eds.), *APA handbook of testing and assessment in psychology* (Vol. 3, pp. 355–368). American Psychological Association.

Abedi, J., Lord, C., & Hofstetter, C. (1998). *Impact of selected background variables on students' NAEP math performance*. National Center for Research on Evaluation, Standards, and Student Testing.

Adie, L. (2013). The development of teacher assessment identity through participation in online moderation. *Assessment in Education: Principles, Policy & Practice, 20*(1), 91–106. https://doi.org/10.1080/0969594X.2011.650150

Afflerbach, P., Kapinus, B., & DeLain, M. T. (1995). Reading assessment: Equity and performance-based assessment: An insider's view. *The Reading Teacher, 48*(5), 440–442. https://www.jstor.org/stable/20201461

Airasian, P. W. (2001). *Classroom assessment: Concepts and applications*. McGraw-Hill.

Alonso-Tapia, J., & Panadero, E. (2010). Effects of self-assessment scripts on self-regulation and learning. *Infancia y Aprendizaje, 33*(3), 385–397. https://doi.org/10.1174/021037010792215145

American Educational Research Association. (2000, July). *Position statement on high-stakes testing.* https://www.aera.net/About-AERA/AERA-Rules-Policies/Association-Policies/Position-Statement-on-High-Stakes-Testing

American Educational Research Association, American Psychological Association, & National Council on Measurement in Education. (Eds.). (2014). *Standards for educational and psychological testing.* American Educational Research Association.

Andrade, H., Huff, K., & Brooke, G. (2012). *Assessing learning* (The Students at the Center series). Jobs for the Future. http://studentsatthecenter.org/topics/assessing-learning

Andrade, H., & Valtcheva, A. (2009). Promoting learning and achievement through self-assessment. *Theory Into Practice, 48*(1), 12–19. https://doi.org/10.1080/00405840802577544

Andrade, H. L. (2019). A critical review of research on student self-assessment. *Frontiers in Education, 4*, 87. https://doi.org/10.3389/feduc.2019.00087

Ansari, D. (2012). Culture and education: New frontiers in brain plasticity. *Trends in Cognitive Sciences, 16*(2), 93–95. https://doi.org/10.1016/j.tics.2011.11.016

Arcuria, P., & Chabaan, M. (2019, February 8). *Best practices for designing effective rubrics.* Teach Online. https://teachonline.asu.edu/2019/02/best-practices-for-designing-effective-rubrics/

Aronson, B., & Laughter, J. (2016). The theory and practice of culturally relevant education: A synthesis of research across content areas. *Review of Educational Research, 86*(1), 163–206.

Artiles, A. J., Rueda, R., Salazar, J. J., & Higareda, I. (2005). Within-group diversity in minority disproportionate representation: English language learners in urban school districts. *Exceptional Children, 71*(3), 283–300. https://doi.org/10.1177/001440290507100305

Assessment for Learning Project. (2019). *Assessment for learning principles.* https://kumu.io/moonbeammachine/assessment-for-learning-principles#alp-assessment-for-learning-principles

Baas, D., Castelijns, J., Vermeulen, M., Martens, R., & Segers, M. (2015). The relation between assessment for learning and elementary students' cognitive and metacognitive strategy use. *The British Journal of Educational Psychology, 85*(1), 33–46. https://doi.org/10.1111/bjep.12058

Bailey, J. M., & Guskey, T. R. (2001). *Implementing student-led conferences.* Corwin.

Baker, E. L., & O'Neil, H. F. (1994). Performance assessment and equity: A view from the USA. *Assessment in Education: Principles, Policy & Practice, 1*(1), 11–26. https://doi.org/10.1080/0969594940010102

Baker, E. L., O'Neil, H. F., & Linn, R. L. (1993). Policy and validity prospects for performance-based assessment. *American Psychologist, 48*(12), 1210–1218.

Bell, Y. R., & Clark, T. R. (1998). Culturally relevant reading material as related to comprehension and recall in African American children. *Journal of Black Psychology, 24*(4), 455–475. https://doi.org/10.1177/00957984980244004

Bishop, R., & Glynn, T. (1999). *Culture counts: changing power relations in education.* Dunmore Press.

Black, P., Harrison, C., Lee, C., Marshall, B., & Wiliam, D. (2004). Working inside the black box: Assessment for learning in the classroom. *Phi Delta Kappan, 86*(1), 8–21. https://doi.org/10.1177/003172170408600105

Black, P. J., & Wiliam, D. (1998). Inside the black box: Raising standards through classroom assessment. *Phi Delta Kappan, 80*(2), 139–148.

Black, P., & Wiliam, D. (2006) Developing a theory of formative assessment. In J. Gardner (Ed.), *Assessment and learning* (pp. 81–100). Sage Publications.

Black, P., & Wiliam, D. (2009). Developing the theory of formative assessment. *Educational Assessment Evaluation and Accountability, 21*(1), 5–31. https://doi.org/10.1007/s11092-008-9068-5

Bloom, B. S. (1978). New views of the learner: Implications for instruction and curriculum. *Educational Leadership, 35*(7), 563–568, 570–576.

Boudett, K. P., City, E. A., & Murnane, R. J. (Eds.). (2013). *Data wise: A step-by-step guide to using assessment results to improve teaching and learning.* Harvard Education Press.

Brookhart, S. M. (2004). *Grading.* Merrill Prentice Hall.

Brookhart, S., Moss, C., & Long, B. (2008). Formative assessment that empowers. *Educational Leadership, 66,* 52–57.

Brown, S., Race, P., & Smith, B. (2004). *500 Tips on assessment.* Routledge. https://doi.org/10.4324/9780203307359

Bulkley, K. E., & Henig, J. R. (2015). Local politics and portfolio management models: National reform ideas and local control. *Peabody Journal of Education, 90*(1), 53–83.

Butler, R. (1987). Task-involving and ego-involving properties of evaluation: Effects of different feedback conditions on motivational perceptions, interest, and performance. *Journal of Educational Psychology, 79*(4), 474–482. https://doi.org/10.1037/0022-0663.79.4.474

Butler, R. (1988). Enhancing and undermining intrinsic motivation: The effects of task-involving and ego-involving evaluation of interest and performance. *British Journal of Educational Psychology, 58*(1), 1–14. https://doi.org/10.1111/j.2044-8279.1988.tb00874.x

Cardelle, M., & Corno, L. (1981). Effects on second language learning of variations in written feedback on homework assignments. *TESOL Quarterly, 15*(3), 251–261. https://doi.org/10.2307/3586751

Carjuzaa, J., & Ruff, W. G. (2010). When Western epistemology and an Indigenous worldview meet: Culturally responsive assessment in practice. *Journal of the Scholarship of Teaching and Learning, 10*(1), 68–79.

Civil, M., & Hunter, R. (2015). Participation of non-dominant students in argumentation in the mathematics classroom. *Intercultural Journal, 26*(4), 296–312.

Clark, I. (2011). Formative assessment: Policy, perspectives and practice. *Florida Journal of Educational Administration & Policy, 4*(2), 158–180.

Collier, V., & National Clearinghouse for Bilingual Education. (1995). *Acquiring a second language for school.* National Clearinghouse for Bilingual Education, U.S. Dept. of Education, Office of Educational Research and Improvement, Educational Resources Information Center.

Collier, V. P., & Thomas, W. P. (2004). The astounding effectiveness of dual language education for all. *NABE Journal of Research and Practice, 2*(1), 1–20.

Crooks, T. J. (1988). The impact of classroom evaluation practices on students. *Review of Educational Research, 58*(4), 438–481. https://doi.org/10.3102/00346543058004438

Cummins, J. (1981). Age on arrival and immigrant second language learning in Canada: A reassessment. *Applied Linguistics, 2*(2), 132–149.

Cumming, J. J., & Van der Kleij, F. M. (2016). *Effective enactment of assessment for learning and student diversity in Australia.* Springer. https://acuresearchbank.acu.edu.au/item/8v533/effective-enactment-of-assessment-for-learning-and-student-diversity-in-australia

Damon, W., & Phelps, E. (1989). Critical distinctions among three approaches to peer education. *International Journal of Educational Research, 13*(1), 9–19. https://doi.org/10.1016/0883-0355(89)90013-X

Dixon-Roman, E. J., Everson, H. T., & McArdle, J. J. (2013). Race, poverty and SAT scores: Modeling the influences of family income on Black and White high school students' SAT performance. *Teachers College Record, 115*(4), 1-33.

Donovan, M. S., & Cross, C. T. (2002). *Minority students in special and gifted education.* National Academies Press.

Dunn, L. M. (1968). Special education for the mildly retarded—is much of it justifiable? *Exceptional Children, 35*(1), 5-22. https://doi.org/10.1177/001440296803500101

Durán, R. P. (2011). Ensuring valid educational assessments for ELL students: Scores, score interpretation, and assessment uses. In M. Basterra, E. Trumbull, & G. Solano-Flores (Eds.), *Cultural validity in assessment: Addressing linguistic and cultural diversity* (pp. 115–142). Routledge.

Elawar, M. C., & Corno, L. (1985). A factorial experiment in teachers' written feedback on student homework: Changing teacher behavior a little rather than a lot. *Journal of Educational Psychology, 77*(2), 162–173. https://doi.org/10.1037/0022-0663.77.2.162

Emler, T. E., Zhao, Y., Deng, J., Yin, D., & Wang, Y. (2019). Side effects of large-scale assessments in education. *ECNU Review of Education, 2*(3), 279–296. https://doi.org/10.1177/2096531119878964

Estrin, E. T. (1993). *Alternative assessment: issues in language, culture, and equity* (Knowledge Brief Number 11). Far West Laboratory.

Fraile, J., Panadero, E., & Pardo, R. (2017, June). Co-creating rubrics: The effects on self-regulated learning, self-efficacy and performance of establishing assessment criteria with students. *Studies in Educational Evaluation, 53,* 69–76.

Gall, M. D., Borg, W. R., & Gall, J. P. (1996). *Educational research: An introduction.* Longman Publishing.

Green, P. C., Bruce, B., & Oluwole, J. (2009). *Achieving racial equal educational opportunity through school finance litigation* (SSRN Scholarly Paper ID 1411918). Social Science Research Network. https://papers.ssrn.com/abstract=1411918

Guskey, T. R. (2007). Closing achievement gaps: Revisiting Benjamin S. Bloom's "Learning for Mastery." *Journal of Advanced Academics, 19*(1), 8–31. https://doi.org/10.4219/jaa-2007-704

Guskey, T. R. (2018). Does pre-assessment work? *Educational Leadership, 75*(5), 52–57.

Guskey, T. R. (2019). Grades versus comments: Research on student feedback. *Phi Delta Kappan, 101*(3), 42–47.

Haager, D. (2007). Promises and cautions regarding using response to intervention with English language learners. *Learning Disability Quarterly, 30*(3), 213–218.

Hakuta, K., Butler, Y. G., & Witt, D. (2000). *How long does it take English learners to attain proficiency?* (Policy Report 2000-1). The University of California Language Minority Research Institute.

Halliday, M. A. K. (1977). *Learning how to mean: Explorations in the development of language.* Elsevier.

Hammond, Z. (2015). *Culturally responsive teaching and the brain: Promoting authentic engagement and rigor among culturally and linguistically diverse students.* Corwin.

Harlen, W., & Deakin Crick, R. (2002). *A systematic review of the impact of summative assessment and tests on students' motivation for learning.* EPPI-Centre, Social Science Research Unit, Institute of Education, University of London.

Hattie, J. (1999). Influences on student learning. *Inaugural lecture given on August, 2*(1999). University of Auckland, New Zealand.

Hattie, J., & Timperley, H. (2007). The power of feedback. *Review of Educational Research, 77*(1), 81–112. https://doi.org/10.3102/003465430298487

Heritage, M., & Wylie, E. (2018). Reaping the benefits of assessment for learning: Achievement, identity, and equity. *ZDM, 50*(4), 729–741.

Hood, S. (1998a). Culturally responsive performance-based assessment: Conceptual and psychometric considerations. *The Journal of Negro Education, 67*(3), 187–196. https://doi.org/10.2307/2668188

Hood, S. (1998b). Introduction and overview: Assessment in the context of culture and pedagogy: A collaborative effort, a meaningful goal. *The Journal of Negro Education, 67*(3), 184–186. https://doi.org/10.2307/2668187

Howard, T. (2001). Powerful pedagogy for African American students: A case of four teachers. *Urban Education, 36*(2), 179–202. https://doi.org/10.1177/0042085901362003

Kachchaf, R. R., Noble, T., Rosebery, A. S., O'Connor, C., Warren, B., & Wang, Y. (2016). A closer look at linguistic complexity: Pinpointing individual linguistic features of science multiple-choice items associated with English language learner performance. *Bilingual Research Journal, 39*(2), 152–166.

Kagawa-Singer, M. (2012). Applying the concept of culture to reduce health disparities through health behavior research. *Preventive Medicine, 55*(5), 356–361.

Kang, H., Thompson, J., & Windschitl, M. (2014). Creating opportunities for students to show what they know: The role of scaffolding in assessment tasks. *Science Education, 98*(4), 674–704. https://doi.org/10.1002/sce.21123

Kelley, H. M., Siwatu, K. O., Tost, J. R., & Martinez, J. (2015). Culturally familiar tasks on reading performance and self-efficacy of culturally and linguistically diverse students. *Educational Psychology in Practice, 31*(3), 293–313. https://doi.org/10.1080/02667363.2015.103361

Kim, K. H., & Zabelina, D. (2015). Cultural bias in assessment: Can creativity assessment help? *International Journal of Critical Pedagogy, 6*(2), 129–148.

Kirova, A., & Hennig, K. (2013). Culturally responsive assessment practices: Examples from an intercultural multilingual early learning program for newcomer children. *Power and Education, 5*(2), 106–119.

Koelsch, N., Estrin, E., & Farr, B. (1995). *Guide to developing equitable performance assessments* (ED397125). ERIC. https://files.eric.ed.gov/fulltext/ED397125.pdf

Krulwich, R. (2011, February 22). *Circling themselves to death.* Krulwich wonders: Robert Krulwich on science. https://www.npr.org/sections/krulwich/2011/02/22/133810924/circling-themselves-to-death

Kuh, G. D., Gambino, L. M., Ludvik, M. B., & O'Donnell, K. (2018). *Using ePortfolio to document and deepen the impact of HIPs on learning dispositions* (Occasional Paper No. 32). University of Illinois. https://learningoutcomesassessment.org/documents/Occ%20paper%2032Final.pdf

Ladson-Billings, G. (1994). What we can learn from multicultural education research. *Educational Leadership, 51*(8), 22–26.

Linn, R. L. (1994). Performance assessment: Policy promises and technical measurement standards. *Educational Researcher, 23*(9), 4–14.

Litchfield, B. C., & Dempsey, J. V. (2015). Authentic assessment of knowledge, skills, and attitudes. *New Directions for Teaching and Learning, 2015*(142), 65–80. https://doi.org/10.1002/tl.20130

Lukin, L. E, Bandalos, D. L., Eckhout, T. J, & Mickelson, K. (2004). Facilitating the development of assessment literacy. *Educational Measurement, Issues and Practice, 23*(2), 26–32.

Macias, C. J. (1989, August). American Indian academic success: The role of Indigenous learning strategies. *Journal of American Indian Education,* pp. 43–52. https://www.jstor.org/stable/44466406

Madaus, G. (1994). A technological and historical consideration of equity issues associated with proposals to change the nation's testing policy. *Harvard Educational Review, 64*(1), 76–96. https://doi.org/10.17763/haer.64.1.4q87663roj76rwv1

Mandinach, E. B., & Gummer, E. S. (2016). Every teacher should succeed with data literacy. *Phi Delta Kappan, 97*(8), 43–46. https://doi.org/10.1177/0031721716647018

McLaughlin, T. F. (1974). Effects of written feedback in reading on behaviorally disordered students. *Journal of Educational Research, 85*(5), 312–316.

McMillan, J. H., & Hearn, J. (2008). Student self-assessment: The key to stronger student motivation and higher achievement. *Educational Horizons, 87*(1), 40-49.

Montenegro, E., & Jankowski, N. A. (2017, January). *Equity and assessment: Moving towards culturally responsive assessment* (Occasional Paper #29). National Institute for Learning Outcomes Assessment.

Moschkovich, J. (2007). Bilingual mathematics learners: How views of language, bilingual learners, and mathematical communication impact instruction. In N. S. Nasir & P. Cobb (Eds.), *Improving access to mathematics: Diversity and equity in the classroom* (pp. 89–104). Teachers College Press.

Muñoz, M. A., & Guskey, T. R. (2015). Standards-based grading and reporting will improve education. *Phi Delta Kappan, 96*(7), 64–68.

Nerlove, S. B., & Snipper, A. S. (1981). Cognitive consequences of cultural opportunity. In R. L. Munroe, R. H. Munroe, & B. B. Whiting (Eds.), *Handbook of cross-cultural human development* (pp. 440–446). Garland STPM Press.

Nicol, D., & McFarlane-Dick, D. (2006). Formative assessment and self-regulated learning: A model and seven principles of good feedback practice. *Studies in Higher Education, 31*(2), 199–218.

Noble, T., Rosebery, A., Suarez, C., Warren, B., & O'Connor, M. C. (2014). Science assessments and English language learners: Validity evidence based on response processes. *Applied Measurement in Education, 27*(4), 248–260.

Noonoo, S. (2018, January 10). *Can a test ever be fair? How today's standardized tests get made.* EdSurge News. https://www.edsurge.com/news/2018-01-10-can-a-test-ever-be-fair-how-today-s-standardized-tests-get-made

Nortvedt, G. A., Wiese, E., Brown, M., Burns, D., McNamara, G., O'Hara, J., Altrichter, H., Fellner, M., Herzog-Punzenberger, B., Nayir, F., & Taneri, P. O. (2020). Aiding culturally responsive assessment in schools in a globalising world. *Educational Assessment, Evaluation and Accountability, 32*(1), 5–27. https://doi.org/10.1007/s11092-020-09316-w

Organisation for Economic Co-operation and Development. (2005). *Policy Brief: Formative assessment: Improving learning in secondary classrooms.* http://www.oecd.org/education/ceri/35661078.pdf

O'Hara, J., McNamara, G., & Harrison, K. (2015). Culture changes, Irish evaluation and assessment traditions stay the same? Exploring peer- and self-assessment as a means of empowering ethnic minority students. In S. Hood, R. Hopson, & H. Frierson (Eds.), *Continuing the journey to reposition culture and cultural context in evaluation theory and practice* (pp. 205–231). Information Age Publishing.

Overton, T. (1996). *Assessment in special education: An applied approach* (2nd ed.). Merrill, Prentice-Hall.

Oyserman, D., Novin, S., Flinkenflögel, N. H., & Krabbendam, L. (2015). Rethinking the culture-brain interface: Integrating culture-as-situated-cognition and neuroscience prediction models. *Culture and Brain, 2014*(2), 1–26. https://doi.org/10.1007/s40167-014-0016-6

Panadero, E., Andrade, H., & Brookhart, S. (2018). Fusing self-regulated learning and formative assessment: A roadmap of where we are, how we got here, and where we are going. *The Australian Educational Researcher, 45*(1), 13–31. https://doi.org/10.1007/s13384-018-0258-y

Panadero, E., & Jönsson, A. (2013, June). The use of scoring rubrics for formative assessment purposes revisited: A review. *Educational Research Review, 9*, 129–144. https://doi.org/10.1016/j.edurev.2013.01.002

Panadero, E., Tapia, J. A., & Huertas, J. A. (2012). Rubrics and self-assessment scripts effects on self-regulation, learning and self-efficacy in secondary education. *Learning and Individual Differences, 22*(6), 806–813. https://doi.org/10.1016/j.lindif.2012.04.007

Park, D. C., & Huang, C.-M. (2010). Culture wires the brain: A cognitive neuroscience perspective. *Perspectives on Psychological Science, 5*(4), 391–400. https://doi.org/10.1177/1745691610374591

Patton, M. Q. (2018, Summer). A historical perspective on the evolution of evaluative thinking. *New Directions for Evaluation*, (158), 11–28.

Perie, M., Grigg, W., & Donahue, P. (2005). *NAEP—The nation's report card: Reading 2005: Executive summary*. National Center for Education Statistics. https://nces.ed.gov/nationsreportcard/pubs/main2005/2006451.asp

Piazza, S. V. (2012). Cultural responsiveness and formative reading assessments: Retellings, comprehension questions, and student interviews. *Language and Literacy, 14*(3), 133–149.

Popham, W. J. (1997). What's wrong—and what's right—with rubrics. *Educational Leadership, 55*(2), 72–75.

Rivet, A., & Krajcik, J. (2008). Contextualizing instruction: Leveraging students' prior knowledge and experiences to foster understanding of middle school science. *Journal of Research in Science Teaching, 45*(1), 79–100. https://doi.org/10.1002/tea.20203

Rogoff, B. (2003). *The cultural nature of human development*. Oxford University Press.

Sealey-Ruiz, Y. (2007). Wrapping the curriculum around their lives: Using a culturally relevant curriculum with African American adult women. *Adult Education Quarterly, 58*(1), 44–60. https://doi.org/10.1177/0741713607305938

Shepard, L. A. (2000). The role of assessment in a learning culture. *Educational Researcher, 29*(7), 4–14. https://doi.org/10.3102/0013189X029007004

Singer-Freeman, K., & Bastone, L. (2016). *Pedagogical choices make large classes feel small* (Occasional Paper 27). National Institute for Learning Outcomes Assessment.

Solano-Flores, G., & Trumbull, E. (2008). In which language should English language learners be tested? In R. J. Kopriva (Ed.), *Improving testing for English language learners: A comprehensive approach to designing, building, implementing, and interpreting better academic assessments* (pp. 169–200). Routledge.

Speece, D. L., & Walker, C. Y. (2007). What are the issues in Response to Intervention research? In D. E. Haager, J. E. Klingner, & S. E. Vaughn (Eds.), *Evidence-based reading practices for response to intervention* (pp. 287–301). Paul H. Brookes.

Spindler, G., and Spindler, L. (2013). *The American cultural dialogue and its transmission*. Routledge.

Spradley, J. P. (1980). *Participant observation*. Holt, Rinehart and Winston.

Staton, J. (1988). ERIC/RCS report: Dialogue journals. *Language Arts, 65*(2), 198–201. http://www.jstor.org/stable/4140554

Stiggins, R. (2004). New assessment beliefs for a new school mission. *Phi Delta Kappan, 86*(1), 22–27.

Stiggins, R., & Chappuis, J. (2005). Using student-involved classroom assessment to close achievement gaps. *Theory Into Practice, 44*(1), 11–18.

Stobart, G. (2008). *Testing times: The uses and abuses of assessment*. Routledge.

Tai, J., Ajjawi, R., Boud, D., Dawson, P., & Panadero, E. (2018). Developing evaluative judgement: Enabling students to make decisions about the quality of work. *Higher Education, 76*(3), 467–481.

Trumbull, E., & Nelson-Barber, S. (2019). The ongoing quest for culturally-responsive assessment for indigenous students in the U.S. *Frontiers in Education, 4*, 40. https://doi.org/10.3389/feduc.2019.00040

Trumbull, E., Nelson-Barber, S., & Huang, C. W. (April, 2016). *Exploring the role of linguistic factors in the performance of English learners on science assessments* [Paper presentation]. Annual meeting of the American Educational Research Association, Washington, D.C.

van Leusen, P. (2013, August 13). *Assessments with rubrics.* Teach Online. https://teachonline.asu.edu/2013/08/assessments-with-rubrics/

Vygotsky, L. S. (1978). *Mind in society.* Harvard University Press.

Walqui, A. (2006). Scaffolding instruction for English language learners: A conceptual framework. *International Journal of Bilingual Education and Bilingualism, 9*(2), 159–180. https://doi.org/10.1080/13670050608668639

Ware, F. (2006). Warm demander pedagogy: Culturally responsive teaching that supports a culture of achievement for African American students. *Urban Education, 41*(4), 427–456. https://doi.org/10.1177/0042085906289710

Wiggins, G. P. (1998). *Educative assessment: Designing assessments to inform and improve student performance.* Jossey-Bass.

Wiggins, G. P., & McTighe, J. (2005). *Understanding by design* (Expanded 2nd ed.). Association for Supervision and Curriculum Development.

Wiliam, D. (2006). Formative assessment: Getting the focus right. *Educational Assessment, 11*(3–4), 283–289.

Wiliam, D. (2011). What is assessment for learning? *Studies in Educational Evaluation, 37*(1), 3–14.

Winerman, L. (2006, February). *The culture-cognition connection.* https://www.apa.org/monitor/feb06/connection

Wolf, M., Farnsworth, T., & Herman, J. (2008). Validity issues in assessing English language learners' language proficiency. *Educational Assessment, 13*(2/3), 80–107.

Xu, Y., & Brown, G. T. L. (2016). Teacher assessment literacy in practice: A reconceptualization. *Teaching and Teacher Education, 58*, 149–162. https://doi.org/10.1016/j.tate.2016.05.010

Zimmerman, B. J., & Schunk, D. H. (2011). Self-regulated learning and performance: An introduction and overview. In H. Schunk (Ed.), *Handbook of self-regulation of learning and performance* (pp. 1–14). Routledge.

Zurcher, R. (1998). Issues and trends in culture-fair assessment. *Intervention in School and Clinic, 34*(2), 103–106. https://doi.org/10.1177/105345129803400206

Zwick, R., & Green, J. G. (2007). New perspectives on the correlation of SAT Scores, high school grades, and socioeconomic factors. *Journal of Educational Measurement, 44*(1), 23–45. https://doi.org/10.1111/j.1745-3984.2007.00025.x

CHAPTER 4

Culturally and Linguistically Responsive Instructional Practices

Susan Chambers Cantrell and Tiffany R. Wheeler

TEACHERS HAVE AN immense responsibility for what students experience each and every school day within the walls of their classrooms. They make a multitude of decisions about what students learn, how instruction is structured, who gets to speak and when, what questions are asked, what students do, and how students show what they know. Amid all these decisions, teachers who want to serve all their students equitably through culturally and linguistically responsive instructional practices critically evaluate traditional practices and their impacts on students. Rather than maintain the status quo, they work to design and implement instruction that builds on, honors, and sustains the cultural backgrounds, experiences, and identities of their students in diverse classroom settings.

It can be challenging for teachers to implement culturally and linguistically responsive practices within educational systems created in the context of racism and White supremacy. Although the term *White supremacy* conjures up notions of extremist groups such as the Ku Klux Klan, Robin DiAngelo (2018) maintains that White supremacy is "a descriptive and useful term to capture the all-encompassing centrality and assumed superiority of people defined and perceived as [W]hite and the practices based on this assumption" (p. 28). Historically, the U.S. education system has reflected the racism and White supremacy that occurs in the larger society. At its inception, schooling in the United States was reserved for privileged White males, and other groups have had to advocate diligently for their right to a high-quality education (Love, 2019).

Traditionally, schools have not been concerned about building on and sustaining students' languages and cultures but, rather, have been designed to eliminate them. Spring (2016) suggests that schools have been used to eradicate the cultures of persons of color and other disenfranchised populations by encouraging them to acquire the linguistic and cultural knowledge of those in power. During periods of massive immigration, an important goal of schooling was to "Americanize" newcomers so that they could become effective workers in a hegemonic economy. For example, in the 1800s, Native Americans were torn from their families and sent to boarding schools where they were forced to speak English and assimilate into White society, thus stripping them of their languages and cultures. Due to legal segregation and Jim Crow laws, African Americans were required to attend segregated schools in the South and were subjected to inferior "separate but equal" schooling until the *Brown v. Board of Education* ruling in 1954. Hispanic Americans also have a history of attending segregated schools in the Southwest and have experienced discriminatory policies that have required them to abandon their native language and culture in order to become "Americanized" (Spring, 2016). Hence, for decades, historically marginalized groups have been rendered invisible in our schools. As a result, students of color and other students who have been marginalized and discriminated against continually have been deprived of an equitable education and have experienced underachievement in U.S. schools.

Given that U.S. teachers are disproportionately White and middle class, they often do not consider the ways in which the educational system, and the classroom instruction therein, serves to perpetuate inequities and disenfranchise students of color (Sensoy & DiAngelo, 2017). Often, well-meaning teachers seek to implement culturally and linguistically responsive practices but only so far as those practices align with helping students attain monocultural and monolingual outcomes. As teachers implement classroom instruction that promotes greater equity and achievement for all, they must actively work to sustain the languages and cultural practices of their students of color and other historically marginalized students (Paris, 2012). This requires that teachers are constantly engaged in critical analysis of curricular policies, instructional practices, and desired outcomes as they plan for and enact instruction so as to resist perpetuation of practices and outcomes that inherently elevate White, Eurocentric, monolingual ideology.

Culturally and linguistically responsive instructional practices are rooted in a belief that the differences that students bring into the classroom are assets that can enhance learning for all students. As outlined in the Culturally Responsive Instruction Observation Protocol (CRIOP; Powell et al., 2017), teachers adhere to a set of asset-oriented principles in culturally responsive classrooms: (1) instruction is contextualized in students' lives, experiences, and individual abilities; (2) students engage in active, hands-on, meaningful learning tasks, including inquiry-based learning; (3) the teacher focuses on developing students' academic language; (4) the teacher uses instructional techniques that scaffold student learning; and (5) students have choices based on their experiences, interests, and strengths. Through instructional practices that build on students' experiences, questions, language, knowledge, interests, and strengths, culturally responsive teachers enable students to reach their highest potential.

Certainly, academic achievement is an important purpose of culturally and linguistically responsive instruction (Ladson-Billings, 1994), and it is critical that historically marginalized students are provided instruction and opportunities that enable them to achieve success on a range of measures. However, there are other outcomes that are foundational to culturally and linguistically responsive practices. Milner (2011) identifies that culturally responsive pedagogy:

> EMPOWERS students to:
> - Examine educational content and processes
> - Create and construct and deconstruct meaning
> - Succeed academically and socially
> - See contradictions and inequities in local and larger communities
>
> INCORPORATES student culture in:
> - Curriculum and teaching
> - Maintaining it [student culture]
> - Transcending negative effects of the dominant culture
>
> CREATES classroom contexts that:
> - Are challenging and innovative
> - Focus on student learning (and consequently academic achievement)
> - Build cultural competence
> - Link curriculum and instruction to sociopolitical realities (p. 70)

As this list reflects, culturally and linguistically responsive instruction is quite complex. Such teaching requires teachers to know deeply the lives and backgrounds of their students so students' cultures can be incorporated in learning. Culturally and linguistically responsive teachers must understand inequities in the social, economic, and political structures and challenge those inequities with their students. Most important, teachers need to maintain high expectations for students' academic outcomes while providing appropriate opportunities and supports for student success.

As we have worked with teachers and teacher candidates who spanned the gamut in terms of their thinking about working in diverse classrooms with students from various cultural and linguistic backgrounds, we have seen teachers grow and develop in their work as culturally/linguistically responsive and antiracist teachers. We have experienced our own growth and development as teacher educators and scholars from different racial/ethnic backgrounds on different paths along the journey. Although we recognize that culturally and linguistically responsive teaching is much broader and encompasses far more than what teachers plan and enact in classrooms, in this chapter, we focus on classroom-based instructional practices that make a difference in *all* students' engagement, academic achievement, and social-emotional development. In the first part of this chapter, we present research that supports and illuminates culturally responsive instructional practices, and in the second part, we present specific examples of the ways in which teachers have enacted culturally responsive instructional practices in classrooms in our state and beyond.

What Does the Literature Tell Us About Instruction That Is Culturally Responsive?

Research suggests that intentionally connecting instruction to students' backgrounds, experiences, and cultural identities affects their learning; thus, creating a classroom environment that views students' cultural knowledge as an asset and affirms students' racial, ethnic, and gender identities is an important part of culturally responsive instruction. There is also evidence in the literature that providing hands-on, meaningful learning experiences that offer opportunities for students to be actively engaged in learning positively impacts student engagement. Instructional practices that include inquiry learning, student choice in learning activities, and scaffolding students' acquisition of new skills and concepts are impactful for all students but are particularly important in facilitating high levels of learning in diverse classrooms. In addition, there is a rather large body of research that is specific to English learners (ELs) that documents instructional practices that are beneficial to this particular population. In this section, we discuss the impacts of culturally responsive instructional practices on student achievement and student engagement. Furthermore, we review research that illustrates the power of linking instruction to students' lives and identities and providing meaningful and choice-based learning experiences. Finally, we focus on teaching academic language and scaffolding students' learning to promote ELs' language acquisition and achievement.

Impacts of Culturally Responsive Instructional Practices on Student Outcomes

Implementing practices that are responsive to students' backgrounds, cultures, linguistic heritages, and out-of-school lives can make positive differences in the academic achievement and engagement of students who have been historically marginalized in schools. Over the past decade, researchers have responded to calls for empirical evidence that culturally responsive practices translate to higher student outcomes (Sleeter, 2012). Aronson and Laughter (2016) conducted an extensive review of research examining the impact of culturally responsive educational practices on student outcomes, focusing their review across multiple disciplines. Although the reviewers noted that the studies that have been conducted on culturally responsive practices are primarily small in scale, they found evidence for the efficacy of culturally responsive instructional practices across content areas. For example, in mathematics, studies have indicated that teachers' connections of math concepts to students' everyday lives resulted in positive impacts on student learning (Civil & Kahn, 2001), and building mathematics instruction around social justice issues that impact students resulted in deeper mathematical thinking and improved academic achievement (Gutstein, 2003). Similarly, Lipka and colleagues (2005) examined a culturally based mathematics program in their work with Yup'ik elders and teachers. Working with both teachers who were "insiders" or "outsiders," the researchers found that the curriculum, which was grounded in the cultural context, was effective in increasing students' mathematics performance.

More recently, Abdulrahim and Orosco (2020) conducted a review of research on culturally responsive practices in mathematics between 1993 and 2018 and documented the value of culturally responsive teaching on student outcomes. The researchers identified themes across the studies and found a number of threads in teacher practices that resulted in positive outcomes for students: a focus on cultural identity, instructional engagement, high expectations, student critical thinking, social justice, and collaboration. The results of this review indicated that culturally responsive curricula and interaction patterns, such as storytelling, the use of native languages, and real-world projects built positive student identities. Furthermore, the studies showed that culturally responsive practices resulted in higher student engagement and mathematics achievement.

In addition to mathematics, the positive impacts of culturally responsive instruction have been demonstrated in science classrooms. For example, in a study of urban high school students who focused on social justice issues within their science curriculum, student interview and focus group data reflected high student engagement (Dimick, 2012). In addition, Carlone et al. (2011) conducted a comparative ethnography in which they illustrated how differences in the ways in which teachers engage students in learning science (i.e., inquiry learning, generative thinking, and productive exchange of ideas) can impact students' identities as science learners, particularly students of color.

As the research in this section suggests, culturally and linguistically responsive instructional practices do impact students' academic, emotional, and social outcomes in positive and powerful ways. In the remaining sections of the first half of this chapter, we examine what we perceive as the most critical dimensions of culturally and linguistically responsive instruction. These dimensions are the foundation for the CRIOP Instructional Practices indicators operationalized in the second half of the chapter.

Students' Lives and Identities as Instructional Foundations

The primary purpose of culturally responsive instructional practices is promoting educational equity through student empowerment (Gay, 2010, 2015). Students are empowered when teachers view their life experiences as assets rather than problematic and when their learning is rooted in their lives and identities. In culturally responsive classrooms, teachers honor and value students' lives outside of school and embed their experiences within curricular and instructional activities, as opposed to presenting a traditional curriculum disconnected from students' homes and families. Using curricula and instructional strategies that honor and build on diversity validates students' cultures and makes the content of the curriculum more relevant to students (Gay, 2010). Empowering students requires replacing deficit perspectives of students, their families, and their communities with notions that students bring unique and valuable sets of knowledge into the classroom (Gay, 2013).

In the research that follows on using students' lives and experiences as foundational for classroom activities, teachers position themselves as learners. First, teachers learn *about* students' lives, backgrounds, and experiences outside of the classroom. It is important that teachers are aware of students' cultural and linguistic knowledge so that this knowledge can be utilized and extended. Teachers also learn *with* their students. This means posing questions together and seeking answers to those questions as a collective community. Finally, teachers learn *from* their students. This learning occurs when the teacher shows a genuine interest in gaining knowledge about students' specialized expertise and their families' funds of knowledge, or "the historically accumulated and culturally developed bodies of knowledge and skills essential for household or individual functioning and well being" (Moll et al., 1992, p. 133). Understanding the funds of knowledge of students' families extends beyond learning about students' lives to enhance instruction and seeks to position students as holding important knowledge and expertise from which others can learn.

In Chapter 1, Walker-Dalhouse suggests incorporating morning meetings in the regular classroom routine as a way to learn about students' lives outside the classroom. In Chapter 2, Perry documents several ways for getting to know students and their families, for example, family visits, family journals, and the like. Here, we emphasize that a culturally competent educator uses this information to plan for instruction. Embedding students' and families' cultural knowledge in instruction simultaneously affirms that knowledge and makes new information more comprehensible for students.

A number of studies illustrate the ways in which teachers can frame instruction within the context of students' lives and identities. Machado et al. (2017) conducted a case study in a seventh-grade classroom in which they documented the use of poetry to help students explore their own cultural identities and the identities of their peers. The teacher, Mr. Coppola, engaged students in exploring and critiquing different aspects of their cultures as they read and studied varied forms of poetry. Students culminated their work by writing and performing spoken-word poems rooted in their own lives and identities. Students explored dimensions of their ethnic, cultural, religious, and family affiliations, including how those affiliations played out in their lives. Instead of teaching poetry in a more traditional way or even having students write poems about cultural heroes, events, or holidays, Mr. Coppola honored and sustained students' cultural identities and practices by centering the study of poetry within students' lives. He learned about and with his students, and the students learned from one another. The researchers documented high student engagement and increased linguistic play. The researchers concluded that, through this experience, students were able to better understand the fluid nature of culture in a way that was culturally sustaining and identity affirming.

In another classroom-based qualitative study, Milner (2011) used observations and interviews to examine the ways in which a middle school teacher learned about, with, and from his students and expanded his own cultural competence. The teacher in this study, Mr. Hall, used his teaching of personal narratives to both expand his own cultural knowledge and maximize student learning opportunities. Mr. Hall shared his own life with his students in an urban classroom, including writing his own personal narratives that included information about his wife and his children and siblings. He used his growing knowledge of his students through their shared writing and interactions to grapple with issues of identity and race in an urban setting. Milner (2011) demonstrated the ways in which these classroom interactions provided a foundation for culturally responsive pedagogy. Through getting to know his students, Mr. Hall developed his own cultural competence that facilitated effective teaching and built critical relationships with his students. Milner suggests that such mutual identity-focused learning resulting in "cultural and racial convergence seemed necessary (at least as a foundation) for academic success" (2011, p. 87).

Studies of incorporating students' cultural and household knowledge into the classroom curriculum (reviewed in depth in Chapter 2) illustrate how teachers can position students as experts from which others can learn. For example, Moll and colleagues (1992) conducted a study in working-class Mexican communities in Tucson, Arizona, in which a teacher and researcher conducted interviews with families in their homes and then used the knowledge gained about families' funds of knowledge to create units of study. One teacher learned that an entrepreneurial student bought and sold candy that he acquired on his many visits to Mexico. She worked with her students to create a candy-focused unit in which students developed research questions and investigated to find answers to those questions using a variety of sources. The teacher engaged the students in drawing on their social contacts outside of the classroom, and an expert parent came into the classroom to teach students how to make *pepitoria*, a Mexican candy. In this example, the teacher capitalized on students' diverse experiences and perspectives and built on students' cultural knowledge and expertise to extend learning and promote student engagement.

A central aspect of students' background and identity is language, and an important consideration for culturally responsive classrooms is ensuring that students' home language is honored and centralized. Baker-Bell et al. (2017) conducted a collaborative research project in Jackson's high school classroom in which they explored with students the use and role of Black Language (BL) in students' lives. The researchers spent extensive time critically evaluating how their own lives and experiences shaped their thinking about BL, and they asked the students to deconstruct racialized deficit views of BL that result from theories of White linguistic superiority. The students viewed and analyzed video of court testimony in the George Zimmerman trial for the killing of Trayvon Martin and subsequent news commentary that focused on BL. They read articles on BL, including one that focused on President Barack Obama's flexible use of BL. Through rich discussions, the teacher, researchers, and students explored the cultural value of BL and the ways in which BL is inappropriately devalued in a society that elevates White, middle-class norms. Students deepened their understanding of how linguistic flexibility, or using "multiple languages and varieties of language depending on your audience and your purposes" (2017, p. 372) can empower individuals and sustain valuable cultural practices.

Engagement in Learning What's Worth Knowing

In addition to an intentional focus on students' own lives and identities, research suggests that culturally responsive instructional practices engage students in purposeful, hands-on, inquiry-oriented work geared toward social change (Aronson & Laughter, 2016). Milner (2011) points out that culturally responsive practices "prepare students with skills to question inequity and to fight against the many -isms and -phobias that they encounter while allowing students to build knowledge and to transfer what they have learned through classroom instructional/learning opportunities to other experiences" (p. 69). As they consider the ways in which the world works, students are encouraged to pose questions and find answers to their questions using a variety of resources.

Howell et al. (2019) provide an example of this level of engagement in their description of a middle school teacher who challenged his students to investigate the practice of redlining, which is the discriminatory practice of refusing to offer credit or insurance in a particular community and is most often based on race or ethnicity of the residents. The students, who were concerned about redistricting in their own community, began by asking questions about the origins of and rationale for redlining in their city. They read historical news articles and viewed maps that showed homeownership and property values over time. They had discussions, wrote essays, crafted letters to the city council, and prepared presentations for a local school board meeting. Students in this class were engaged in grade-level, standards-based language arts instruction and activities in the context of curriculum that was relevant to students' lives and enabled them to critically examine and directly confront an unjust social practice rooted in racism. They read, wrote, spoke, and listened for authentic audiences and were motivated by knowing that their work was important, and not just for the sake of task completion for the teacher.

An action-oriented approach is evident in research on the Indigenous framework of culturally responsive instruction that undergirds teaching and learning in the Hawaiian-focused charter schools first studied by Kathryn Au nearly four decades ago (Keehne et al., 2018). The framework included five elements: (1) literacy in Indigenous languages; (2) community connections; (3) a shared vision that encompasses culture, academic proficiency, and community; (4) authentic assessment; and (5) teaching grounded in culture and higher level thinking. Students' work was organized in project-based thematic units that were "outward-looking and action-oriented" (Keehne et al., 2018, p. 160). Students were encouraged to look beyond the walls of the classroom and use their growing knowledge and skills to uplift their community. Units were on topics central to students' cultural identities and communities and included a focus on community issues such as access to ancestral lands, restoration of water rights, and preservation of ecosystems. Students learned mainstream strategies and content through instruction that was rooted in their cultural identities first and foremost and focused on revitalizing their language, culture, and environment. Such action-oriented, real-world inquiries provided engaging and hands-on opportunities for students to apply content in meaningful ways.

These examples of critically examining a relevant issue and taking action to change it are representative of the kind of sociopolitical consciousness that is at the heart of culturally and linguistically responsive instruction (Ladson-Billings, 1995). It is important here to note that this aspect of instruction is so essential that there is an entire element of the CRIOP that focuses on critical consciousness. See Chapter 6 for a discussion of this component of culturally responsive practices and additional examples of critical consciousness in classrooms.

Effective Teaching of Language for Bi-/Multilingualism

In culturally and linguistically responsive classrooms, teachers use a wide range of strategies to ensure that students understand the content. For students who are emerging as bilingual or multilingual, teachers need to ensure that the language used to teach the content is comprehensible to the students. Teachers need to be cognizant of and appropriately adjust their rate of speech and their use of unfamiliar terms, idioms, or colloquialisms. Acting out words, using gestures, and facial expressions can be helpful in aiding students' understanding of unfamiliar language (Gersten & Geva, 2003).

It is also important that teachers provide background knowledge, link new concepts to prior experiences and content, and provide extensive scaffolding of students' cognitive strategies and linguistic development (August & Shanahan, 2006). For students who are learning English, using their first language as a bridge to learning English can be helpful. In a study that illustrates the efficacy of encouraging students to use their native language, Nykiel-Herbert (2010) documented achievement outcomes for Iraqi refugees who were assigned to mainstream classes and participated in an intervention that encouraged the use of students' native language for communication and cooperation. According to Nykiel-Herbert, students who participated in the intervention made better progress as measured by a language assessment posttest than students who received traditional instruction in an English as a second language (ESL) pullout program.

One of the instructional aspects of culturally and linguistically responsive instruction that is beneficial to all students, regardless of cultural and linguistic backgrounds, is a focus on academic language. Research on instruction for ELs emphasizes the need for students to learn the vocabulary, language structures, and conversational conventions that are foundational to school learning (August & Shanahan, 2006). However, it is critical that teachers not take a deficit approach to helping students acquire English (Brown & Souto-Manning, 2008). As teachers support students' comprehension and acquisition of language and content, it is also important that they help students maintain their home languages by building on the language that they already know (August & Shanahan, 2006; Nykeil-Herbert, 2010).

August et al. (2005) reviewed research on vocabulary development for ELs and suggested three instructional practices that were beneficial for building vocabulary knowledge. The first practice is to take advantage of students' first language. Students who are literate in their first language are more likely to gain proficiency in English, and often, students can draw on their knowledge of their first language to discern the meanings of English words. This is particularly true if the native language and English share cognates, or the same linguistic derivation. Cognates in Spanish and English (e.g., *domestic—doméstico, celebration—celebración*) are often similar in spelling and meaning and can be helpful for students as they are learning new content (Jiménez et al., 1996). A second recommended practice is ensuring ELs know the meanings of basic words. Researchers have documented the benefits of explicitly teaching essential vocabulary through multiple activities and with supports (Baker et al., 2014). The third practice emphasizes review and reinforcement. Instruction that enables students to use new vocabulary in meaningful contexts through reading, writing, and discussion reinforces the new knowledge and empowers students for further learning.

Taffe et al. (2009) conducted a review of research that suggested the teaching of vocabulary is best carried out in a concept-rich, language-rich, and word-rich environmental context whereby students have opportunities to learn strategies for figuring out the meanings of words on their own. Key academic vocabulary and language structures are identified prior to a study or investigation, and teachers build on what students already know. It is important to choose words to teach that are central to understanding the text, used frequently in the text, may be used across content areas, have multiple meanings, or have affixes that can be generalized to other words (Baker et al., 2014). Teaching word-learning strategies that students can use to figure out words on their own can help students expand their vocabularies. Most important, however, is that students have many opportunities to use new vocabulary in multiple modalities and contexts. It is the actual use of vocabulary that enables students to internalize and then build on word knowledge (Beck et al., 2013).

The use of visuals, including multimedia, can support vocabulary learning and comprehension for students who are ELs. Silverman and Hines (2009) studied the use of multimedia resources to enhance read-aloud science vocabulary instruction for ELs in preschool through second grade. The study compared traditional read-aloud instruction to read-aloud instruction that also utilized video clips that used the vocabulary. The researchers found a positive effect for ELs on a researcher-designed measure and a general vocabulary knowledge measure. Using the videos closed the gap between ELs and native English speakers in the knowledge of the targeted vocabulary words. Also, the gap in general vocabulary knowledge was narrowed. Other ways of incorporating visuals in instruction are presented later in this chapter.

Researchers who have conducted experimental studies have demonstrated the effectiveness of vocabulary instruction and instructional scaffolds. Vaughn and colleagues (2017) conducted a randomized control trial that demonstrated the effects of providing comprehension support, preteaching essential vocabulary, knowledge building, and team-based learning in social studies classes. Both ELs and non-ELs who were in the treatment group outperformed students in the control group on measures of content knowledge and reading comprehension. In another experimental study that supports the explicit teaching of language, August and colleagues (2009) assessed the effectiveness of an intervention designed to develop the science knowledge and academic language of middle school ELs. In addition to the regular instructional curriculum and materials, the intervention included extensive hands-on experimentation and instructional scaffolds (i.e., visuals, illustrations of key vocabulary, and graphic organizers). Students in the treatment group (both ELs and non-ELs) significantly outperformed students in the control group on measures of science and vocabulary achievement.

Culturally Responsive Instruction: From Research to Practice

The second half of this chapter focuses on ways that teachers can operationalize the culturally and linguistically responsive practices that we have highlighted in our earlier review of the research. This section is organized according to the indicators in the Instructional Practices element of the CRIOP. We focus on contextualizing instruction in students' lives, experiences, and individual abilities; engaging students in active, hands-on, meaningful learning tasks, including inquiry-based learning, developing students' academic language, using instructional techniques that scaffold student learning, and giving students choices based on their experiences, interests, and strengths.

Rooting Instruction in the Lives of Students

Where I am From
By Afton Richardson, 4th Grade

I am from games
From candles and pictures
I am from a house that is always
Loud and smells like outdoors
I am from the roses
I am from a laundry system
From Gabrielle and Darryl
I am from playing rough
And a competitive family

I am from use manners,
Clean your room and church songs
I am from Lexington, my favorite granny, soup and meat
From my brother tearing his ACL after
Getting in an argument
I am from my great granny's grave in a fenced in area whose support I know
I will always have.

There are many ways to connect learning to students' lives outside the classroom. As the research reviewed in the preceding section illustrates, writing can be a powerful tool for making these connections. One example of how teachers can engage students in writing about their lives is through "Where I'm From" poems like the one by Afton Richardson that introduces this section. Writer George Ella Lyons's (1999) poem "Where I'm From" serves as a mentor text and provides a framework for students in constructing their own poems about their lives. Students reflect on their histories, their cultures, and their experiences and brainstorm significant elements of their identities that they might include in the poem. They examine the poetic devices in the mentor text and think about how they can incorporate poetic devices in similar ways. Lyons herself has initiated a Where I'm From project, which has resulted in the submission of countless poems from all over the world (see http://www.georgeellalyon.com/where.html). In the fourth-grade classroom where Afton wrote his poem, students practiced their speaking skills by reading their poems aloud and got feedback from their peers prior to presenting them to parents. Final versions of the poems were displayed on cut-out silhouettes of the students' faces posted as a hallway display.

Although it might seem natural for students to write about their lives in language arts, it can seem more challenging to make other content areas relevant to students. In our own work, we have seen teachers get creative in linking even the most personally distant content to students' lives and experiences. In the example provided in Classroom Scenario 4.1, an eighth-grade science teacher asked students to consider how the major geological events in the Earth's history might serve as metaphors for aspects of students' lives. Students engaged in a number of whole-group and individual activities that required them to think about the significant facts related to each event and how those facts metaphorically paralleled with events from their own lives. Sometimes it takes effort to figure out ways to make content personally relevant to students, but as the vignette shows, the payoff is big in terms of student engagement and learning.

Classroom Scenario 4.1.:
Connecting Geologic and Biologic History to Students' Lives
Brittany Manion

My eighth-grade science classes are filled with diverse groups of students. As a Title 1 school, I have students of all socioeconomic backgrounds, ethnicities, reading levels, and different first languages. Such diversity provides opportunities to think about ways to make instruction more culturally responsive. If you are like me, you are a science nerd, but the study of geologic and biologic history has never been something I have been too interested in. I noticed this same feeling coming from my students in years past. So I wanted to make a change. I wanted my students to connect this seemingly mundane content to their lives in the hope that they would be able to comprehend the history of our Earth. I also hoped that my students would make connections with one another in the process.

I began this project by creating several graphic organizers to help support student learning throughout the project. The first activity allowed students time to converse with one another on how specific geologic and biologic events we have been studying related to an event in their lives. For example, for the geologic event "Formation of the Earth," students related this event to "being born," "first day of school," or "the start of a new me." There were nine total Earth events, and for each event, students related it to an event in their own lives. The nine Earth events were written on large poster boards around the room, and the students moved through the stations to write down their connected life event. This gave the students an opportunity to see other students' ideas and record those on their graphic organizer if it was significant to them. Before moving forward in the project, I took time to show my students a completed example of this project to use as a mentor text. I think this really helped them grasp the depth of knowledge and connection I was expecting from them.

The second part of this project was more of a shift to individual student thought. Each student was to pick one Earth event that was personally salient to them. The second page of the graphic organizer contained sentence starters and charts to keep their work organized. Once students chose their Earth and life event, they shared with their group members why they chose those events. This provided students an opportunity to form connections with one another. After the group was finished sharing, students started to work on finding evidence for the Earth event of their choosing and made even more connections to their life event. This process took several days as students were to use their notes and resources to research their specific Earth event. Once the students were finished gathering evidence, they used their research to create a formal writing piece.

This was the first year I did this project after teaching this content for 4 years prior. I saw noticeable differences in the results. I noticed higher levels of student engagement and classroom participation. Students were speaking with one another about content but were making revelations when they related it to their own lives. By providing opportunities for students to have conversations throughout the project, they were able to learn about one another and form connections. By providing the graphic organizers and support along the

> *way, students were able to create excellent writing pieces that surpassed the quality of those from previous years. One student related supercontinent Pangaea to her family reunions when her family from all over the world came together. Another student explained that the Ice Age reminded him of a time when his family was snowed in and could not leave their home. My students were able to take a mundane topic in Earth history and relate it to an important aspect of their lives in very creative ways!*

The prior example focused on a middle-level classroom, but we also have seen elementary teachers work hard to anchor instruction in students' lives and experiences. In kindergarten classrooms, we have seen student-created alphabet walls constructed around students' names and supported with items, pictures, and words brought in from their homes. Students brought in cereal boxes, magazine photos of favorite toys, and digital photos of favorite foods, such as empanadas. Both English and Spanish spellings of each word were prominently displayed on the word wall. Children can more easily internalize letter sounds and beginning sight words if they are connected to what is familiar. We have found that phonics anchor charts that use environmental print, cognates, and logos are particularly effective. The photo in Figure 4.1 shows an example of pictures of familiar logos that students used as anchors for learning letter–sound relationships (Mm—McDonald's logo).

Figure 4.1. *Using familiar logos can help ELs acquire phonics knowledge.*

Focusing on cognates can also be helpful for students who are new to English. For languages that have a common etymological origin to English, creating a class book of cognates associated with each letter sound can provide a way for young ELs to link letter sounds to familiar words. As discussed previously, there are many Spanish–English cognates that young children know. Too often, teachers use unfamiliar English words to teach phonics, which is problematic for students who do not know the English words. Figure 4.2 shows an alphabet book with Spanish-English cognates that a teacher with whom we worked used to reinforce phonics concepts.

To create instruction centered on students' lives, teachers must get to know students, their families, and their experiences. As discussed in Chapter 2, one powerful way to get to know students is to learn about families' "funds of knowledge" (González et al., 2005). Each family is unique in its practices, skills, and expertise, and this cultural knowledge is often rooted in a family's cultural identity. Teachers can invite parents and caregivers into the classroom to read in their native language, share their household practices and foods, educate students about different religions, teach students about games and other recreational activities, and expose students to an array of jobs. In one kindergarten classroom

Figure 4.2. *Sample page from an alphabet book using English–Spanish cognates.*

that was studying transportation, a father who earned a living as a truck driver brought his rig to the school parking lot. The students were thrilled to explore the truck and to ask questions about what it is like to spend so much time on the road. The students wrote explanatory sentences and drew pictures of the truck and the father, thereby connecting social studies concepts with literacy learning.

Another excellent way to connect to students' lives and experiences is to bring their language and cultural practices into the classroom. One approach that serves as an example is reality pedagogy (Emdin, 2016). Reality pedagogy is

> an approach to teaching and learning that has a primary goal of meeting each student on his or her own cultural and emotional turf. It focuses on making the local experiences of the students visible and creating contexts where there is a role reversal of sorts that positions the student as the expert in his or her own teaching and learning, and the teacher as the learner. It posits that while the teacher is the person charged with delivering the content, the student is the person who shapes how best to teach that content. Together, the teacher and students co-construct the classroom space. (p. 27)

Simply put, in reality pedagogy, students' cultural language, traditions, and routines are a natural part of classroom activities. A central feature is open dialogues, which Emdin (2016) refers to as "cogenerative dialogues," or simply "cogens." These small-group cogens between teachers and students help them bridge cultural divides and deepen students' understanding of concepts and contributions to classroom culture. In these dialogues, students and the teacher discuss what is occurring in the classroom and decide on a single pressing issue that needs to be addressed. Students then each develop a specific plan of action that they will enact in the classroom. In his research (Emdin, 2008), students videotaped their science classrooms, and the videos were later used to facilitate conversations about specific lessons. Teachers and students also "co-constructed the classroom space" by implementing co-teaching whereby the students would conduct lessons for their peers or would teach in pairs or small groups. Emdin (2008, p. 775) writes that "In some cases, the teachers became students themselves. . . . Teachers would take notes on the analogies, words, or examples that students employed when teaching other students and use them in their own lessons."

Another aspect of reality pedagogy that utilizes students' cultural and language practices to engage students in higher levels of learning is creating a classroom ethos in which students' language patterns and practices are utilized by teachers and students alike (Emdin, 2016). For example, a teacher may utilize call-and-response, which is a prominent feature within hip-hop music and the Black church. Specifically, "a classic hip-hop lyric like 'Can I proceed?' followed by the response 'Yes indeed' can positively transform classrooms" (Emdin, 2016, p.114). This type of exchange helps teachers to determine if students understand the concepts being taught, and it also allows students to see aspects of their culture and language reflected in the classroom. Utilizing students' cultural and language practices in authentic ways is an important facet of the first CRIOP Instructional Practices indicator, which is focused on contextualizing instruction in students' lives, experiences, and abilities.

Authentic, Hands-On, and Inquiry Learning

Centering learning within students' lives, interests, and identities is easier when tasks have authentic purposes and audiences. In culturally responsive classrooms, students are engaged in active, hands-on learning. For instance, in Elizabeth Morgan's kindergarten classroom, students enjoyed creating their own fast-food restaurant. They decided together what food, drinks, and desserts they wanted to sell and created a menu of items along with their prices. Then, students practiced taking orders from peers and doing addition problems to determine the amount of the final bill. (See Figure 4.3.) This authentic learning station created opportunities for both literacy and math development and students enjoyed "playing restaurant" during daily center rotations.

A natural tool for incorporating authentic, hands-on, inquiry learning is a camera. Photography incorporates visual literacy, or the ability to create and interpret visual

Figure 4.3. *Real-life learning stations in early primary can reinforce important literacy and math skills.*

images, and is a powerful way to connect instruction to students' out-of-school lives while engaging them in active, hands-on learning (Allen, 2010). Jennerjohn (2020) described a camera project in which young elementary students worked with their families to create culturally sustaining texts. Teachers arranged meetings with students and their families in students' neighborhoods and took photographs of the students and families as they interacted. Using a language experience approach in which students' language about each photograph was dictated, the students created a page for each of the pictures. Digital tools were used to polish and duplicate the finished books so that students could take the books home and share them with their families. The project enhanced the teacher's knowledge of students' communities and lives, and they built relationships with their students' families. Student engagement was exceptionally high as they created authentic and relevant texts directly connected to their lives

Cameras can also provide a hands-on way for students to explore content in active, real-world contexts. In a kindergarten classroom in which we worked, students compared the heights of people throughout their school building. Students took digital photos of the pairs of people they examined and used the photos to write about the differences they observed. Students used content vocabulary, such as *taller, shorter, height, left, right, measure, feet,* and *inches* as they wrote about the photos. All the students were completely engaged as they went about studying measurement in such a hands-on and active way. In a fourth-grade classroom, students used cameras to take pictures of items that used fractions and decimals (e.g., drill bits, food cans, etc.). They created a hallway display with pictures and labels showing the many ways that these math symbols are used in the real world. (Our favorite is "We use fractions to make mac and cheese.") In yet another example, a fourth-grade teacher had her students photograph images in the home that represented various geometrical elements, for example, shapes, angles, dissecting lines, and so on. These were used as a visual display to reinforce important vocabulary and concepts in geometry.

An important characteristic of culturally and linguistically responsive instructional practices is that students have many opportunities to engage in meaningful learning tasks that include inquiry-based learning. A number of years ago, Rebecca Powell and I (Susan) had the opportunity to interview fourth-grade students who had spent the entire year engaged in inquiry learning around mountaintop removal (Powell et al., 2001). From their social studies textbook, the students had been excited to learn about Black Mountain, the highest peak in their state of Kentucky. One day their teacher, Sandy Adams, presented her students with a dilemma: Coal companies planned to engage in mountaintop removal through strip mining, which would mean that Black Mountain would no longer be the highest mountain in the state. The students were alarmed and decided they wanted to dive deeper into learning about the mountain and its historical and ecological significance. The class ultimately enlisted the entire fourth grade, and students sought to get answers to their questions from research, field trips, interviews of miners, and conversations with eastern Kentucky environmental activists. Eventually, students decided to take action to prevent strip mining on Black Mountain. They wrote letters, raised money, and even helped organize a rally with students from eastern Kentucky. Several students developed proposals and made presentations to the state legislature. Alongside other activist groups, the students' efforts ultimately contributed to an agreement that preserved part of Black Mountain and created a conservation area. Through this inquiry project, Ms. Adams taught all the English/language arts standards in a hands-on, meaningful way that produced an exceptionally high level of student engagement and academic achievement.

Empowering Students With Language

To support students' content learning, culturally and linguistically responsive teachers focus on the most critical vocabulary for learning the content and give students many opportunities to explore meanings, make connections, and use the language in meaningful reading and writing. One teaching process that is especially effective is the Generative Vocabulary Matrix (GVM; Larson, 2014). The GVM is a public classroom space in which vocabulary is generated, displayed, categorized, manipulated, and revised over the course of a unit of study. Students use content text sets to generate domain-specific words, general academic vocabulary, and language structures that students use to make connections among the concepts and link to their prior knowledge. There are four major steps that comprise the GVM: (1) students self-collect words, (2) teacher and students arrange words meaningfully on a classroom wall or bulletin board, (3) conceptual categories of words are created and labeled, and (4) semantic structures are added as they are identified in texts and conversations about the concepts. The GVM is dynamic in that words are added and moved around and new categories are created as students go deeper with content throughout the unit. An example is provided in Figure 4.4 that shows a GVM focused on the mathematical concept of fractions. In addition to students' questions, processes, and key vocabulary related to fractions, there is a section of the matrix labeled "Words Mathematicians Use" that lists the content-specific academic vocabulary essential for effective communication and comprehension in the discipline.

Figure 4.4. *Example of a Generative Vocabulary Matrix.*

In culturally and linguistically responsive classrooms, teachers promote a love of language, and students aspire to have rich vocabularies. A few years ago, friend and colleague Victor Malo-Juvera taught in an urban Miami eighth-grade English/language arts classroom where students' state assessment scores were among the lowest in Florida. Vocabulary was at the center of Mr. Malo-Juvera's curriculum (see Malo-Juvera, 2011). Hundreds of complex words that students had learned were categorized semantically and posted around the classroom. Malo-Juvera chose two sets of words for students to learn each week. The first 20 word lists were groups of synonyms for words students already knew. For example, he introduced words like *myriad, cornucopia, plethora, copious,* and *profuse* for the well-known phrase *a lot.* He also introduced students to what he called Funky Fly Fresh words, or high-level words that many adults do not know. He selected words that students could easily use in school or at home, such as *draconian, diatribe, vituperative,* and *lambaste.*

Students were charged with using these words in their writing and in their conversations. When a visitor entered the room, Malo-Juvera's students played a game called "Stump the Visitor," whereby students quizzed the visitor on their vocabulary knowledge. The students took great pleasure when school administrators and other often highly educated visitors were unable to define words that were very familiar to the students. Malo-Juvera taught the students strategies for studying and memorizing the words, including acronyms and double-sided index cards, and he asked students to use the vocabulary in poetry or rap pieces that they wrote and performed aloud. At the end of Malo-Juvera's fourth year of teaching, his students' state writing assessment scores were among the highest in the state. State and district administrators were so shocked by the high performance of Malo-Juvera's students—believing that students from historically underachieving populations are not capable of such a stellar performance—that he and his teammate were investigated and later exonerated for cheating on the state test.

Although vocabulary development is essential in facilitating students' academic competence, it is important to reemphasize here that the focus for students, especially ELs, should be on maintaining their native languages and vernaculars (Escamilla, 2009; Paris, 2012). As students are becoming more competent with English, it is essential that their bilingualism/multilingualism be reinforced and sustained. We have seen students participating in student-led parent conferences who are unable to share what they are learning with their parents, who only speak their home language, because the students have learned new concepts and vocabulary only in English. We believe that, as students are learning new words and concepts in English, their teachers should provide multiple and rich opportunities to expand their bi-/multilingualism to encompass the new knowledge that students are acquiring. One way that teachers can provide these opportunities is to include vocabulary words in both English and students' native languages on word walls and concept maps such as the GVM. We have found the glossaries provided by the New York State Statewide Language Regional Bilingual Education Resource Network to be very valuable for acquiring content-specific words in multiple languages: https://steinhardt.nyu.edu/metrocenter/resources/glossaries.

Exposing students to multiple language forms and varieties is important for honoring their own language practices and expanding their knowledge of bi-/multilingualism and bidialectalism. Contrastive analysis is one approach that has been effective in helping students make connections between their own language and other languages and dialects (Boutte & Johnson, 2013). Contrastive analysis involves "the explicit comparison and contrast of the communication styles of mainstream and nonmainstream language systems" (Boutte & Johnson, 2013, p. 138). Teachers can use contrastive analysis to help students recognize important features of language and navigate between multiple communication styles. For example, teachers can encourage students to pay attention to elements of their home and school languages during read-alouds and storytelling (Boutte, 2007; Boutte & Johnson, 2013). Students can also practice translating their home languages and dialects into mainstream or "school" language. For example, they can translate books and other texts written in African American Language (AAL) or African American Vernacular English (AAVE) into mainstream or Standard English (SE). However, Boutte and Johnson (2013) note that it is important for students to gain practice in not just translating AAL to SE, but they should also translate texts in SE to AAL.

In culturally and linguistically responsive classrooms, teachers scaffold students' language development, as needed. One helpful scaffold is the use of sentence stems or paragraph frames that provide a linguistic structure for students (Rodriguez-Mojica & Briceño, 2018). Sentence stems can provide support for students in writing and in discussions. Simple sentence starters, such as "I predict _______" can serve to provide the conceptual language that enables students to participate in the discussion and embed the language into their schemas. Similarly, paragraph frames that include the syntactic language and connecting words can provide genre-specific structures for students to be successful. As students grow in linguistic competence, the stems and frames are gradually diminished until the student no longer needs the support.

Even older students can benefit from using sentence stems as they practice specific strategies. Table 4.1 shows sentence stems that we have used with middle school students to help them summarize complex texts. We use a Read–Pair–Share (Herrell & Jordan, 2016) approach whereby students work in pairs to read small sections of a text. Students take turns using the stems to summarize and clarify the text.

Table 4.1. *Summarizing Stems: Read–Pair–Share.*

Partners read a complex text divided into small, manageable sections. After reading each section . . .	
1. One partner summarizes:	2. The other partner adds on or clarifies:
"The basic idea here is . . ."	Add on
"The key information is . . ."	"To add to what you said . . ."
"In summary, this says that . . ."	"I would also say . . ."
"First . . . Next . . . Then . . . Finally . . ."	Clarify
	"To clarify what you said . . ."
	"What did you mean by _______?"

While learning the language of school is important for students who have been historically marginalized in our educational institutions, we agree with Escamilla (2009) that it is a mistake to take a deficit view that assumes native English speaking, middle-class students are highly adept with language and English learners need to "catch up." In our own work in classrooms, we have found that most students need support with complex content vocabulary and academic conversation to achieve their highest potential. It is for this reason that we encourage culturally and linguistically responsive teachers to have specific language objectives in addition to content objectives for the lessons that they plan. Having specific goals in mind for students' linguistic output enables the teacher to articulate expectations for language use and for students to internalize and apply the relevant vocabulary and language structures. For example, in a mathematics lesson on fractions, a teacher might say, "I want you to use the words *numerator* and *denominator* in your discussion" or "I expect you to explain your thinking in complete sentences." Figure 4.5 shows an example of an objective that clearly specifies the use of language. A written statement such as "I can explain the steps I used to find the product using math language" can draw students' attention to the kind of vocabulary that teachers want students to internalize and use. Including language targets in lesson planning and being explicit about language expectations reinforces language learning and teaches all students to embed academic language in their expressions of learning (Echevarria et al., 2008). Additional examples of language objectives are included in Chapter 5.

Figure 4.5. *Example of a language objective used in Ryan Arbuckle's fifth-grade mathematics class.*

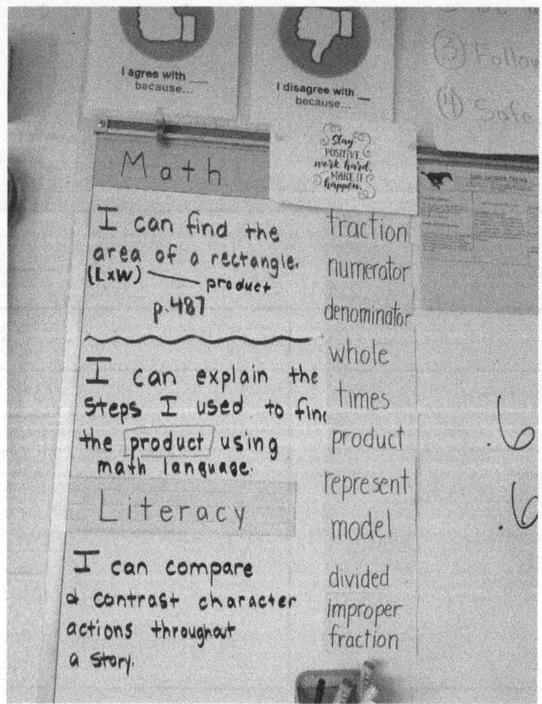

Scaffolds That Provide Access

Promoting students' academic competence is an important dimension of instructional practices in CLR classrooms (Ladson-Billings, 1994). It is essential, then, to ensure the content is accessible to all students and to provide supportive scaffolds that enable students to show what they know. In this section, we provide several scaffolds that culturally responsive educators can use to assure student success.

Picture Word Inductive Model

As mentioned in the earlier research section, a useful strategy for supporting students who are developing linguistically is the use of visuals (Silverman & Hines, 2009). An instructional structure for incorporating visuals into content-area instruction is Picture Word Inductive Model (PWIM; Calhoun, 1999). PWIM uses pictures to introduce concepts and engages students in identifying what they see in the pictures. The purpose of PWIM is to connect new content and language to students' background knowledge and experiences through visual supports and content vocabulary. Students develop their vocabulary and concept knowledge in preparation for diving deeper into content learning. Through an inductive process, students play with words, sentences, and paragraphs as they link new learning to their background knowledge and experiences. Teachers use pictures that connect to content area units and facilitate writing about the content. Implementing PWIM involves a number of instructional steps:

1. Select a picture.

2. Ask students to identify what they see in the picture.

3. Label the picture parts identified. (Draw a line from the identified object or areas, say the word, write the word; ask students to spell the word aloud and then to pronounce it).

4. Read and review the picture word chart aloud.

5. Ask students to read the words using the lines on the chart if necessary and to classify the words into a variety of groups. Identify common concepts, for instance, beginning consonants, rhyming words, etc. to emphasize with the whole class.

6. Read and review the picture word chart (say the word, spell it, and say it again).

7. Add words, if desired, to the picture word chart and to the word banks.

8. Lead students into creating a title for the picture word chart. Ask students to think about the information on the chart and what they want to say about it.

9. Ask students to generate a sentence, sentences, or a paragraph about the picture word chart. Ask students to classify sentences; model putting the sentences into a good paragraph.

10. Read and review the sentences and paragraphs.

(Calhoun, 1999, p. 23)

We have seen PWIM implemented effectively with both very young elementary-aged students and with upper middle grades students. In the "kindness" unit showcased in Chapter 1, the first-grade teachers introduced the study with pictures of children being kind in various ways. The children generated vocabulary related to the unit and wrote about what it meant to be kind. In a kindergarten classroom, a teacher used the strategy as part of a unit on life cycles. A picture of hatching chickens elicited vocabulary words that students used to write a paragraph about how a baby chick hatches from an egg. In an eighth-grade social studies classroom, the teacher introduced her unit on revolution by displaying an image of the painting *Liberty Leading the People* by Eugène Delacroix commemorating the July Revolution of 1830. Students generated vocabulary inspired by the painting, classified the vocabulary, and used the words to compose a quick write as an activity to build background knowledge. One major advantage of PWIM is that it provides vocabulary for writing and making content connections. Providing the language on which to build new knowledge is especially important for ELs and other students who may not know the foundational vocabulary. Figure 4.6 shows a class using PWIM to support their writing about a field trip experience.

Figure 4.6. With PWIM, young students can use picture labels and sentence frames to write their own sentences.

Classroom Scenario 4.2.: PWIM
Emily D. Banks

So there I was, fresh off hours of professional development in culturally responsive teaching with a head full of strategies I wanted to use with my new class of third graders. Which strategy would I use first? Which approach would be the best to meet the needs of my 17 Spanish- and Swahili-speaking students? I work in a small rural school that services an urban community and allows me to teach a diverse population of students. In my past 6 years of teaching at this school, I have not had a majority of on-grade-level, White, English-speaking students. So again, there I was, feeling more prepared than in the past to service this group of diverse learners.

As the year began, I used strategies I had learned to build a class culture of respect and eagerness to learn. I built safe spaces for students to share and question and talk openly about who they are and where they come from. I was feeling like I was on a roll with this class. I was seeing their confidence shine. My biggest challenge was how to adapt the required districtwide reading program for my English learners.

This was not my first year working with our districtwide reading program. I enjoyed the program and all the supplemental resources that came with it. The year prior had allowed me to build my confidence in teaching this program, and I knew this year would be even better. Naturally, with my confidence in my abilities, I hit the ground running with the program. I was introducing eight designated vocabulary words a week, in addition to all of the background building and contextual information I was providing for my students about the reading. I introduced new reading strategies and plugged along teaching the state standards all while watching the eagerness and excitement for learning wane in my students' eyes. They were interested in the stories, and they participated during reading lessons, but I felt that my students were simply being complacent rather than invested in their own learning. I wanted them to be able to take those eight new vocabulary words, build connections in their brain to the words, and be able to use those words in their personal vocabulary. This is when I reflected on my hours of summer professional development and thought about using Emily Calhoun's (1999) Picture Word Inductive Model (PWIM) I had learned about.

The PWIM is a strategy that allows students to look at a picture with familiar objects or scenes and draw out words from their speaking and listening vocabularies. Often my students would know how to say a word or would know what a word sounds like but were unsure of that same word when reading it. The teacher's job is to record the words that students are using to describe what they see in the picture. This strategy allows teachers to create active engagement and gather formative assessment data at the same time.

I used the PWIM with my vocabulary teaching for our district program. The program has vocabulary cards with real-world pictures associated with the vocabulary words. This gave me a great opportunity to use the PWIM strategy to aid in vocabulary acquisition.

First, I introduced the PWIM to my students without using the vocabulary component. This allowed me to develop procedures for students to follow when using this strategy in our classroom. I used pictures of cultural events that many of my students had ties to so that they could feel the connections to the content and would be able to share words that they knew how to say but did not always know how to write. One of the first few times practicing this strategy I used a picture of a group of African girls dancing. I had a very shy and quiet student who recently came to our community from the Congo. She lit up and quickly made connections to the picture. She shared words and memories of dancing in the same way. The rest of the class was hooked on what she was sharing and eagerly asked questions, wanting to know more. I felt that sense of natural engagement and knew this strategy would aid in my students' vocabulary acquisition.

After establishing the procedures for this strategy, my students became familiar with how the process worked. They knew to look at the picture, have quiet think time, and then share. Once we were ready, I added the next step of introducing an unfamiliar vocabulary word with the picture on the card. I used vocabulary words that most closely connected to or would aid in their understanding of the reading content for that week.

For example, we did a week of reading about investigating and inventing. These were the main vocabulary words for the week, so I started with the word investigation to aid my students in their learning. I covered the word on the card and began the process we had practiced many times. The picture associated with the word investigation is a young boy holding a magnifying glass up to his eye, looking very closely at something outside in the grass. My students went into their quiet think time and made personal connections to what they saw. When we began to share, words and phrases like science, magnifying glass, looking for, looking close at something, and trying to find something came out. These are all pieces of the definition for investigation, and my students knew it already. Next I introduced the word investigation to them. We practiced saying it a few times together, broke it into syllables, and I used it in a sentence for them.

Me: "Juan did a careful investigation of a spider web in his back yard. What do you think the word investigation means?"

Student A: "He is looking really really close at it, so like looking at something close?"

Student B: "Yea, like in science when we use the magnifying glass, we look at things really careful."

We continued to share our thinking and form connections to the word investigation. Then I posed a question to my class: "Can you think of a time when you had to do some kind of investigation?" Students' hands went up, and they talked about times when they had to look at things in science or when they wanted to know the answer to something they had to look for it. This gave my students the ability to generalize what we read regarding investigating problems and form connections to build understanding.

> *I continued using PWIM throughout the year. I added more layers, like having my students respond in writing to questions posed about the pictures. We kept several of our class-generated anchor charts, and I placed them in the area we used for our small-group writing center. I asked questions about the posters, and my students used the language we had generated during the whole-group discussion to respond in writing. I incorporated this strategy in my small-group literacy rotations for students to visit daily. In addition to students working with this strategy independently, I was able to increase students' language use by giving them opportunities for conversation centered on the words they were using. This allowed students to transfer their vocabulary knowledge across all four domains of language: reading, writing, speaking, and listening. Through using the PWIM, my students continued to have that eagerness for learning new words and generalizing their vocabulary and knowledge.*

Graphic Organizers

Another set of tools that can serve as important scaffolds for student learning are graphic organizers, which help students access and learn content more effectively (Baker et al., 2014). Tools such as Venn diagrams, concept maps, text structure charts, and paragraph frames can help students make sense of content and organize ideas. As part of a unit on colonialism, eighth-grade teacher Aimee Graham asked her students to create a presentation, including images, that argued whether it was ethical to make forced contact with Indigenous peoples who were intentionally isolating themselves from the outside world. She found her students struggling with a number of things: articulating a thesis, sticking with that thesis throughout their preparations, finding and organizing evidence to support the thesis, and selecting appropriate images. Midway through students' preparation of their presentations, Aimee decided to give her students an organizer to help them structure their argument-based presentations (see Figure 4.7 on the following page). Students completed the organizer and then transferred the information to well-structured presentations.

Graphic organizers that visually show relationships between concepts and ideas can help students make connections and internalize information. A concept map is a specific type of graphic organizer that uses labeled nodes and lines or arrows to show relationships among concepts. Concept maps are well recognized for their usefulness in teaching content (Nesbit & Adesope, 2006). Semantic feature analysis matrix is another graphic organizer that can help students, including Els, make sense of content (Filippini et al., 2012). Figure 4.8 on the following page shows a feature analysis matrix that a second-grade teacher created to help students better understand concepts and ideas related to ecosystems.

Students Supporting Each Other

In addition to providing tools to scaffold students' learning, culturally and linguistically responsive teachers understand how students can serve as support for one another. In Chapter 1, Walker-Dalhouse discussed the importance of students working together to create a cohesive classroom community that values the contributions of every student.

Figure 4.7. *Organizer for an opinion or argument presentation.*

Argument Presentation Planning Worksheet

My position (Thesis):		

Reason #1	*Evidence* for Reason #1	Image for Reason #1
Reason #2	*Evidence* for Reason #2	Image for Reason #2
Reason #3	*Evidence* for Reason #3	Image for Reason #3

My conclusion:		

Figure 4.8. *Second-grade graphic organizer for the study of ecosystems.*

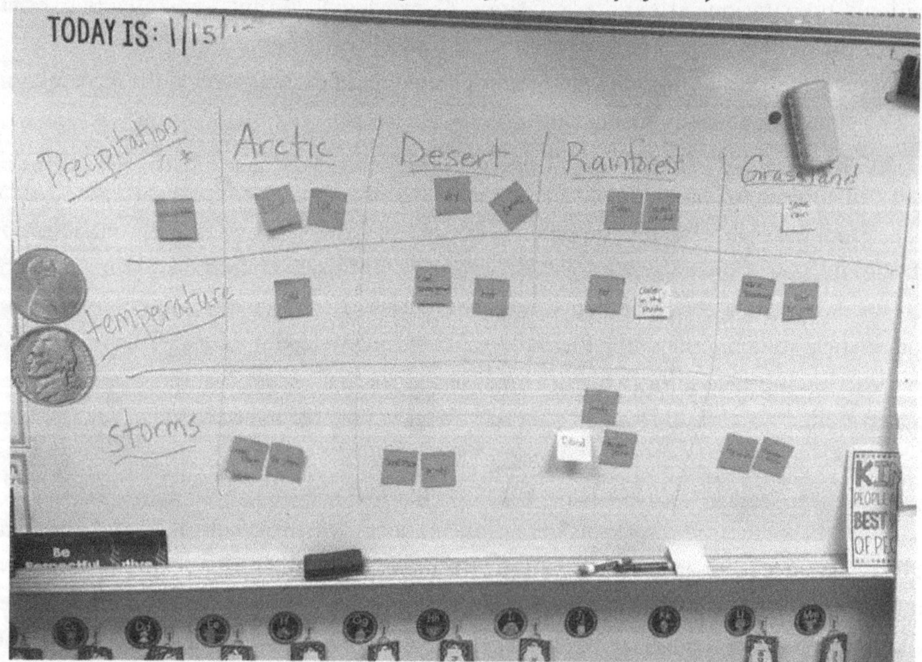

Here, we discuss the value of providing opportunities for students to partner with one another to promote academic achievement. As part of a "reality pedagogy" approach described earlier, Emdin (2016) explores the concept of "cosmo duos," for example, "two students (duo) who work together to ensure that each of them can support the other in their times of challenge (p. 116). Teachers invite students who have participated in the co-generative dialogues (discussed previously) to partner in two-student duos to support each other in the classroom. Students explore their strengths and weaknesses with their partners and find ways to help each other overcome their challenges.

In cosmo duos, teachers encourage students to reveal their strengths and needs regarding classroom content, classroom performance, and general comfort with the classroom environment. The students in the cosmo duos make presentations to the larger classroom about how their two-person partnerships are working for them, how often they meet outside of school to work on content, and any practices they participate in regularly together. The cosmo duos create plans of action for capitalizing on their strengths and teaching content to one another. Based on the cosmo duos' ongoing presentations and discussions about their strengths and challenges, teachers consider the specific needs of their students and encourage high performing students to partner with lower performing students. However, cosmo duos may be reconfigured at different times because students may demonstrate expertise on certain topics but not others. Emdin (2016) maintains that "it is important for youth to know and see that everyone can be an expert and/or need help as the class moves from one topic to another" (p. 121). In this student-centered way, youth are positioned as co-teachers, who utilize their own understanding of the content to scaffold the learning of their peers.

The Power of Choice

Another student-centered indicator of culturally and linguistically responsive instructional practices is giving students choices in what they learn and how they show what they know. Wlodkowki (1999) applied a motivational theory to culturally responsive instruction that posits that culture is inseparable from motivation and engagement. For students to be engaged, the work must be personally relevant, include their perspectives and values, and incorporate choice. For example, Slack (2001) used a multigenre research paper as an example of the power of giving students choices in the topics they investigate and the forms in which they exhibit their learning. Rather than assigning a traditional research paper, Slack asked her eighth-grade students to compose multigenre papers about a political movement of their own choosing and gave them a wide range of genre options for showing the results of their work. Students chose topics such as Mothers Against Drunk Driving, the abolitionist movement, animal rights, anti-smoking, special education, the pro-choice movement, and Title IX. They chose to express their learning through multiple forms, including letters, essays, poems, and dramatizations. Students prepared brief factual speeches as introductions to their projects, and some were brought to tears as they conveyed the passion they felt for the topic they chose. When Slack surveyed her students about the experience, they indicated that the choice-focused assignment required more from them in terms of their time, research, and creativity than with teacher-directed assignments. Still, students overwhelmingly preferred the multigenre approach to a traditional research paper and felt they gained a better understanding of the topic and were better able to add their own voices to the product.

We have experienced firsthand the passion that students bring to self-selected topics. When middle school social studies teacher Annabeth Edens, (highlighted in Chapter 6) asked her seventh-grade students to create multimodal products to illustrate their learning about a social issue, students were excited to share their representations. Susan (first author) was working with Annabeth as a CRIOP coach, and during one classroom visit, students were sharing their projects with one another and giving feedback. Students' projects took many forms: posters depicting victims of police brutality, letters to the school superintendent regarding safety from gun violence, and sketches with captions urging the protection of endangered species. One especially enthusiastic student shared an extensive handbook on youth mental illness and suicide prevention that she had created for the school guidance counselor to use to help students in their building. Each page of the book was carefully illustrated and inserted into a three-ring binder organized with sheet protectors for durability. As this example conveys, when students compose for authentic purposes and audiences and have some ownership over the topic, their engagement in the activity and their concern for the quality of the final product is increased.

One elementary school in which we have worked has regular family Exhibition Nights. Students throughout the school generally have a choice in terms of what they want to study and how they want to display their learning. For instance, fifth-grade students choose topics for their civil rights unit and decide how they will present what they learned. Some create dramatizations, some write essays and develop brochures, and some choose to write speeches. ELs are encouraged to develop their exhibitions in both English and their native languages so that their parents can understand their presentations.

A few years ago in this same school, second-grade teachers implemented an economics unit where students chose a business they wanted to create and decided how they would demonstrate their learning to stakeholders. They visited several local small businesses, interviewed the owners, and wrote a summary of what they had learned. Then they decided on a business for their classroom that would "open" on Exhibition Night and developed various teams (product managers, marketing, accounting, design, and production). Students completed job applications and were assigned jobs based on their top choices. They then wrote letters to potential "investors" to have funds to purchase the materials for their projects. The businesses they created were all different: Mrs. Baird's Magical Books; Sweet Treats Bakeria (baked goods); The World of Games (student-created games to play and purchase); The Snack and Drink Attack; Kirk's Creations (student-made toys); and even Witt's Little Sketchers (student-created artwork). Through this project, the students were not only extremely motivated, but they also learned all of the elements of creating a business, from keeping ledgers to principles of marketing. (For a more detailed description of this project, see https://www.kentuckyteacher.org/leadership/guest-columns/2017/06/second-graders-learn-how-to-create-a-business/).

Conclusion

For teachers to empower the students in their increasingly diverse classrooms to achieve their highest potential, instructional practices must be responsive to students' cultural and linguistic backgrounds. This means designing and delivering instruction that is contextualized in students' lives and experiences; meaningful, hands-on, and rooted in inquiry and student choice; focused on honoring students' language while supporting multilingualism; and providing scaffolded support so that all students have access to content learning. Creating instruction that is culturally and linguistically responsive and sustaining requires that teachers know their students well and value their students' backgrounds and experiences as assets. We believe there is no more important work than ensuring equity within the walls of the classroom so that all students can achieve and contribute to the world in powerful ways.

References

Abdulrahim, N. A., & Orosco, M. J. (2020). Culturally responsive mathematics teaching: A research synthesis. *The Urban Review, 52*(1), 1–25.

Allen, J. (2010). *Literacy in the welcoming classroom.* Teachers College Press.

Aronson, B., & Laughter, J. (2016). The theory and practice of culturally relevant education: A synthesis of research across content areas. *Review of Educational Research, 6*(1), 163–206.

August, D., Branum-Martin, L., Cardenas-Hagan, E., & Francis, D. J. (2009) The impact of an instructional intervention on the science and language learning of middle grade English language learners. *Journal of Research on Educational Effectiveness, 2*(4), 345–376.

August, D., Carlo, M., Dressler, C., & Snow, C. (2005). The critical role of vocabulary development for English language learners. *Learning Disabilities Research & Practice, 20*(1), 50–57.

August, D., & Shanahan, T. (2006). *Developing literacy in second-language learners: Report of the national literacy panel on language minority children and youth.* Erlbaum.

Baker, S., Lesaux, N., Jayanthi, M., Dimino, J., Proctor, C. P., Morris, J., Gersten, R., Haymond, K., Kieffer, M. J., Linan-Thompson, S., & Newman-Gonchar, R. (2014). *Teaching academic content and literacy to English learners in elementary and middle school* (NCEE 2014-4012). National Center for Education Evaluation and Regional Assistance, Institute of Education Sciences, U.S. Department of Education. http://ies.ed.gov/ncee/wwc/publications_reviews.aspx

Baker-Bell, A., Paris, D., & Jackson, D. (2017). Learning Black language matters: Humanizing research as culturally sustaining pedagogy. *International Review of Qualitative Research, 10*(4), 360–377.

Beck, I. L., McKeown, M. G., & Kucan, L. (2013). *Bringing words to life: Robust vocabulary instruction.* Guilford Press.

Boutte, G. S. (2007). Teaching African American English speakers: Expanding educator and student repertoires. In M. E. Bris (Ed.), *Language, culture, and community in teacher education* (pp. 47–70). Routledge.

Boutte, G. S., & Johnson, G. L. (2013). Do educators see and honor biliteracy and bidialectalism in African American Language speakers? Apprehensions and reflections of two grandparents/professional educators. *Early Childhood Education Journal, 41*(2),133–141.

Brown, S., & Souto-Manning, M. (2008). "Culture is the way they live here": Young Latin@s and parents navigate linguistic and cultural borderlands in US schools. *Journal of Latinos and Education, 7*(1), 25–42.

Calhoun, E. F. (1999). *Teaching beginning reading and writing with the Picture Word Inductive Model.* Association for Supervision and Curriculum Development.

Carlone, H. B., Haun-Frank, J., & Webb, A. (2011). Assessing equity beyond knowledge-and skills-based outcomes: A comparative ethnography of two fourth-grade reform-based science classrooms. *Journal of Research in Science Teaching, 48*(5), 459–485.

Civil, M., & Khan, L. H. (2001). Mathematics instruction developed from a garden theme. *Teaching Children Mathematics, 7*(7), 400–405.

DiAngelo, R. (2018). *White fragility: Why it's so hard for White people to talk about racism.* Beacon Press.

Dimick, A. S. (2012). Student empowerment in an environmental science classroom: Toward a framework for social justice science education. *Science Education, 96*(6), 990–1012.

Echevarria, J., Vogt, M., & Short, D. (2008). *Making content comprehensible for English learners: The SIOP Model.* Pearson/Allyn & Bacon.

Emdin, C. (2008). Outstanding dissertation award: The three C's for urban science education. *Phi Delta Kappan, 89*(10), 772–775.

Emdin, C. (2016). *For White folks who teach in the hood . . . and the rest of y'all too.* Beacon Press.

Escamilla, K. (2009). Review of "English language learners: Developing literacy in second-language learners"—Report of the National Literacy Panel on Language-Minority Children and Youth edited by Diane August and Timothy Shanahan. *Journal of Literacy Research, 41*(4), 432–452.

Filippini, A. L., Gerber, M. M., & Leafstedt, J. M. (2012). A vocabulary-added reading intervention for English Learners at-risk of reading difficulties. *International Journal of Special Education, 27*(3), 14-26.

Gay, G. (2010). *Culturally responsive teaching: Theory, research and practice* (2nd ed.). Teachers College Press.

Gay, G. (2013). Teaching to and through cultural diversity. *Curriculum Inquiry, 43*(1), 48–70.

Gay, G. (2015). Teachers' beliefs about cultural diversity. In H. Fives & M. Gregorie Gill (Eds.), *International handbook of research on teachers' beliefs* (pp. 453–474). Routledge.

Gersten, R., & Geva, E. (2003). Teaching reading to early language learners. *Educational Leadership, 60*(7), 44–49.

González, N., Moll, L., & Amanti, C. (Eds.). (2005). *Funds of knowledge: Theorizing practices in households, communities, and classrooms.* Erlbaum.

Gutstein, E. (2003). Teaching and learning mathematics for social justice in an urban, Latino school. *Journal for Research in Mathematics Education, 34*(1), 37–73.

Herrell, A. L., & Jordan, M. (2016). *50 Strategies for teaching English language learners* (5th ed.). Pearson.

Howell, P. B., Cantrell, S. C., & Rintamaa, M. (2019). Setting the stage for action: Teaching social justice in the middle school classroom. *The Clearing House: A Journal of Educational Strategies, Issues and Ideas, 92*(6), 185–192.

Jennerjohn, A. (2020). School–family partnerships for culturally sustaining texts. *The Reading Teacher, 73*(5), 657–661.

Jiménez, R. T., García, G. E., & Pearson, P. D. (1996). The reading strategies of bilingual Latina/o students who are successful English readers: Opportunities and obstacles. *Reading Research Quarterly, 31*(1), 90–112.

Keehne, C. N., Sarsona, M. W., Kawakami, A. J., & Au, K. H. (2018). Culturally responsive instruction and literacy learning. *Journal of Literacy Research, 50*(2), 141–166.

Ladson-Billings, G. (1994). *The dreamkeepers: Successful teachers of African American children.* Jossey-Bass.

Ladson-Billings, G. (1995). Toward a theory of culturally relevant pedagogy. *American Educational Research Journal, 32*(3), 465–491.

Larson, S. C. (2014). Using a generative vocabulary matrix in the learning workshop. *The Reading Teacher, 68*(2), 113–125.

Lipka, J., Hogan, M. P., Webster, J. P., Yanez, E., & Adams, B. (2005). Math in a cultural context: Two case studies of a successful culturally based math project. *Anthropology & Education Quarterly, 36*(4), 367–385.

Love, B. L. (2019). *We want to do more than survive: Abolitionist teaching and the pursuit of educational freedom.* Beacon Press.

Lyons, G. E. (1999). *Where I'm from: Where poems come from.* Absey & Co.

Machado, E., Vaughan, A., Coppola, R., & Woodard, R. (2017). "Lived life through a colored lens": Culturally sustaining poetry in an urban literacy classroom. *Language Arts, 94*(6), 367 381.

Malo-Juvera, V. (2011). Vocabulary instruction in diverse classrooms. In R. Powell & E. Rightmyer (Eds.), *Literacy for all students: An instructional framework for closing the gap* (pp. 173–175). Routledge.

Milner, H. R. (2011). Culturally relevant pedagogy in a diverse urban classroom. *Urban Review, 43*(1), 66–89.

Moll, L. C., Amanti, C., Neff, D., & González, N. (1992). Funds of knowledge for teaching: Using a qualitative approach to connect homes and classrooms. *Theory Into Practice, 41*(2), 132–141.

Nesbit, J. C., & Adesope, O. O. (2006). Learning with concept and knowledge maps: A meta-analysis. *Review of Educational Research, 76*(3), 413–448.

Nykiel-Herbert, B. (2010). Iraqi refugee students: From a collection of aliens to a community of learners—The role of cultural factors in the acquisition of literacy by Iraqi refugee students with interrupted formal education. *Multicultural Education, 17*(3), 2–14.

Paris, D. (2012). Culturally sustaining pedagogy: A needed change in stance, terminology, and practice. *Educational Researcher, 41*(3), 93–97.

Powell, R., Cantrell, S. C., & Adams, S. (2001). Saving Black Mountain: The promise of critical literacy in a multicultural democracy. *The Reading Teacher, 54*(8), 772–781.

Powell, R., Cantrell, S. C., Malo-Juvera, V., & Correll, P. (2017). *Culturally Responsive Instruction Observation Protocol: A training manual* (2nd ed.) [Unpublished instrument].

Rodriguez-Mojica, C., & Briceño, A. (2018). Sentence stems that support reading comprehension. *The Reading Teacher, 72*(3), 398–402.

Sensoy, O., & DiAngelo, R. (2017). *Is everyone really equal?: An introduction to key concepts in social justice education* (2nd ed.). Teachers College Press.

Silverman, R., & Hines, S. (2009). The effects of multimedia-enhanced instruction on the vocabulary of English-language learners and non-English-language learners in pre-kindergarten through second grade. *Journal of Educational Psychology, 101*(2), 305–314.

Slack, D. B. (2001). Fusing social justice with multigenre writing. *The English Journal, 90*(6), 62–66.

Sleeter, C. E. (2012). Confronting the marginalization of culturally responsive pedagogy. *Urban Education, 47*(3), 562–584.

Spring, J. (2016). *Deculturalization and the struggle for equality: A brief history of the education of dominated cultures in the United States* (8th ed.). Routledge.

Taffe, S. W., Blachowicz, C. L. Z., & Fisher, P. J. (2009). Vocabulary instruction for diverse students. In L. M. Morrow, R. Rueda, & D. Lapp (Eds.), *Research on literacy and diversity* (pp. 320–337). Guilford Press.

Vaughn, S., Martinez, L. R., Wanzek, J., Roberts, G., Swanson, E., & Fall, A. M. (2017). Improving content knowledge and comprehension for English language learners: Findings from a randomized control trial. *Journal of Educational Psychology, 109*(1), 22–34.

Wlodkowski, R. J. (1999, Summer). Motivation and diversity: A framework for teaching. *New Directions for Teaching and Learning,* (78), 7–16.

CHAPTER 5

Discourse and Culturally Responsive Instruction

Pamela Knuckles Correll

> All intellectual growth relies heavily on conversation as a form of assisted performance in the zone of proximal development. When teaching through conversation occurs, classrooms and schools are transformed into "the community of learners" that they can become "when teachers reduce the distance between themselves and their students by constructing lessons from common understandings of each others' experience and ideas" and make teaching a "warm, interpersonal and collaborative activity" (Dalton, 1989). (Tharp & Gallimore, 1991, p. 7)

SCHOLARS HAVE EMPHASIZED the critical nature of discourse, or the ways in which we communicate, in the development of language, knowledge, and literacy (Cummins, 1999; Krashen, n.d.; Vygotsky, 1986). Yet, in many classrooms, opportunities for students to engage in substantive academic conversations are limited (Backer, 2017; Lingard et al., 2003; Nystrand et al., 2001). Teacher talk often takes precedence over student speech, and the predominant mode of questioning practiced by teachers across the US during classroom instruction continues to follow forms of Initiate–Respond–Evaluate (IRE), whereby a teacher asks a question, a student responds, and the teacher evaluates the response as correct or incorrect and moves on (Cazden, 2001; Delpit, 2008). These patterns of classroom interactions, which emphasize a transfer of information from teacher to student and a focus on providing the "correct" answer, fail to support students' critical thinking and expressions of diverse perspectives. Moreover, the high level of teacher talk in many U.S. classrooms frequently results in silence among students throughout the school day, as teachers commonly ask that students work independently and quietly while reading, writing, and completing academic tasks. Students often are discouraged from talking with their peers, and opportunities to engage in collaborative discussions are limited.

Furthermore, the language practices of students from culturally and linguistically diverse backgrounds are often criticized, neglected, and undervalued (Alim & Paris, 2017; Bucholtz et al., 2017; Escamilla et al., 2010; Ladson-Billings, 1995; Lee & Walsh, 2017; Purcell-Gates, 2008). When mainstream standards of instruction and behavior guide school practices, students from diverse backgrounds encounter difficulties in learning due to the lack of congruence to their cultural standards and values (Au, 2011). It is critically important that teachers affirm students' cultures, languages, and home lives in classroom settings (Gay, 2002; Ladson-Billings, 1994; Paris, 2012). Teachers who practice culturally responsive instruction embrace approaches that respect and validate students' linguistic and cultural backgrounds and utilize students' prior experiences to guide curriculum, classroom learning events, and opportunities for engagement through discourse (Powell et al., 2016). Through culturally responsive discourse approaches, teachers build positive relationships with their students while enhancing student engagement and prompting deeper learning.

What Does the Literature Tell Us About Discourse?

Discourse as Social Practice

Learning language is a social endeavor. Halliday (1993) underscored the social foundations of language development as a process of making meaning and generating learning through his observations that individuals learn by interpreting signs and symbols in their surroundings. Communication through language and print is central to social institutions, including schools, and speech is the most commonly practiced form of communication. The process of language development also has been linked with conceptual learning through social interactions and experiences; as children make connections among the cultural, historical, and individual experiences of their social groups, they develop knowledge of language and literacy practices (de Saussure, 2004; Gee, 2004; Vygotsky, 1986). According to Cummins (1999), "all children acquire their conceptual foundation (knowledge of the world) through conversational interactions in the home" (p. 4). As children use language for communicative purposes at home, through social practices and interactions, conceptual learning occurs (Vygotsky, 1986).

Theorists point out that language, social interaction, and intellectual growth are interconnected. As Vygotsky (1986) notes,

> thought development is determined by language, i.e., by the linguistic tools of thought and by the sociocultural experience of the child. . . . The child's intellectual growth is contingent on his mastering the social means of thought, that is language. (p. 94)

Essentially, language is a process of making meaning. According to Bakhtin (1986), language learning is social-cultural; we learn language as we hear and reproduce speech through authentic oral communications with others. Krashen (n.d.) further elaborated on language development as he differentiated language *learning* with language *acquisition* and posited that children develop proficiency in languages through input and exposure to language in social interactions that occur independent of specific instruction.

Findings from the work of psychologists, anthropologists, and linguists clearly demonstrate the connections between students' cultural backgrounds, social interactions, prior experiences, and their language practices (Bakhtin, 1986; Cummins, 1981; Hymes, 1974; Wodak, 2011). In addition, prior schooling and planned instruction also may influence how students use language (Heath, 1982; Krashen, n.d.; Ladson-Billings, 2008). Theories related to the functionality of language point to the purposes of language used by individuals for specific tasks and to accomplish goals (Halliday, 1993). As students engage in learning events involving conversations for specific purposes, they experience deeper learning and enhanced language development, a vital consideration for instructing linguistically diverse students. Labov's (1972) research with the language practices of urban Black children underscores sociocultural theories of language development as he observed the powerful influence of social situations on children's verbal communication. Our discourses are created intrinsically by our languages, actions, values, symbols, objects, tools, and places that form our identities, along with relationships with others and institutions (Bloome et al., 2008; Bové, 1995; Gee, 2011).

Learning is not an isolated experience; as students participate in conversations, they are enabled to construct meaning. "Authentic thinking, thinking that is concerned about *reality*, does not take place in ivory tower isolation, but only in communication" (Freire, 2002, p. 77). In addition, increased learning results when tasks occur within the *zone of proximal development*, when individuals are able to solve problems and achieve higher levels of understanding with assistance from more capable others (Vygotsky, 1978). Through conversations with teachers and peers, individuals reach higher levels of thinking and understanding, as engagement in verbal interactions with others requires abstract thought and logic and enables critical thinking (Freire, 2002; Street, 1984). Moreover, true education cannot occur without dialogue, the objective of discourse is not to impose one's viewpoints about a topic on others but to dialogue about individually held views (Freire, 2002).

Language and Culture

Language is inextricably intertwined with culture, and it is essential that teachers value and respect the language practices students bring to school. Heath (1983) illustrated the interconnection of cultural and linguistic practices, stating that "the place of language in the cultural life of each social group is interdependent with the habits and values of behaving shared among members of that group" (p. 11). Because home language practices are intricately linked to the foundations of their culture, as teachers validate students' home languages, students' pride and respect for their cultural and linguistic resources are enhanced. Culturally responsive practitioners aim to minimize the incongruities between home and school cultures and to avoid viewing students' home languages as deficient, inappropriate, or an educational disadvantage (Heath, 1982; Paris, 2012; Stubbs, 2008).

The mismatch between home and school language expectations and experiences can be problematic if teachers are unaware of these differences or view home language experiences as deficient. In her ethnographic study, Heath (1983) described the contrasting language expectations for students from diverse backgrounds as illustrated by her explanation of children from lower income families, which she denoted as groups from Trackton and Roadville. Children in these communities had varying communication modes due to differing "social legacies and ways of behaving in face to face interactions" (Heath, 1983, p. 5) and learned to use language according to family structures, accepted community roles, and child-rearing practices. Some of these students had little experience with fantasy stories or with books involving fictional accounts of animals. Thus, teachers in the community focused on adjusting their instruction to make connections to students' cultural backgrounds and build on students' literacy strengths while maintaining high standards.

When Trackton and Roadville children go to school, they meet very different notions of

> truth, style, and language appropriate to a "story" from those they have known
> at home. They must learn a different taxonomy and new definitions of stories.
> They must come to recognize when a story is expected to be true, when to stick
> to the facts, and when to use their imaginations. (Heath, 1983, p. 294)

In another example, Au and Mason (1981) found that effective teachers of Native Hawaiian children conducted classroom conversations using communication patterns employing *talk story*, which students practiced in their interactions with families and friends outside of school. As teachers supported students in their co-narrations and overlapping conversations during classroom discussions, students maintained their cultural and linguistic identities and were more engaged in reading lessons, responded more often, and experienced higher levels of learning.

Hence, it is important to recognize and value students' cultural backgrounds and linguistic practices in school and classroom communities. When students are discouraged from using their home languages in classrooms, their linguistic histories are marginalized or excluded. Teachers must engage in self-reflection to ensure that they view students' home language practices as assets, rather than as deficiencies, or *less than*, Standard English (SE) or formal language. When students' language practices are continually critiqued, students begin to shut down and are silenced from participating fully as members of the classroom community. Teachers who are committed to culturally responsive approaches welcome students' language assets and contributions in classrooms as "they support young people in sustaining the cultural and linguistic competence of their communities while simultaneously offering access to dominant cultural competence" (Paris, 2012, p. 95).

Affirming and validating students' home languages also reduces the alienating factors English learners (ELs) often experience in school contexts. As suggested by Krashen (n.d.), affective factors, or filters, related to increased anxiety, stress, or tension, may constrain students' language acquisition. When teachers respect, welcome, and support students' uses of their home languages, the effects of affective filters are reduced, and students acquire new language practices more readily (Delpit, 2008; Krashen, n.d.).

Thus, all students benefit from experiences that engage them in using their home language practices in situationally appropriate contexts. Furthermore, as I discuss later, research shows that students also benefit from explicit instruction in formal language structures as they acquire standard linguistic forms.

The Perpetuation of Deficit Perspectives

As noted previously, language is a social process, and culture and language are integrally related. Sociolinguists suggest that language dialects, or language varieties "used in a particular geographical region or by a particular social group" (Stubbs, 2008, p. 72), are influenced by social factors and involve language conventions, systems, and rules of grammar (Heath, 1982; Street, 1984). While *dialect* refers to varied vocabulary preferences, pronunciations, or grammar usage among groups, differences in pronunciation only, when vocabulary and grammar are shared, are considered to be *accents*. Acceptable and prestigious dialectical features and variants are based on the social status of speakers and their economic success, power, and influence (Gee, 1993). In their discourses, speakers are motivated and influenced by desires for social status, to show solidarity with their peers, or to demonstrate group membership or identity (Gee, 1993).

In fact, Gee (2011) suggests that one's language, as used within particular social contexts, can be considered to be a type of "identity kit." He differentiates between "discourse," utilizing oral language for communicative purposes, and "Discourse," that is, a "way of saying, doing, and being" (p. 30). He writes:

> A Discourse with a capital 'D" is composed of distinctive ways of speaking/listening and often, too, writing/reading coupled with distinctive ways of acting, interacting, valuing, feeling, dressing, thinking, believing, with other people and with various objects, tools, and technologies, so as to enact specific socially recognizable identities. (p. 37)

In this sense, the language we use through our Discourses enables us to take on a certain identity (Gee, 1990). Furthermore, our Discourses signify our membership in social groups with others who share common backgrounds, interests, beliefs, or goals and are shaped through the linguistic practices of social and cultural groups, which may include ethnic groups, academic disciplines, professions, and cultures, among others (Gee, 1992, 2011). Gee (2011) contended that individuals may be members of different social groups simultaneously; as individuals interact with others, they use language for purposes of signifying affiliation or membership with various groups.

For students in classrooms who represent diverse cultures, backgrounds, and social practices, the recognition and affirmation of the language practices of their Discourses is a critical factor in developing positive classroom relationships and creating safe classroom environments. Paris (2012) has recommended that teachers implement culturally sustaining pedagogies, which maintain that students' languages are important facets of their identities. Thus, culturally responsive pedagogy needs to include the affirmation and use of students' native languages. Consider that when teachers hold deficit perspectives of students' languages and vernaculars, they are conveying that their sociocultural identities are also deficient. Because language is an integral part of our identity, it is crucial that teachers affirm the home languages of students who are learning English as a second language. As teachers aim to sustain students' native language practices and multilingualism, they prepare students to be successful in our demographically evolving world.

Theorists have asserted linguistic practices are among the strongest features of social class and may afford or constrain educational opportunities (Heath, 1982; Purcell-Gates, 2008). While language use and cultural practices are intricately intertwined and reinforced, language practices and dialects also function as social markers, as evidenced by the common acceptance of dialects of individuals who hold positions of power and disdain for dialects from individuals of color or from groups who have been historically marginalized (Heath, 1982; Paris, 2012). The effects on the educational opportunities for students is profound as "socio-politically driven attitudes toward the language that people speak, think with, and learn with" have resulted in "a class difference in learning and achievement" (Purcell-Gates, 2008, p. 134).

As Fairclough and Wodak (1997) suggest, "discursive practices may have major ideological effects—that is, they can help produce and reproduce unequal power relations between (for instance) social classes, women and men, and ethnic/cultural majorities and minorities through the ways in which they represent things and position people" (p. 258). That is, perceptions of language use actually can reinforce and contribute to unequal power relations in schools and society (Baker-Bell et al., 2017; D. Martinez, 2017; Paris, 2012). As a result, members of groups with lower social status or fewer economic resources are more likely to experience negative perceptions of their intelligence, knowledge, and abilities as compared to students from cultural and social groups with higher status and sociopolitical power, and these conditions exist both in the United States and in underdeveloped countries (Purcell-Gates, 2008).

Failure to use forms of SE may result in correction, and schools commonly enforce dichotomies of *acceptable* and *unacceptable* language uses; due to social prejudices, nonstandard forms of English may be viewed as inferior (Gee, 1993; Purcell-Gates, 2008). These deficit views have had profound adverse effects on the literacy achievement and academic success of students from culturally and linguistically diverse backgrounds. Children who are raised in economically advantaged homes with parents with higher levels of formal schooling enter school prepared to use school-based forms of English, as practiced in their homes, while children from homes with limited access to quality schools or long-term education are challenged by using language in new ways (Gee, 1993; Purcell-Gates, 2008). For example, in elementary classrooms, teachers from predominantly middle-class backgrounds often fail to recognize Black students' narratives, which follow discourse patterns used in students' homes and communities, because they utilize different chronological structures than those practiced in middle-class homes (Gee, 1992). Additionally, teachers may fail to recognize the language creativity exhibited through storytelling, puns, jokes, and word games that students use in conversation (Ford et al., 2000). Research findings from observations in classrooms where teachers overcorrected students' uses of dialects differing from Standard American English have revealed how such practices have led to student frustration, disengagement, and resentment (Delpit, 1995). Furthermore, these teachers tended to devalue the contributions offered by children using nonmainstream forms of English.

It is also important to note that, since printed texts function as codes of language, students who are discouraged or forbidden to use their home languages and to adopt different forms of language when reading or writing are hindered in developing print literacy (Purcell-Gates, 2008). ELs are more engaged and participate more readily in classrooms where teachers bridge differences between home and school literacies by making connections to students' backgrounds and experiences (August & Shanahan, 2006; Escamilla et al., 2010). However, research findings related to classroom interventions and uses of students' home languages and effects on student literacy and academic outcomes are limited, and more studies are needed (Escamilla et al., 2010).

Developing Students' Linguistic Competence

Because language is part of one's identity, teachers have an important role in validating and sustaining students' vernaculars and languages. Yet scholars acknowledge that SE is the language of power, and thus acquiring SE must be emphasized to enable students to develop literacy practices "recognized by the larger society" (Au, 2011, p. 72). Paris (2012) advocates that teachers should aim to help students maintain their language and cultural practices while expanding these repertoires to include dominant languages and literacies. Hence, it is necessary that students learn to exercise multilinguistic flexibility.

Encouraging multilinguistic flexibility includes helping students understand the ways in which different language forms provide access to social capital in varying contexts. According to Bourdieu's (1991) theories of language, "speakers lacking the legitimate competence are *de facto* excluded from the social domains in which this competence is required, or are condemned to silence" (p. 55). If we are to help prepare children to function as productive members of an equitable society, it is imperative that educators practice pedagogies that support students' acquisition of dominant language and cultural competence (Paris, 2012).

For many, if not most students, the formal language is what Gee (2011) refers to as "secondary discourses," that is, various language forms that allow us to function within a variety of social contexts. These secondary discourses can be acquired through explicit teaching in schools. Gee (1993) defined *communicative competence* as "the capacity of people to select and recognize the language variety appropriate to the occasion" (p. 349). Consider, for example, the flexibility in language use of individuals such as former president Barack Obama, who is capable of using both formal language structures and the Black vernacular, depending on which is most appropriate for the context. In classrooms, students may learn and practice using appropriate registers of language through planned instructional experiences, collaborative projects, and learning events.

Consistent with Gee's (2011) theory of Discourse, communicative competence not only involves the language forms used by members of a particular group but also addresses group norms for speaking rights of group members; relevant knowledge sources; and acceptable ways of displaying one's information and self (Bloome & Bailey, 1990). In other words, Discourses are more than simply language; they also involve acceptable norms for *what* and *how* information is shared. Thus, to acquire secondary discourses, students must be given opportunities to practice those discourses in authentic contexts. Although it is important that teachers value and affirm students' home languages, it is critical that students learn and practice various registers of language in multiple contexts. Students develop linguistic dexterity and communicative competence as they participate in specific speaking events and use language for varied purposes.

In culturally responsive classrooms, teachers recognize and affirm students' uses of their native languages and dialects, while also teaching code-switching, or using specific language styles depending on context or purposes. As Delpit (2008) observed, students readily utilize code-switching, particularly when they identify with those who speak in varied language forms. In her study of effective teachers of African American students, Ladson-Billings (1995) found as African American students were affirmed in their ability to code-switch, or to "move with facility, in language between African American language and a standard form of English," they were "supported in the attempts at role-switching between school and home" (p. 482).

Danny Martinez and colleagues (2017) advocate using students' home language abilities to provide access to the dominant language and literacy practices. For example, Ramón Martinez (2010) leveraged sixth graders' use of Spanglish to prompt higher levels of students' academic language and literacy. In another study in a school with a predominantly Hispanic/Latino population, eighth-grade students self-produced videos of language interactions that demonstrated their uses of language at school and at home (Orellana et al., 2012). These researchers observed that the teacher leveraged students' uses of Spanish, Spanglish, and English in varied contexts to expand students' linguistic repertoires in both classroom and home settings.

As students benefit from using their home languages when they participate in informal conversations, paired discussions, and small group interactions, they also profit from using formal language in a variety of ways. In a study of African American high school students' perceptions of using SE or African American Vernacular English (AAVE) in English classes, researchers found that students demonstrated awareness of using code-switching and described expectations for using appropriate registers of language in various contexts while differing in their opinions of using SE or AAVE in school (Godley & Escher, 2012). Findings of the study revealed that most participating students believed classrooms should be safe spaces where students can practice SE without judgment. Researchers also recommended that educators discuss with students how they adapt their language in various spaces and role-play appropriate language uses for differing situations (Godley & Escher, 2012).

Just as vernacular speakers need to learn how to code-switch, students who speak languages other than English need to acquire proficiency in their native languages. According to the National Literacy Panel on Language-Minority Children and Youth report, oral language proficiency and literacy development in students' home languages prompt English-language acquisition and achievement for linguistically diverse students (August & Shanahan, 2006). Furthermore, findings from research studies indicate that linguistically diverse students' language development is enhanced through opportunities to engage in academic and social conversations both in English and in students' dominant languages (August & Shanahan, 2006). Educators must recognize the value of bilingualism as the new global norm and avoid viewing ELs as not *normal* or *behind* their grade-level peers (Escamilla et al., 2010).

An important way to help students develop linguistic competence is through academic conversations. By having specific language outcomes in mind and using various language supports, students learn formal discourse by communicating in structured settings with peers. I turn now to the research on this topic.

Discourse in Classroom Settings

As students interact with each other in small-group discussions, they construct meaning (Bloome & Bailey, 1990). Students who engage in academic conversations consider diverse perspectives, create meanings through speech, and experience enhanced understandings of concepts. However, in some classrooms, opportunities for students to engage in higher level academic conversations with their peers are limited, although the results of research point to higher levels of student engagement, deeper understanding, and increased learning through student verbal interactions (Cazden, 2001; Gee, 2004; Michaels et al., 2016).

Cazden's (2001) findings that teachers commonly implement IRE forms of classroom questioning point to patterns of limited use of authentic classroom discourse. These types of school-based questioning structures are used to test individual student knowledge. However, the IRE questioning pattern is inauthentic and inconsistent with student conversation structures in settings apart from school and thus results in limited student engagement and participation. In addition, rather than promoting authentic forms of students' home discourse and native languages, teachers often limit the opportunities for students to develop academic language proficiency by assigning speaking rights to specific students. In contrast, culturally responsive discourse protocols consistently engage students in speaking events that encourage academic conversations and meaningful dialogue, and when provided with guidance and support, these conversations enable students to learn and use the academic language of school. In addition to linguistic benefits, peer conversations also have important cognitive benefits. Rich conversations in classrooms enable students to compare and contrast perspectives more deeply and reflectively and promote greater reasoning (Gee, 2004).

The theories on language development that have been discussed thus far have critical implications for teachers who strive to support the English-language development and academic achievement of students learning English as an additional language. Cummins (1999) differentiated between the language used for basic interpersonal communication skills (BICS), or verbal forms of communication used by individuals for social interactions in their everyday lives, and cognitive academic language proficiency (CALP), the language used for academic purposes and in classroom contexts. It typically requires up to 3 years to develop proficiency in BICS, whereas CALP often requires from 5 to 7 years. Although these two types of language overlap, they remain "conceptually distinct" (Cummins, 1999, p. 4). Students who have higher levels of BICS and use English proficiently for social purposes may have lower CALP and struggle with formal uses of academic language. For classroom teachers with linguistically diverse students, planning challenging learning and language objectives and integrating content-specific instruction with language learning lead to enhanced development of students' CALP (Cummins, 1999).

Academic conversations in classrooms provide rich opportunities for teaching academic language structures, not just for ELs but for all students. With explicit goals and appropriate linguistic support, students can grow in their use of formal linguistic structures. To help ELs develop linguistic proficiency, teachers are encouraged to incorporate language objectives into their lesson planning and to emphasize building academic vocabulary throughout their instruction to foster academic success (Echevarria et al., 2006). Among elements of sheltered instruction are recommendations that teachers provide sentence frames and models to guide students as they discuss academic concepts with their peers (Goldenberg, 2013). Examples of language supports are provided in the next section.

A lack of specific instruction in academic language can have particularly devastating effects on ELs. It is particularly important that teachers avoid "one size fits all" approaches to instruction and that they recognize the unique strengths and assets of ELs as emerging bilinguals. According to Au and Raphael (2010), "a major reason for the poor progress shown by ELLs [English language learners] as a group is that they seldom receive the high-quality instruction necessary to build their knowledge of literate discourse" (p. 209). In the United States, approximately 80% of teachers are White, and many are monolingual with few experiences with linguistically diverse students, while students of color make up approximately 48% of students (National Center for Educational Statistics, 2019). Contributing to the issue of a lack of quality instruction for ELs are assertions of inadequate teacher preparation for meeting the language and learning needs of culturally and linguistically diverse students (Au & Raphael, 2010; Li & Protacio, 2010; Lucas et al., 2008; Mueller et al., 2006). A large body of research has confirmed that ELs benefit from instructional modifications based on students' proficiency in English (Escamilla et al., 2010; Goldenberg, 2010; Harper & de Jong, 2004; Lucas et al., 2008).

Classroom practices that include opportunities for ELs to participate in classroom discourse, verbal interactions, and academic conversations support language and literacy development, as well as conceptual learning (Center for Research on Education, Diversity, and Excellence, 2020; Echevarria & Vogt, 2010). Participating in classroom academic conversations, verbal interactions with linguistically diverse and native English-speaking peers, and other forms of classroom discourse leads to enhanced proficiency in English and higher levels of learning for ELs (Echevarria & Vogt, 2010; Thomas & Collier, 2002). As asserted by Garcia and Garcia (2010), "a child's linguistic, cognitive, and social characteristics are fundamentally connected and interrelated" (p. 49). Thus, students benefit when teachers bridge language differences between home and school contexts to increase participation and engagement in classroom learning events. In arranging grouping patterns for peer conversations, varied combinations of small groups that consider students' language backgrounds, interests, and mixed ability levels are recommended as students collaborate to achieve common learning goals.

The effects of limited proficiency in academic English become more evident when students reach about the third-grade level, and demands on reading comprehension increase with higher levels of content-specific vocabulary. As noted in the previous chapter, vocabulary development is important for students at all grade levels but is particularly crucial for ELs at higher grade levels, and educators are encouraged to provide direct vocabulary instruction, activities to support content-area knowledge, and opportunities for oral language practice (Goldenberg, 2010; Harper & de Jong, 2004). Varied forms of visual representations related to concepts and vocabulary, and verbal activities including poems, songs, and repeated readings are recommended strategies for students learning English as an additional language (Goldenberg, 2010). Because bilingualism and biliteracy are cognitive assets (Escamilla et al., 2010), ELs benefit from strategies such as using students' native languages for restating or clarifying and comparing English with students' native languages.

Discourse: From Research to Practice

For students to participate fully in classroom discourse, their language variations must be celebrated, rather than negated, corrected, or ignored. As discussed earlier, when schools build classroom communities that incorporate the language and cultures of students from diverse backgrounds, students are empowered and supported in learning (Au, 2011; Cummins, 1994). Accordingly, teachers are encouraged to adopt culturally responsive pedagogies that utilize students' home languages in learning and to focus on supporting students' linguistic metacognition and increasing their language abilities. In the following sections, I discuss the Culturally Responsive Instruction Observation Protocol (CRIOP) indicators for the Discourse element to describe how teachers can utilize strategies throughout their instruction to encourage students to participate in classroom speaking events.

Active Student Engagement Through Discourse Practices

In culturally responsive classrooms, teachers consistently provide opportunities for student conversations to prompt engagement and participation in classroom learning events. Discourse can be integrated into a lesson to enhance instruction and understanding. Through varied grouping configurations of student pairs, small groups, and whole-class discourse activities, teachers can encourage student talk and verbal interactions throughout literacy and content-area instruction. Teachers should consider encouraging extended conversations and equitable participation through their instructional planning. Through shared participation in classroom discussions, students practice formulating and expressing their ideas while strengthening classroom relationships and building supportive classroom communities. In her study of successful teachers of Black students, Ladson-Billings (1995) observed opportunities for students to participate in shared discourse through varied formal and informal configurations of student paired activities, buddy systems, and small groups. These shared student conversations encouraged mutuality and reciprocity, building communities of learners in which students learned collaboratively and supported each others' academic success.

Partner or paired discourse protocols such as Think–Pair–Share (Lyman, 1981) and Think–Pair–Square (Fisher & Frey, 2014), in which students are asked to think about a prompt or respond to a question, discuss their responses with a partner or partners, and then share their answers in a whole-class discussion, allow all students in the class to engage in discourse. Students may also participate in dialogues with a partner in Stand Up/Pair Up as they verbalize their ideas, compare responses, or share impressions about a particular concept or topic. In another adaptation, students may respond to a question or prompt by writing in a journal or by jotting their answers on a sticky note. Students then share their written responses with a partner or a small group prior to sharing in a whole-class discussion. Read–Write–Pair–Share (Fisher & Frey, 2014) follows the same procedures after students have read a text or viewed a video or other visual.

Teachers may also incorporate opportunities for whole-class discourse through strategies such as call and response and choral response. For example, fourth-grade teacher Madeline Todd used a call–response format to review the previous chapter of a novel they were reading:

The characters in this chapter were _____ (students respond together).

The setting was _____ (students respond together).

The first thing that happened was _____ (students respond together).

We have also seen call and response used as a classroom management strategy to get students' attention. ("When I say 'burger,' you say 'fries.' Teacher: 'Burger!' Students: 'Fries!'") Bohn (2003) found that African American students responded positively to their teacher's use of call and response, along with teacher modeling of SE, embedding choral responses in classroom discussions, and using chants and role-play within her instruction to prompt student engagement and participation.

Novel Ideas Only (Fisher & Frey, 2014) is a whole-class discourse strategy in which teachers provide a question or prompt that may have multiple responses. After students individually have written at least three ideas for the question, all students stand; as each student shares one of their listed ideas, others in the class cross off any answers on their lists stated by another student, continuing until all novel ideas have been shared. Students remain standing until all their responses have been eliminated. As students listen to diverse responses from their peers, they reach higher levels of understanding, and teachers may use students' responses to assess any misconceptions or to address any gaps in learning.

Students can serve as powerful resources for one another during instruction. To share an example of what a quality small-group discussion might look like in an elementary school, I observed in a kindergarten classroom with Spanish-speaking ELs as part of a study of teachers' preparation for teaching linguistically diverse students (Correll, 2016). The teacher in this classroom consistently allowed her native Spanish-speaking students to sit next to each other during whole-class, small-group, and independent activities. These young students actively participated in collaborative activities and often translated and explained the teacher's directions to their linguistically diverse peers, resulting in students' greater understandings of tasks, increased learning of conceptual knowledge, and higher levels of English-language development. By providing opportunities for ELs to communicate with their Spanish-speaking peers, the teacher demonstrated her recognition and affirmation of students' bilingualism as ELs engaged in social and academic conversations that led to increased levels of language development and learning. In a math lesson that I observed in another school, third grade students engaged in role-playing an "on-the-scene newscast" conducted by a "television reporter," played by the teacher (Correll, 2016). All students appeared to be engaged in conversations around the classroom as they met in groups in corners of the room and debated the difference between intersecting and perpendicular lines before participating in the mock television news report. The teacher, speaking in a "news re-porter" voice and holding a pretend microphone, questioned a spokesperson from each group as if she were interviewing people on the street for a feature during a newscast. Each spokesperson answered the teacher's geometry-related questions for their group and drew a diagram on the SMART Board to illustrate. The teacher prompted students at times with responses such as "Interesting! Will you show me what you mean?" As one student explained, he went to the SMART Board, drew intersecting lines with points of intersection, and marked right angles and points of intersection. The teacher then asked, "If intersecting lines don't have a right angle, are they perpendicular?" Students in the class answered aloud in unison. By participating in this role-play scenario, students engaged in academic discourse to explain mathematics concepts.

Equitable and Culturally Sustaining Discourse Practices

The Discourse element of the CRIOP supports discourse practices that are congru-ent with students' ways of using language and that sustain students' native languages. In culturally responsive classrooms, students from culturally and linguistically diverse backgrounds are recognized as resources who can help their teachers and peers learn more about culture, language, and living as global citizens. Culturally responsive teachers provide myriad opportunities for students to use community speech patterns and their home languages in classroom tasks as they collaborate with their peers. To encourage student discourse and participation in dialogic experiences, it is critical that teachers recognize and validate students' cultural and linguistic backgrounds and strengths as they plan content-area instruction and language objectives.

As classroom teachers learn about their students' home language practices, they need to familiarize themselves with "the linguistic structures of various ethnic com-munication styles as well as contextual features, logic and rhythm, delivery, vocabulary usage, role relationships of speakers and listeners, intonation, gestures, and body move-ments" (Gay, 2002, p. 111). This becomes particularly important when considering that students from culturally and linguistically diverse backgrounds are uncomfortable participating in some discourse structures such as peer discussions, debates, or criti-cal questioning due to cultural norms and beliefs. For example, in some cultures, the teacher is seen as an authority figure, so questioning authority is viewed as disrespectful. Therefore, teachers must be knowledgeable of students' cultural and linguistic norms to interpret attitudes and behavior (Li, 2013).

By utilizing community speech patterns congruent with students' cultural back-grounds and recognizing students' use of home discourse structures, which may involve overlapping speech and co-narration during culturally congruent conversations, teachers help bridge gaps between home and school settings (Au, 2011). In her work with Native Hawaiian students, Au (2011) reported that using talk story–like participation structures resulted in higher levels of student engagement and increased textual references and inferences. With talk story, students cooperatively produce a response, which is in contrast to the typical classroom discourse structure whereby a teacher poses a question and expects a single student to respond. Thus, although the focus is still on comprehension, the rules for participation are very different. Au and Kawakami (1985) write that

> there are very few times during talk story when just one child monopolizes the right to speak. This is because what seems to be important to Hawaiian children in talk story is not *individual performance* in speaking, which is often important in the classroom, but *group performance* in speaking. . . . This value attached to group rather than individual performance seems to be consistent with the importance in Hawaiian culture of contributing to the well-being of one's family or circle of friends, rather than working only for one's personal well-being. (p. 409; emphasis in original)

To encourage active participation in classroom speaking events, teachers may use a variety of strategies. At the same time, one of the problems in small-group interaction is that some students tend to dominate the conversation. Turn-taking, share circles, and using talking sticks are examples of strategies that encourage equitable participation in verbal interactions (Cazden, 2001). Share circles are used by some teachers as a form of a daily class meeting and, as noted in Chapter 1, can help develop a positive classroom community (Schwab & Elias, 2014). Students sit in a circle and are encouraged to make eye contact with the speaker. As students share their experiences and feelings, they build supportive, caring relationships with their peers, offer suggestions for classroom routines and management, and engage in group problem-solving.

Teachers can also use share circles for sharing students' thoughts about a particular topic. For instance, students can respond to a prompt in writing journals and then read their responses in a share circle, building on one another's ideas during their discussion. Sitting in a circle makes for a more natural conversational structure, and when students are permitted to respond spontaneously to the ideas of others, this arrangement can be particularly useful for students from cultures that tend to prefer overlapping discourse forms.

The talking stick has been used by Native Americans for hundreds of years to assure that all voices are heard within the circle. Individuals who hold the talking stick are permitted to speak without interruption. Once they have expressed all their thoughts and ideas, they pass the stick on to the next individual. We have used a similar technique by tossing a ball or beanbag to students, thereby giving them speaking rights while other students listen.

The "talking sticks" strategy is somewhat different in that two or three sticks are distributed equally to each student. Students are directed to turn in a stick each time they wish to speak. After their sticks have been used, they may not speak again. With this type of discourse structure, only the person holding the artifact is permitted to speak. Another way to ensure that all students have speaking opportunities involves teachers distributing a certain number of chips to each student. Every time students give a response, they must put a chip in the middle of the circle and stop after their chips have been used. Some teachers also use the "build a tower" strategy with LEGOs or other tokens, in which students are given a certain number of tokens and contribute to the tower until their tokens are used up. Teaching accountable talk frames to children also helps assure more equitable participation in group conversations. Accountable talk is discussed later in this section.

To celebrate the linguistic diversity within classrooms, teachers may infuse a myriad of practices designed to encourage the development of students' native languages and literacies. Teachers may include learning opportunities for students to write narratives, poems, and songs in their home languages or to translate texts into their home dialects (Delpit, 1995; Lee & Walsh, 2017). Teachers may embed linguistic diversity as part of their curricula, and students can teach each other about their languages. Some teachers we have known have designated certain students "language experts," asking them to state ideas and concepts in their native languages so that others can learn from them.

Figure 5.1. *To affirm the home language of some of her students, Kelsey Davis directed her third graders to use Spanish vocabulary in their math problems.*

Another way to celebrate students' native languages is to label items in the classroom in those languages. As Walker-Dalhouse suggests in Chapter 1, seeing one's native language throughout the classroom can go a long way in affirming students' cultural and linguistic identities. In one school I visited with a large population of Spanish-speaking students, a number of teachers labeled classroom fixtures (e.g., desk, chair, bookshelf, calendar, clock, etc.) in both English and Spanish. Posters of numbers, colors, and geometric shapes in primary classrooms were labeled in Spanish and English. In addition, some of the classroom libraries included books with texts printed in both Spanish and English or books with embedded Spanish terms. Other teachers in our project have used translation sites to create labels in the various languages of their families. We recall the change in Tanish, for example, when he came into his kindergarten classroom one morning and saw several items labeled in his native language of Hindi.

Ideally, teachers would be able to communicate with students in their native languages throughout the day, both to communicate new concepts and to establish relationships. In our multilingual classrooms, however, this is not always possible. Teachers can, however, learn greetings and simple phrases in ELs' home languages such as *hello, good-bye*, and *good job*, and use the phrases in their interactions with students. In one class I observed, a teacher with several ELs from Spanish-speaking families included comments such as *Gracias, Muy bien*, and *Bueno* often in her conversations with students. Teachers may also incorporate words in students' native languages in math problems (e.g., Figure 5.1) and use books that include words from students' home languages for class read-alouds. In another school, a primary grade teacher with several Spanish-speaking ELs carried a small Spanish–English dictionary with her throughout the school day to use as a reference as she conversed with her young students. When teachers become learners of students' languages, they convey to them that their cultural/linguistic identity is significant and valued.

Research strongly supports the use of bilingualism in instruction, which includes encouraging students to discuss new concepts in their native languages. For instance, during a mathematics lesson in one kindergarten classroom I observed, the teacher put students into small groups to discuss and collaboratively solve math problems. At one table, a group of five native Spanish speakers spoke animatedly together in Spanish as they discussed counting problems with one another and wrote numbers on a math worksheet. Although the teacher was monolingual and did not speak Spanish, she recognized bilingualism as an asset and affirmed students' use of their home languages as she encouraged her young students to speak in their home language with their peers to complete the task.

In another example, fifth-grade students prepared biographical presentations on a famous civil rights leader for their school's Exhibition Night. Two students who were native Spanish speakers chose to research the life of César Chávez and present their findings in both English and Spanish. Through this activity, they not only acquired academic vocabulary in Spanish (which is essential for developing and sustaining their native language), but they were also able to share their findings with family members who had limited English proficiency.

Providing Structures That Promote Academic Conversation

As noted previously, participation in academic conversations promotes student engagement and facilitates learning. A consistent theme throughout this book is that when teachers ground their instruction in students' cultural backgrounds, language practices, and interests, students are more likely to feel connected to school, with new concepts, and with academic language. Through their instructional practices, teachers may provide opportunities for students to increase their conceptual understandings and linguistic proficiencies. Research findings have shown that participating in academic conversations facilitates student participation and higher levels of achievement (Johnson, 2011; Morrell & Duncan-Andrade, 2002: Stovall, 2006).

Academic conversations also enable teachers to discern students' uses of academic language. As teachers listen to students' responses and infer intended meanings, teachers assess student understanding and conceptual misunderstandings and adjust their instruction to facilitate student comprehension and learning. Teachers who regularly set concrete language targets for students' academic vocabulary and language use can listen to students' conversations to determine whether those language targets are being met. Formative assessment during classroom discussions also enables teachers to encourage the expression of diverse perspectives and make connections to current issues.

As they promote classroom academic conversations through opportunities for paired and small-group learning opportunities, teachers enable students to engage in deep thinking, to use academic vocabulary in authentic ways, and to apply critical thinking in discussions revolving around authentic, real-world issues. Teachers who practice culturally responsive instruction (CRI) at high levels consistently provide discourse structures that allow students to verbalize their learning using a variety of oral language strategies. Theories of language and learning recognize that "learning occurs through social interaction" (Hammerberg, 2004, p. 655), and learning also occurs when students are empowered and their languages are affirmed.

Students may engage in whole-class academic discussions, or conversations with a partner/buddy, in student-led groups, or in teacher-led small groups. Strategies for implementing *instructional conversations* involve providing explicit instruction for conducting shared speaking experiences, encouraging extended student responses, and prompting students to provide evidence to support their views. Furthermore, teachers need to set rigorous and challenging learning and language goals—a topic I discuss in more detail later. It is often useful to provide prompts such as sentence frames or conversation cards to guide students' paired or small-group discussions. These are illustrated in Figures 5.2 and 5.3.

One strategy that works well for promoting academic conversations about texts is paired book conversations. Teachers pair up students based on reading proficiency and other factors (e.g., language, who they feel can work together productively). Through teacher modeling, students are taught to read a short portion of the text (such as a

Figure 5.2. Sentence frames such as this one used in Melissa Collins's first-grade math class can be beneficial to students in structuring their conversations.

Figure 5.3. In upper grades, conversation cards can be used with student pairs or small groups to guide their discussions. This conversation card includes vocabulary, sentence starters, and partner questions.

paragraph or half a page) and then have a conversation with their partner. To begin this process, the teacher demonstrates how to have both productive and nonproductive conversations about the text, as illustrated in the following excerpt:

> Teacher and partner choose who will read first, and he or she reads a short portion of the text orally. After reading, they have a conversation that might go something like this:
>
> Teacher: So, did you watch the game last night?
>
> Partner: Yeah, wow, what did you think about that touchdown in the last minute of the game!
>
> Teacher: Oh that was so exciting! I really thought we were going to lose. So let's read some more.
>
> This is followed by a discussion with the class about what *not* to do during a book conversation. (Teachers should feel free to insert any behaviors that they might anticipate from their students!) Next, they model an effective reading/conversation that focuses on the text, and students are directed to listen and watch carefully. Specific behaviors and language are noted on a chart, which is revisited often as students "try out" paired book reading with a partner. The chart would typically note behaviors such as stay on topic, refer to the book, build on what your partner says, and so on. The language might include I agree, I disagree because . . . , What did you think about ______? I can make a connection to (something in my life; another book); Do you know what ______ means? and so on.

Several tasks are embedded in student conversational reading. Students are directed to find unfamiliar vocabulary words and mark them with sticky notes as they read. During a whole-class review, students share their vocabulary words and use the context to try to determine the word's meaning. When studying specific comprehension skills such as inferencing or visualizing, students are asked to apply them to their reading ("Find an inference in your reading today." "Mark a place where you visualized.") Many teachers initially believe this strategy will not work with their students because it requires a good deal of self-monitoring, but once they try it, they are pleasantly surprised at the animated conversations and high level of student engagement. Students particularly enjoy partner reading because they have control and choice in the vocabulary words they select, how much they read, and the topics of their conversations.

In classrooms, utilizing varied grouping configurations (e.g., pairs and small groups, teacher-selected groups, student-interest groups, book clubs, literacy circles, others) prompts student participation and optimizes learning. Teaching skills like *accountable talk* helps students have effective conversations that include all students and result in higher levels of learning (Resnick, 1999). Guidelines for accountable talk include focusing on the topic, contributing accurate information related to the topic, and deep thinking about the statements of others. Teachers lead students to engage in accountable talk through questioning, guiding discussions, and modeling effective academic conversations as they "press for clarification and explanation, require justification of proposals and challenges, recognize and challenge misconceptions, demand evidence for claims and arguments, or interpret and 'revoice' students' statements" (Michaels et al., 2016, p. 3). Examples of conversation stems used with accountable talk that promote productive student conversations include "I believe _______ because _______"; "I have a question about _______"; "I disagree with _________ because _______; and "I wonder what would happen if _______" (Ross et al., 2009). Figure 5.4 illustrates accountable talk stems that can be used with children as young as kindergarten.

Figure 5.4. *Even young children can be taught to use simple accountable talk frames when having conversations with peers.*

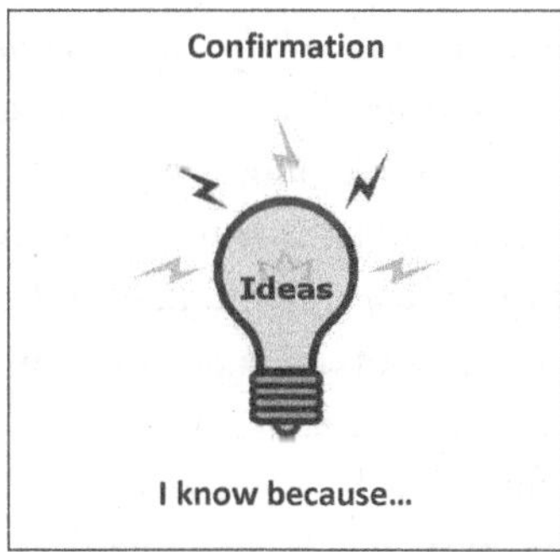

When classroom talk is accountable to the learning community, students listen to one another, not just obediently keeping quiet until it is their turn to take the floor but also attending carefully so that they can use and build on one another's ideas. Students and teachers paraphrase and expand on one another's contributions. If speakers aren't sure they understood what someone else said, they make an effort to clarify. They disagree respectfully, challenging a claim, not the person who made it. Students move the argument forward, sometimes with the teacher's help, sometimes on their own. (Michaels et al., 2016, p. 4). Classroom Scenario 5.1 illustrates the use of accountable talk.

Classroom Scenario 5.1.:
Implementing Accountable Talk in the Elementary Classroom
Ashley Mangum

At the elementary school where I teach, we believe that "through collaboration, celebration, and communication we will ensure confidence in student learners." As a school, we refer to these as the "four C's." Teachers strive to plan lessons, activities, units, and projects for their classes that focus on helping students grow in the way that they collaborate, communicate, and celebrate one another with confidence. Our school is a Title 1 school with 450 students, with 52 of the students receiving English as a second language services.

As I began teaching fifth grade in 2016, I noticed that students seemed to love collaborating with one another as they learned new content. Working together gave students the opportunity to gain ideas and new perspectives. However, I quickly realized their interactions did not go beyond surface-level conversations. I had four English learners (ELs) that year, and several other students from various backgrounds and socioeconomic statuses. Overall, my students did not know how to effectively communicate with one another. I wanted them to go deep in their understanding, ask one another meaningful questions, and gain insight into what their peers felt and believed, but they did not know how to find reasoning to support their opinion, ask one another higher level questions, or respectfully disagree when they found an area of tension in their answers or responses. I found that their writing reflected this as well. I strongly believe that if students cannot converse with their own peers about something, they will not be able to write about it independently. I knew I needed to make a change.

I believe that a key component in ensuring that students are confident learners is effective communication Thus, teachers need to research ways to help students communicate deeply with one another. As I researched, I found several articles online about "accountable talk," a strategy in which students are given sentence stems to guide their conversations and help organize their thinking. Accountable talk refers to talk that is meaningful, respectful, and mutually beneficial to both the speaker and listener. Accountable talk stimulates higher order thinking and helps students learn, reflect, and communicate their knowledge and understanding with their peers. These conversations can happen when two or more students share and explain their thinking. Accountable talk can be used in and outside of the classroom. Accountable talk also gives all students an entry point for conversing with one another, which was perfect for giving my EL students language they could use to enter the conversation with their classmates.

After reading several articles, books, and resources regarding accountable talk, I knew I wanted to try it in my classroom. First, I taught my students several sentence stems such as "I agree with you because . . . ," "I respectfully disagree with you because . . . ," "Can you clarify what you meant by . . . ," and so on. Because my students were in fifth grade, I started with only giving stems for agreeing, disagreeing, clarifying, confirming, questioning, and extending their thinking. We began with having conversations in morning class meetings, practicing using the accountable talk sentence stems from nonacademic topics such as sports, food, or their favorite television shows. Not only did this help build our classroom community, but the spoken words I listened to immediately went from surface level to rich, meaningful conversations that my students wanted to continue to have past the "ding" of my attention-grabbing bell—even if they were about random topics that my students enjoyed. I was amazed. All students were conversing with one another, not just one group. My ELs were engaging in conversations with their peers and showed a new confidence in their language skills.

We continued practicing using the sentence stems for about a week during morning meetings to help students become familiar with the language in the stems. It was also essential that during our meetings, we discussed the importance of having conversations and being able to communicate effectively with our peers on a variety of topics. As a class, we brainstormed when it would be appropriate to clarify, confirm, or question during a conversation and how to politely agree or disagree with our peers. Once students showed they had grasped the concept of communicating using accountable talk within morning meetings, I knew it was time to take it to our academic subjects.

I found that students naturally transitioned using accountable talk from their everyday conversations to their academic conversations. They no longer had 20-second chitchats when I posed an open-ended question about the novel we were reading; rather, they were engaged in forming opinions, respectfully disagreeing with one another, and building off each other's thinking. In math, they were asking each other questions about how they arrived at a certain answer or why they chose specific strategies and how that helped them problem-solve through a challenging task. To my surprise, the accountable talk stems were even used on the playground when students disagreed. Parents were emailing me telling me that they had begun to use new phrases at home such as "I respectfully disagree with you because..." with their siblings, and I saw a new confidence in students that I had never seen before. Again, I was amazed! As we continued to use the accountable talk sentence stems in our classroom, I made adaptations as needed. For example, I found that students were showing mastery at using the sentence stems appropriately, but lacked using specific academic vocabulary as they talked. Therefore, I changed the stems for each subject area (cut and displayed in $2 IKEA frames on the student tables) to include vocabulary words that I wanted to hear students using when having their conversations. This practice helped my ELs and non-ELs practice using domain-specific academic vocabulary as they explained their thinking. An example of a talk frame I use in math can be found at the end of this Classroom Scenario. For ELs, including pictures to illustrate the vocabulary is also helpful.

Throughout the years, I have continued to use accountable talk to help my students effectively communicate with one another. Our school has adapted this practice into our common language used throughout the entire school, kindergarten through Grade 5, and it is incredible to watch even the primary students use the thinking stems and have meaningful conversations to deepen their understanding in their academic areas and beyond. Because students are now talking about their thinking, we have also seen a huge improvement in student writing quality and the way they are able to form opinions, back their thinking with reasoning, and even give feedback to one another throughout the editing and revising process. Accountable talk is one simple way that we ensure our students are effectively communicating with confidence to become lifelong learners.

ACCOUNTABLE TALK

Words to use:

Denominator—the number that tells how many equal parts are in the whole

Numerator—the number that tells how many are being considered of the whole

Equivalent Fraction—fractions that name the same amount or part

Mixed Number—a number that is made up of a whole number and a fraction

Improper Fraction—a fraction amounting to more than one whole

Simplest Form—a fraction in which 1 is the only number that can divide evenly into the numerator and denominator

Sum—the answer to an addition problem

Difference—the answer to a subtraction problem

The process to solve this problem is . . .
First you would . . .
Then you would . . .
Finally, you would . . .
The sum difference is . . .

I know your explanation made sense because . . .

Teachers may facilitate productive student conversations through a variety of strategies that include asking open-ended questions, providing talking frames, and setting specific language objectives. For example, if a student asks a challenging question during a discussion, the teacher may respond and ask everyone, "Great question; what do you all think?" to encourage critical thinking and direct students back to the text. To maintain active participation in whole-class conversations, teachers may ask, "Did everyone hear what he said?" "Do you agree or disagree, and why?" and "Who can add to what she just said?" (Michaels et al., 2016). Teachers encourage meaningful dialogues during content area instruction through responses such as the following:

> From what we read, tell me what you know about the turtle's shell.
>
> What did we learn about the seed and the seed casing?
>
> The character, Finn, was thrilled about getting a hot dog. What does thrilled feel like?
>
> We read that the chrysalis turns into a butterfly. Describe what chrysalis is. (Wasik & Iannone-Campbell, 2012, p. 327)

When setting language targets as part of their instructional planning, teachers need to consider the language demands associated with students verbalizing their conceptual learning, along with the language necessary for students to fully engage in the learning event. These considerations of language are particularly essential for ELs. In the following example from a math class, note how the teacher analyzed the language required for students to complete the learning task:

> The math teacher realized that students would need to use different terms and grammatical structures as they worked in small groups to calculate surface area. For example, they needed to use sequence terms (e.g., "first," "second," "finally"), technical vocabulary related to surface area (e.g., "length," "width," "side," "face," "radius," and "circumference"), and explanations (e.g., "To calculate surface area of a pyramid, we need to . . ."). With these language demands in mind, the teacher created two language objectives tied to the content objective. The first language objective was created with her ELLs in mind, and she would assess only the ELLs' progress in this language objective. The second language objective was created with the academic language demands for all her students in mind.
>
> Students will be able to use sequential language in stating procedures for calculating the surface area of their group's object.
>
> Students will be able to use technical geometry terms and explanatory language in their oral presentation of the procedure for calculating surface area of a selected polygon. (Ernst-Slavit & Wenger, 2016, p. 34)

In culturally responsive classrooms designed to promote students' language proficiency, language targets are just as essential as content targets. Students must not only learn important concepts, but they also must be able to articulate their understanding. As with content objectives, language objectives should be measurable. Here are some examples of specific language targets that teachers can assess through students' writing or oral conversations:

- I can use linking words and phrases, such as *therefore* and *also*, in my opinion writing.

- I can write an equation that makes 10. I can read my equation to a partner.

- _____ plus _____ equals 10.

- I can use sequential language in retelling a plot in literature: *first, then, next, finally.*

- I can use technical language in talking about a science experiment with my partner, for example, *hypothesis, experiment, trial.*

- I can use comparison language in making text-to-text connections: *however, in comparison, in contrast.*

- I can use the terms *numerator* and *denominator* when describing how a model matches a fraction. (See Figure 5.5.)

Figure 5.5. *Third-grade teacher Kelsey Davis uses picture frames to display her language objectives for small-group work.*

Opportunities for Students to Develop Linguistic Competence

Culturally responsive teachers understand that in addition to expanding students' knowledge and cognition, one of their main roles is to develop students' linguistic competence. Thus, they provide many opportunities for students to use both written and oral language in meaningful ways. They also guide students in learning about the contextual nature of language and the importance of developing linguistic flexibility. In this section, I provide a number of suggestions for promoting students' linguistic development through authentic uses of language.

Although affirming and building on students' home language practices are essential to sustaining students' identities and promoting student literacy and learning, nonstandard dialects may preclude people from success in formal or academic contexts. Purcell-Gates (2008) emphasized the need for students to learn to adjust their speech to various social contexts as she confirmed that language functions as both "social and political capital" (p. 157). Although students' heritage languages are linguistic assets, SE has been recognized as the language of power in American culture. Thus, abilities to access dominant language and literacy practices and to code-switch are powerful skills for students to acquire (R. Martinez, 2010). Students benefit from learning the features of different registers of language through listening experiences, observing teachers use varied language forms, and making connections in students' personal reading and writing. Culturally responsive teachers help students recognize how different forms of language are used in varied social, academic, formal, and informal settings.

For example, to help students think about different ways of using language for expressing themselves, teachers can develop posters like this: "At school, we say, _______; at home, we say, _______." (At school, we say, "I don't have a pencil." At home, we say, "I ain't got no pencil.") One of the editors worked in a first-grade classroom where the teacher used the book *Flossie and the Fox* (McKissack, 1986) to teach the registers of language. The students were asked the question, "Who is smarter, Flossie (who spoke a nonmainstream vernacular and outwitted the fox) or the Fox (who spoke formal English)?" They compared the language of the two characters and practiced talking both ways (see Figure 5.6). These types

Figure 5.6. Books like Flossie and the Fox *can be used to explore language differences.*

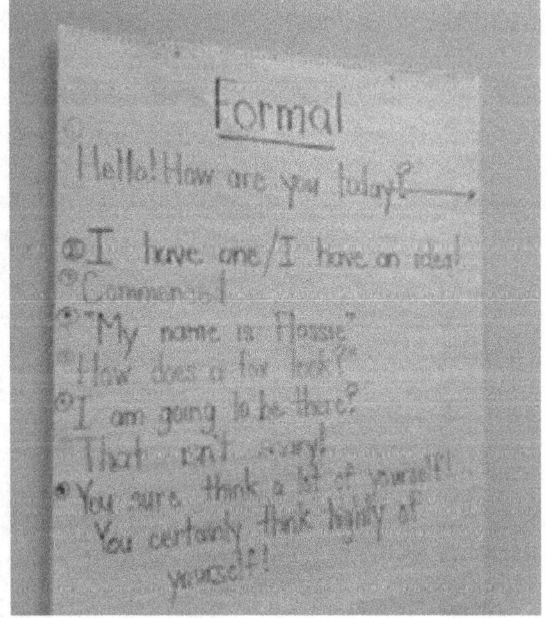

of activities help students develop metacognitive knowledge about language differences and learn when to use different registers of language.

Authentic language use is often embedded in learning experiences that are personally meaningful to students. In one example, a high school teacher with low-income immigrant ELs utilized a social justice orientation to sustain students' cultural and linguistic backgrounds while meeting both learning and socio-emotional needs (Lee & Walsh, 2017). The teacher grounded his instructional practices in students' previous experiences by providing abundant opportunities for student small- and large-group conversations, using students' conversations to address misconceptions and to provide specific vocabulary instruction, and asking students to write conceptual terms on the whiteboard in their home languages, thus developing students' linguistic flexibility. In a unit on immigration, students collaborated to make posters reflecting problems faced within their home communities and families while examining power structures and immigration policies. Through collaborative, dialogic learning events, students addressed real-world issues while building on previous learning, making connections with their communities and homes, and increasing their bilingual abilities as they spoke and wrote in their native languages and in English.

Other suggestions for helping students develop linguistic competence include using mentor texts and dissecting them for effective writing moves, creating a "dead words" wall with synonyms students can use in speaking and writing, using drama, and having students give speeches to authentic audiences. In Megan Willhite's fourth-grade classroom, students watched several speeches delivered by young people and were asked to think about what made the speeches so powerful. They then dissected those oral speeches and the teacher put examples on the wall of various elements of effective speeches from these mentor texts (see Figure 5.7) The students also used highlighters to identify those same elements in a written speech and created synonym lists for common vocabulary words. Using these displays as guides, students wrote their own speeches for a real audience to convince their school's parent–teacher association to contribute to an animal rescue site.

Figure 5.7. *Wall display of the features of effective speeches gleaned from mentor texts.*

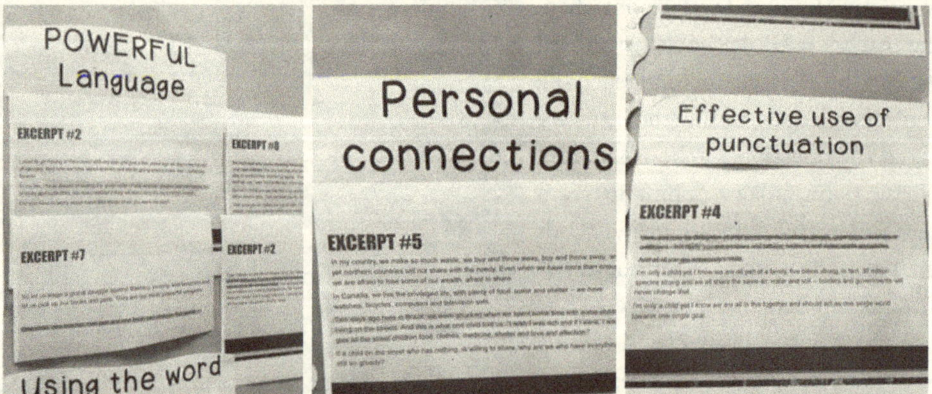

POWERFUL
Language
EXCERPT #2
EXCERPT #8
EXCERPT #7
EXCERPT #2
Using the word
Personal
connections
EXCERPT #5
Effective use of
punctuation
EXCERPT #4

In another example, fifth-grade teacher Amanda Stewart used posters and other displays to help students acquire academic language. For instance, she posted how effective summaries and responses to a literary prompt would be phrased ("According to the text, _____."). Students referred to these as they wrote their own responses. The teacher also had a categorized list of transition words under her whiteboard, including words used to compare/contrast (however, yet, etc.) and words to extend (in addition, furthermore, etc.). In addition, the teacher had posted charts with pictures of headstones with "dead words." Students referred to these posters as reminders to use alternative words for common terms like *bad*, and they created a game where they were assigned points whenever anyone was caught using a "dead word."

Figure 5.8 *Posters and lists of transition words can be helpful to students as they develop academic language competence.*

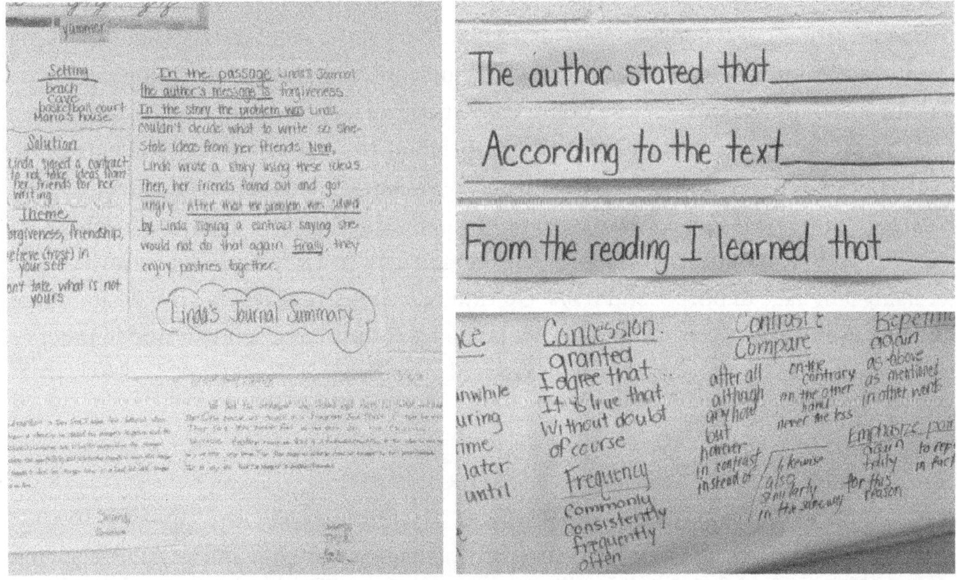

In summary, a variety of language models and supports can be provided to scaffold students' language development: mentor texts, vocabulary walls, excerpts showcasing effective language used with particular genres. Students also benefit from opportunities to have frequent guided conversations with peers. Clarity about language expectations and support in meeting those expectations is key to ensuring students' language development flourishes.

Conclusion

A wide body of research emphasizes the integral relationships between discourse practices and individuals' cultural backgrounds, social interactions, and prior experiences. Discourses serve as an identity kit, as language demonstrates membership in various cultural and social groups with those who share common interests, beliefs, goals, and ways of "saying, doing, and speaking." In addition, language practices are influenced by economic, political, and social factors and hold power. Historically, speakers of standardized language forms experience greater societal acceptance and status, and speakers of nonstandard languages are often marginalized. Thus, it is imperative that classroom teachers avoid critical views of students' linguistic abilities and validate students' language backgrounds while teaching standard forms of English and ensuring that students acquire linguistic competence to use language across various contexts.

Students learn through social interactions. In classroom settings, providing abundant opportunities for students to participate in discourse leads to higher levels of student engagement, enhanced language development, and deeper learning. Culturally responsive teachers work to ensure that all students participate frequently in classroom learning events through whole-class discussions, small-group conversations, and paired dialogues. Students are encouraged to use their home languages in classroom speaking events as appropriate while learning to participate in academic conversations.

In culturally responsive classrooms, teachers view students' home linguistic practices and community speech patterns as assets and promote the development of students' bilingual abilities. Linguistically diverse students are encouraged to sustain and practice their native languages through speaking, reading, and writing. At the same time, teachers are encouraged to teach students skills for engaging in effective academic conversations and for using language in purposeful ways. Culturally responsive teachers provide abundant learning events that allow students to use language in authentic contexts and to practice using registers of language for home and formal purposes.

References

Alim, H. S., & Paris, D. (2017). What is culturally sustaining pedagogy and why does it matter. In D. Paris & H. S. Alim (Eds.), *Culturally sustaining pedagogies: Teaching and learning for justice in a changing world* (pp. 1–21). Teachers College Press.

Au, K. H. (2011). *Literacy achievement and diversity: Keys to success for students, teachers, and schools.* Teachers College Press.

Au, K. H, & Kawakami, A. J. (1985). Research currents: Talk story and learning to read. *Language Arts, 62*(4), 406–411.

Au, K., & Mason, J. (1981). Social organizational factors in learning to read: The balance of rights hypothesis. *Reading Research Quarterly, 17*(1), 115–152.

Au, K. H., & Raphael, T. E. (2010). Using workshop approaches to support the literacy development of ELLs. In G. Li & P. A. Edwards (Eds.), *Best practices in ELL instruction* (pp. 189–206). Guilford Press.

August, D., & Shanahan, T. (Eds.). (2006). *Developing literacy in second-language learners: Report of the National Literacy Panel on Language-Minority Children and Youth.* Erlbaum.

Backer, D. I. (2017). The mass psychology of classroom discourse. *Educational Theory, 67*(1), 67–82.

Baker-Bell, A., Paris, D., & Jackson, D. (2017). Learning Black language matters: Humanizing research as culturally sustaining pedagogy. *International Journal of Qualitative Research, 11*(4), 360–377.

Bakhtin, M. M. (1986). The problem of speech genres. In *Speech genres and other late essays* (V. W. McGee, Trans.; pp. 60–102). University of Texas Press.

Bloome, D., & Bailey, F. M. (1990). Studying language and literacy through events, particularity, and intertextuality. In R. Beach, J. L. Green, M. L. Kamil, & T. Shanahan (Eds.), *Multidisciplinary perspectives on literacy* research (pp. 181–210). National Conference on Research in English and the National Councils of Teachers of English.

Bloome, D., Carter, S. P., Christian, Beth M., Madrid, S., Otto, S., Shuart-Farris, N., & Smith, M. (2008). *Discourse analysis in classrooms: Approaches to language and literacy research.* Teachers College Press.

Bohn, A. P. (2003). Familiar voices: Using Ebonics communication techniques in the primary classroom. *Urban Education, 38*(6), 688–707.

Bourdieu, P. (1991). The production and reproduction of legitimate language. In J. B. Thompson (Ed.), *Language & symbolic power* (G. Raymond & M. Adamson, Trans.) (pp. 43-65). Harvard University Press. (Original work published 1982).

Bové, P. A. (1995). Discourse. In F. Lentricchia & T. McLaughlin (Eds.), *Critical terms for literacy study* (2nd ed., pp. 50–65). University of Chicago Press.

Bucholtz, M., Casillas, D. I., & Lee, J. S. (2017). Language and culture as sustenance. In D. Paris & H. S. Alim (Eds.), *Culturally sustaining pedagogies: Teaching and learning for justice in a changing world* (pp. 43–60). Teachers College Press.

Cazden, C. B (2001). *Classroom discourse: The language of teaching and learning* (2nd ed.). Heinemann.

Center for Research on Education, Diversity, and Excellence. (2020). *The CREDE five standards for effective pedagogy and learning: Instructional conversation.* https://manoa.hawaii.edu/coe/credenational/instructional-conversation/

Correll, P. K. (2016). *Teachers' preparation to teach English language learners (ELLs): An investigation of perceptions, preparation, and current practices* [Doctoral dissertation]. University of Kentucky.

Cummins, J. (1981). *Bilingualism and minority language children.* The Ontario Institute for Studies in Education. https://files.eric.ed.gov/fulltext/ED215557.pdf

Cummins, J. (1994). From coercive to collaborative relations of power in the teaching of literacy. In B. M. Ferdman, R. M. Weber, & A. G. Ramirez (Eds.), *Literacy across languages and cultures* (pp. 295–331). State University of New York Press.

Cummins, J. (1999). *BICS and CALP: Clarifying the distinction* (ED438551). ERIC. https://files.eric.ed.gov/fulltext/ED438551.pdf

de Saussure, F. (2004). Course in general linguistics. In J. Rivkin & M. Ryan (Eds.). *Literary theory: An anthology* (pp. 59–71). Blackwell Publishing.

Delpit, L. (1995). *Other people's children.* The New Press.

Delpit, L. (2008). *No kinda sense.* In L. Delpit & J. Dowdy (Eds.), *The skin that we speak* (pp. 31–48). The New Press.

Echevarria, J., Short, D., & Powers, K. (2006). School reform and standards-based education: A model for English-language learners. *Journal of Educational Research, 99*(1), 195–210.

Echevarria, J., & Vogt, M. (2010). Using the SIOP model to improve literacy for English learners. *New England Reading Association Journal, 46*(1), 8–15.

Ernst-Slavit, G., & Wenger, K. J. (2016). Surrounded by water: Talking to learn in today's classrooms. *Kappa Delta Pi Record, 52*(1), 28–34.

Escamilla, K., Ruiz-Figueroa, O. A., Hopewell, S., Butvilofsky, S., & Sparrow, W. (2010). *Transitions to literacy: Literacy squared* (Final Technical Report). University of Colorado. http://literacysquared.org/ABOUT%20Page/Lit2%20Technical%20Manual%20Phase%20I_2004_2009.pdf

Fairclough, N., & Wodak, R. (1997). Critical discourse analysis. In T. A. van Dijk (Ed.), *Introduction to discourse studies* (pp. 258–284). Sage Publications.

Fisher, D., & Frey, N. (2014). *Checking for understanding: Formative assessment techniques for your classroom* (2nd ed.). ASCD.

Ford, D. Y., Howard, T. C., Harris, J. J., & Tyson, C. A. (2000). Creating culturally responsive classrooms for gifted African American students. *Journal for the Education of the Gifted, 23*(4), 397–427.

Freire, P. (2002). *Pedagogy of the oppressed.* Continuum International Publishing Group.

Garcia, E. E., & Garcia, E. H. (2010). Language development and the education of dual-language-learning children in the United States. In G. Li & P. A. Edwards (Eds.), *Best practices in ELL instruction* (pp. 15–43). Guilford Press.

Gay, G. (2002). Preparing for culturally responsive teaching. *Journal of Teacher Education, 53*(2), 106–116.

Gee, J. P. (1990). *Social linguistics and literacies: Ideology in discourses.* Falmer Press.

Gee, J. P. (1992). *The social mind: Language, ideology, and social practice.* Bergin & Garvey.

Gee, J. P. (1993). *An introduction to human language: Fundamental concepts in linguistics.* Prentice Hall.

Gee, J. P. (2004). *Situated language and learning: A critique of traditional schooling.* Routledge.

Gee, J. P. (2011). *An introduction to discourse analysis: Theory and method.* Routledge.

Godley, A., & Escher, A. (2012). Bidialectical African American adolescents' beliefs about spoken language in English classrooms. *Journal of Adolescent & Adult Literacy, 55*(8), 704–713.

Goldenberg, C. (2010). Improving achievement for English learners. In G. Li & P. A. Edwards (Eds.), *Best practices in ELL instruction* (pp. 15–43). Guilford Press.

Goldenberg, C. (2013). Unlocking the research on English learners: What we know—and don't yet know—about effective instruction. *American Educator, 37*(2), 4–11, 38.

Halliday, M. K. (1993). Towards a language-based theory of learning. *Linguistics and Education, 5*(2), 93–116.

Hammerberg, D. D. (2004). Comprehension instruction for socioculturally diverse classrooms: A review of what we know. *The Reading Teacher, 57*(7), 648–658.

Harper, C., & de Jong, E. (2004). Misconceptions about teaching English-language learners. *Journal of Adolescent & Adult Literacy, 48*(2), 152–162.

Heath, S. B. (1982). What no bedtime story means: Narrative skills at home and school. *Language in Society, 11*(1), 49–76.

Heath, S. B. (1983). *Ways with words: Language, life, and work in communities and classrooms.* Cambridge University Press.

Hymes, D. (1974). *Foundations in sociolinguistics: An ethnographic approach.* University of Pennsylvania Press.

Johnson, C. C. (2011). The road to culturally relevant science: Exploring how teachers navigate change in pedagogy. *Journal of Research in Science Teaching, 48*(2), 170–198.

Krashen, S. D. (n.d.) *Principles and practice in second language acquisition.* http://www.skrashen.com/SL_Acquisition_and_Learning/index.html

Labov, W. (1972). *Language in the inner city.* University of Pennsylvania Press.

Ladson-Billings, G. (1994). *The dreamkeepers: Successful teachers of African American children.* Jossey-Bass.

Ladson-Billings, G. (1995). Toward a theory of culturally relevant pedagogy. *American Educational Research Journal, 32*(3), 465–491.

Ladson-Billings, G. (2008). I ain't writin' nuttin': Permissions to fail and demands to succeed in urban classrooms. In L. Delpit & J. Dowdy (Eds.), *The skin that we speak* (pp. 107–120). The New Press.

Lee, S. J., & Walsh, D. (2017). Socially just, culturally sustaining pedagogy for diverse immigrant youth: Possibilities, challenges, and direction. In D. Paris & H. Alim (Eds.), *Culturally sustaining pedagogies: Teaching and learning for justice in a changing world* (pp. 191–208). Teachers College Press.

Li, G. (2013). Promoting teachers of culturally and linguistically diverse (CLD) students as change agents: A cultural approach to professional learning. *Theory Into Practice, 52*(2), 136–143.

Li, G., & Protacio, M. S. (2010). Best practices in professional development for teachers of ELLs. In G. Li & P. Edwards (Eds.), *Best practices in ELL instruction* (pp. 353–380). Guilford Press.

Lingard, B., Hayes, D., & Mills, M. (2003). Teachers and productive pedagogies: Contextualising, conceptualising, utilising. *Pedagogies, Culture & Society, 11*(3), 399–424.

Lucas, T., Villegas, A. M., & Freedson-Gonzalez, M. F. (2008). Linguistically responsive teacher education: Preparing classroom teachers to teach English language learners. *Journal of Teacher Education, 59*(4), 361–373.

Lyman, F. T. (1981). The responsive classroom discussion: The inclusion of all students. In A. Anderson (Ed.), *Mainstreaming digest* (pp. 109–113). University of Maryland Press.

Martinez, D. C. (2017). Emerging critical meta-awareness among Black and Latina'o youth during corrective feedback practices in urban English Language Arts classrooms. *Urban Education, 52*(5), 637–666.

Martinez, D. C., Morales, P. Z., & Aldana, U. S. (2017). Leveraging students' communicative repertoires as a tool for equitable learning. *Review of Research in Education, 41*(1), 477–499.

Martinez, R. A. (2010). "Spanglish" as literacy tool: Toward an understanding of the potential role of Spanish-English code-switching in the development of academic literacy. *Research in the Teaching of English, 45*(2), 124–149.

McKissack, P. C. (1986). *Flossie and the fox.* Penguin Young Readers Group.

Michaels, S., O'Connor, M. C., Hall, M. W., Resnick, L. B. (2016). *Accountable talk sourcebook: For classroom conversation that works.* Institute for Learning, University of Pittsburgh. https://ifl.pitt.edu/documents/AT-SOURCEBOOK2016.pdf

Morrell, E., & Duncan-Andrade, J. M. (2002). Promoting academic literacy with urban youth through engaging hip-hop culture. *English Journal, 91*(6), 88–92.

Mueller, T. G., Singer, G. H., & Carranza, F. D. (2006). A national survey of the educational planning and language instruction practices for students with moderate to severe disabilities who are English language learners. *Research & Practice for Persons With Severe Disabilities, 21*(3), 242–254.

National Center for Education Statistics. (2019, February). *Spotlight A: Characteristics of public school teachers by race/ethnicity.* https://nces.ed.gov/programs/raceindicators/spotlight_a.asp

Nystrand, M., Wu, L. L., Gamoran, A., Zeiser, S., & Long, D. (2001). *Questions in time: Investigating the structure and dynamics of unfolding classroom discourse.* National Research Center on English Learning and Achievement. https://files.eric.ed.gov/fulltext/ED461119.pdf

Orellana, M. F., Martinez, D. C., Lee, C. II., & Montana, E. (2012). Language as a tool in diverse forms of learning. *Linguistics and Education, 23*(4), 373–387.

Paris, D. (2012). Culturally sustaining pedagogy. *Educational Researcher, 41*(3), 93–97.

Powell, R., Cantrell, S., Malo-Juvera, V., & Correll, P. (2016). Operationalizing culturally responsive instruction: Preliminary findings of CRIOP research. *Teachers College Record, 118*(1), 1–46.

Purcell-Gates, V. (2008). "... As soon as she opened her mouth!": Issues of language, literacy, and power. In L. Delpit & J. Dowdy (Eds.), *The skin that we speak* (pp. 121–150). The New Press.

Resnick, L. B. (1999). Making America smarter. *Education Week, 18*(40), 38–40.

Ross, D., Fisher, D., & Frey, N. (2009, November). The art of argumentation. *Science and Children,* pp. 28–31. http://www.cspinconline.com/resources/2017-Summer/1-Art-of-Argumentation-Science-and-Children-4th-Gr.pdf

Schwab, Y., & Elias, M. J. (2014). From compliance to responsibility: Social-emotional learning and classroom management. In E. Emmer & J. Dowdy (Eds.), *Handbook of classroom management* (2nd ed., pp. 94–115). Routledge.

Stovall, D. (2006). We can relate: Hip-hop culture, critical pedagogy, and the secondary classroom. *Urban Education, 41*(6), 585–602.

Street, B. V. (1984). *Literacy in theory and practice.* Cambridge University Press.

Stubbs, M. (2008). *Some basic sociolinguistic concepts.* In L. Delpit & J. Dowdy (Eds.), *The skin that we speak* (pp. 63–85). The New Press.

Tharp, R. G., & Gallimore, R. (1991). *The instructional conversation: Teaching and learning in social activity.* National Center for Research on Cultural Diversity and Second Language Learning. https://escholarship.org/uc/item/5th0939d

Thomas, W. P., & Collier, V. P. (2002). *A national study of school effectiveness for language minority students' long-term academic achievement.* Center for Research on Education, Diversity and Excellence, University of California–Santa Cruz.

Vygotsky, L. S. (1978). *Mind in society: The development of higher psychological processes.* Harvard University Press.

Vygotsky, L. S. (1986). *Thought and language.* Massachusetts Institute of Technology Press.

Wasik, B. A., & Iannone-Campbell, C. (2012). Developing vocabulary through purposeful strategic conversations. *The Reading Teacher, 66*(2), 321–332.

Wodak, R. (2011). Critical linguistics and critical discourse analysis. In J. Zienkowski, J. Ostman, & J. Verscheuren (Eds.), *Discursive pragmatics* (pp. 50–70). John Benjamins Publishing.

CHAPTER 6

Critical Consciousness

Rebecca Powell and Victor Malo-Juvera

WE ARE WRITING this chapter in the summer of 2020 amid a global pandemic. The first cases of COVID-19 were discovered in Wuhan, China, in January, and the disease quickly spread to other continents, causing businesses and other public spaces to shut down in an effort to contain this deadly virus. In the United States, unemployment has soared and tensions have been high. For many weeks, individual states scrambled to secure personal protective equipment for medical staff, as hospitals in large cities like New York City were overrun with hundreds of coronavirus cases daily. Some citizens held protests to open up the economy, while others were insisting that doing so would cause a spike in COVID-19 cases. In some states, lawsuits were filed on behalf of places of worship to allow in-person services despite the danger of contagion. In stores, there have been clashes with security personnel who insisted that patrons wear masks. In short, there has been a perfect storm of individual rights versus the collective good, and we have remained a divided nation that, regrettably, seems incapable of uniting even during a major catastrophe.

Yet the pandemic is only part of the story. In the midst of this crisis, a 25-year-old Black man, Ahmaud Arbery, was shot and killed while out for a jog near Brunswick, Georgia. A father–son team believed Arbery was a robber and took it upon themselves to mete out justice. It took over 2 months and the release of a video of the incident to arrest the alleged assailants, and protests on social media were intense. In Louisville, Kentucky, officers shot and killed an innocent Black woman, Breonna Taylor, in her own apartment during the execution of a no-knock warrant. Just a few short weeks later, George Floyd, a Black man from Minneapolis, died after being pinned to the ground by a police officer using a knee on Floyd's neck. All these actions have led to widespread protests throughout the United States, from the hollers of Appalachia to small towns in the Midwest to large urban areas. As we write this chapter, there continue to be reports of new clashes with police, along with looting and rioting in some of our nation's cities.

Throughout these crises, President Trump has called on the military to help restore order and has been accused of taking unconstitutional action against protestors in Washington, D.C. (Hsu, 2020). He has also continued with the costly construction of a border wall between the United States and Mexico, which has involved the desecration of native burial grounds (BBC News, 2020; Phippen, 2020). And finally, as most news outlets are focused on the pandemic and racial protests, the federal government has quietly rolled back years of regulations designed to protect the environment (Popovich et al., 2020).

During a national and global crisis, perhaps our divisions have become more evident, yet they have always been a part of our fabric as a nation. From our earliest days, we have struggled with racism, classism, ethnocentrism, and other forms of marginalization (Meacham, 2018). More recently, issues related to the environment and global warming have become paramount, as flooding, drought, and a lack of clean water have touched many areas of the world—including some cities and regions in the United States (Intergovernmental Panel on Climate Change, 2018).

Through all this tension, schools have attempted to remain neutral. Teachers have been advised to adhere to the official core content and to avoid divisive issues that might lead to negative repercussions from the community. Yet, in doing so, teachers impart a partial narrative that ignores the voices of the historically marginalized and oppressed. The reality is that schooling can never be neutral. In teaching the "official knowledge" of the school (Apple, 1993), educators reinforce the dominant perspective and thereby unknowingly (or perhaps knowingly) perpetuate the racial, socioeconomic, and environmental struggles that continue to divide us.

In this chapter, we examine the Critical Consciousness element of the Culturally Responsive Instruction Observation Protocol (CRIOP), in which students are encouraged to explore issues that affect their local, state, and global communities. In examining this element, it is important to acknowledge that the ways in which the CRIOP operationalizes critical consciousness differ somewhat from other conceptualizations in the literature. In their discussions of various measures of critical consciousness, Diemer et al. (2016) suggest that critical consciousness has three main elements: critical reflection, critical motivation (or efficacy), and critical action. Critical reflection involves questioning social structures that marginalize groups of people and the ways that those structures are perpetuated, critical motivation refers to the ability and commitment to address injustice, and critical action involves taking individual or collective action for positive change. Although the Critical Consciousness element of the CRIOP incorporates an examination of social inequities and oppression, it has been operationalized to include issues that are relevant to particular social settings, for example, students' schools and local communities. Recently, we have also begun to include issues relating to climate change under the umbrella of Critical Consciousness, as it is a pressing global concern and one that needs to be addressed. We have found that this broader conceptualization has expanded opportunities for elementary students to take a critical stance on contemporary issues and become agents for change.

Although our research is still very preliminary, it suggests that the Discourse and Critical Consciousness elements might have the greatest effect on student achievement (Cantrell et al., 2017). It has been our experience that students are eager to make a difference, and when they feel their words and actions can have positive consequences, they tend to be motivated to learn and to act. Consider that some of the recent demonstrations have been spearheaded by youth who have organized, marshaled support, and marched in large numbers. For instance, the movement for stricter gun laws has been led by young people whose lives have been forever changed by gun violence (Samuelson, 2018; Yee & Blinder, 2018). Similarly, youth are important voices in fighting climate change, and one of the most renowned global voices is that of Greta Thunberg, who began her international movement at the age of 15 (BBC News Daily, 2020). Moreover, one of the greatest advocates for human rights and the rights of women has been Malala Yousafzai, a young Pakistani woman whose work has garnered international acclaim.

While these youth have had a major impact on our thinking at the national and even international level, there are many smaller transformative acts that students have undertaken that have made a difference in their communities (Jankéliowitch, 2014; Sundem, 2010). Admittedly, this particular element is easier to implement with upper elementary and middle school students, yet even very young children can become involved in projects that can bring about change. In this chapter, we share some of those projects, along with others that have been discussed in the research literature.

Another important component of the element of Critical Consciousness is providing opportunities for students to explore their own biases and taken-for-granted assumptions about the world. Racism, classism, homophobia, and other oppressive ideologies are learned, and if we are ever to have a more just and inclusive world, these ideologies must be actively challenged. To do so, teachers must be willing to explore difficult topics and to have "courageous conversations" with their students about race, power, and privilege (Singleton & Linton, 2006).

Indeed, it takes a conscious effort for Whites to *see color* and to understand how White privilege has defined the way we view the world. It is important to understand that White privilege does not imply that White people never experience oppression; rather, it means that their race does not *contribute to* that oppression. White people do not have to worry about others misconstruing their actions simply because of the color of their skin. They do not have to worry about being denied residence in an upscale neighborhood or being denied employment simply because of the color of their skin. They do not have to worry about teachers believing they are less intelligent or capable simply because of the color of their skin. As Peggy McIntosh (1989) suggests in her seminal essay on White privilege, Whites carry an "invisible knapsack" that provides benefits that persons of color do not have. Although the focus in discussions of privilege and hegemony is often on African Americans, the same principles can be applied to any individuals who have historically been marginalized in our society, such as Native Americans; Latinx individuals; those who are lesbian, gay, bisexual, transgender, and/

or queer (LGBTQ), Appalachians; immigrants; and people in poverty. Being White, heterosexual, and middle/upper class and speaking a standard vernacular afford certain privileges not available to those who have a different reality, and preparing students to live harmoniously in a pluralistic society requires that privilege be deconstructed in all its forms.

At its very core, Critical Consciousness is about educating students for democracy. It involves helping them to understand that we each have a role to play in realizing the ideals of our nation. It also involves encouraging them to see diverse perspectives and to respect ideas that might differ from their own. As future citizens in a democratic society, it is important that students have the capacity to listen to alternative viewpoints and to make decisions based on facts, evidence, and sound reasoning. It is equally important that they have the ability to articulate their ideas and to engage in civil discourse. Clearly, our divided nation cries out for a citizenry that can challenge oppression and injustice and unite around common principles and ideals.

What Does the Literature Tell Us About Critical Consciousness?

Theoretical Foundations

Critical Consciousness is grounded in the critical work of theorists such as Paulo Freire, Henry Giroux, Ira Shor, Donaldo Macedo, Peter McLaren, and others. A central idea of critical consciousness is Freire's (1970/1993) notion of *conscientization*, that is, a process of developing an awareness of social reality through reflection and action. Several themes emerge from these seminal works in critical pedagogy that are relevant to this element. Each of these is discussed in turn.

Theme 1: Education Is Not Neutral

In conversations about curriculum and schooling, many often make the assumption that education is a neutral enterprise, that is, that education is simply the teaching of skills and transmission of accumulated knowledge. Critical theorists, however, argue that education is embedded within a wider culture that endorses a Eurocentric ideology. Freire and Macedo (1987) have written that "literacy and education in general are cultural expressions. You cannot conduct literacy work outside the world of culture because education in itself is a dimension of culture" (p. 53). Schooling is designed to teach dominant customs and beliefs and the historical perspectives of those in power (Apple, 1993), "glossing over or ignoring episodes of the past that challenge American exceptionalism" (Pellegrino et al., 2013, p. 211). Indeed, the decision over whose knowledge should be legitimated in schools is a continuing struggle (Crawford, 2003; Monforti & McGlynn, 2010).

The movement toward a more multicultural perspective in education has been in reaction to this traditionally hegemonic role of schooling. As diverse voices have demanded to be heard, assigned readings in school and even the literary canon have slowly shifted to include more works of authors of color. It is also true that some social studies textbooks have become more inclusive. Yet research has found that these texts still tend to marginalize the experiences of persons of color, either omitting them altogether or relegating them to specific chapters (e.g., civil rights; Montforti & McGlynn, 2010; Wallace & Allen, 2008). Furthermore, textbooks often fail to scrutinize the larger social and political context of historical events and may actually reinforce negative stereotypes (Cruz, 2002; Pellegrino et al., 2013).

Theme 2: A Primary Role of Education in a Democracy Should Be to Promote Civic Engagement and Action

Throughout our history of American education, there has been a tension between those who believe education should prepare students for the workforce, and those who see its primary aim as preparing students for civil responsibility (G. Wood, 1984). Over 100 years ago, John Dewey (1916) argued that schools ought to function as democratic institutions, with democratic versus economic ideals as their goals. For Dewey, students would internalize democratic processes and values if schools became microcosms of democracy (Stevens & Wood, 1992).

Central to this position is an understanding that democracy is not just a product but also a process—one that requires active public engagement and involves resolving conflicts through dialogue and debate (Barber, 1992). Thus, classrooms should be sites where diverse perspectives are encouraged and productive critique is welcomed. Democratic dialogue intentionally seeks diversity of thought and opinion, inviting students to speak from their own experiences, and encouraging them to respond respectfully to the ideas of others. Such open discussion can help us to recognize that our understanding of the world is partial and incomplete and that examining the perspectives of others can lead to an interrogation of our own cultural assumptions and biases (Knoblauch & Brannon, 1993).

Civic engagement also requires linguistic competence. Thus, an important component of critical pedagogy is teaching students how to gather evidence, form an educated opinion, and articulate that opinion to a wider audience. This requires that students acquire the "discourse of power" (Delpit, 1995; Jordan, 1988). At the same time, it is critical to state that students' home/native languages are equally legitimate and should be acknowledged and celebrated in classrooms. Indeed, language is an integral part of one's identity, and schools play an important role in sustaining students' home languages and encouraging bi-/trilingualism (Paris, 2012). Yet it is also important to recognize that proficiency in Standard English is vital for acquiring cultural capital in our hegemonic society. (It is beyond the scope of this chapter to examine the social and political ramifications of language differences. See Chapter 5 for a comprehensive discussion.)

Theme 3: Education Should Lead to Societal Transformation

This principle asserts that education should not simply be about reproducing the status quo; rather, the ideological perspective underlying critical consciousness suggests that education should lead to a more compassionate and just society. Our collective aspirations as a nation include liberty and justice *for all*. It is a vision that is encompassed in our founding documents and has resonated in courtrooms and battlefields since our country's inception. Thus, preparing students for citizenship in a democracy encompasses providing them with the skills and dispositions to help realize these foundational ideals.

Henry Giroux (1988) suggests that teachers should be viewed as "transformative intellectuals" whose role is not only to "empower students by giving them the knowledge and social skills they will need to be able to function in the larger society as critical agents" but also to "educate them for transformative action" (p. xxxiii). Educating students for transformation necessitates a very different curriculum than what historically has been promoted in schools. It requires teaching students about the oppressive forces in our society and encouraging them to be actively engaged in critiquing and challenging those forces of domination.

Research in Critical Pedagogy and Student Outcomes

There is a paucity of research on the impact of critical pedagogy on student outcomes; however, the research that has been conducted shows a positive effect on student achievement, engagement, and conscientization. We begin with a discussion of investigations that support the overall positive benefits of students' development of critical consciousness on academic achievement and then examine some studies that were more limited in scope (and often anecdotal) that have been conducted in the various content areas.

Perhaps the largest investigation to date of the impact of critical pedagogy on student achievement has been a comprehensive analysis of the Mexican American Studies (MAS) program implemented in the Tucson Unified School District (TUSD; Cabrera et al., 2014). The MAS program began in 2002, and by the 2004–2005 academic year, it had expanded to four schools and included both social studies and language arts classes. These classes were rooted in the work of Freire and were designed to encourage collective action through a focus on critical consciousness and self-reflection. Teachers were required to "develop the critical consciousness of the students, make meaningful connections with students and their families, push students to see themselves as intellectuals, and help students become agents of change" (Cabrera et al., 2014, p. 1091). A research team from the University of Arizona collaborated with TUSD and used multiple modeling and sampling strategies in gathering and analyzing data. Results show that there was a strong relationship between participation in the MAS program and increased academic achievement. Furthermore, students who enrolled in the program outperformed those who did not in terms of both the AIMS (Arizona's Instrument to Measure Standards) test passing rate and graduation rate, despite having previous academic performances that were significantly lower (Cabrera et al., 2014).

The work of O'Connor (1997) showed how student empowerment that results from embracing a critical consciousness stance can be linked to student resilience. In her study of six high-performing African American high school students, O'Connor used structured open-ended interviews to determine students' personal histories and sociopolitical awareness. These students were optimistic about their futures, with all aspiring to college and some to graduate school. All, however, were keenly aware of how social inequities constrained their life chances. She noted that these students had experienced struggles that contributed to their resilience which were grounded in a belief in their ability to affect change:

> They . . . learned that through protest, resistance, and collective action subjugated individuals could challenge, modify, and transform structures that oppress them. In other words, they had reason to imagine not only that they could work effectively within the system but also that they could potentially change the system—making it more responsive to their needs and interests. (p. 621)

Researchers have investigated the relationships between theories of motivation and sociopolitical development and their respective effects on students' educational outcomes. Luginbuhl et al. (2016) examined whether sociopolitical development theory contributed significantly to Latina/o students' vocational and educational expectations and school achievement, which was measured by higher grades and fewer office referrals. Sociopolitical development theory is described as the process by which people develop critical consciousness and engage in transformative actions. The researchers found that the predictive power of the motivational theory of self-determination was significantly enhanced when combined with sociopolitical development theory, and hence, they concluded that actions designed to heighten both self-determination and sociopolitical consciousness will lead to positive educational outcomes (Luginbuhl et al., 2016). These actions include

> provision of academic support, culturally inclusive learning environments, acknowledging home and cultural experiences, knowing students' needs and interests, inclusion and engagement of parents, and providing a warm and personal learning environment. . . . Recommended strategies for fostering sociopolitical development among young people include participating in and analyzing current educational, political, civic, and sociocultural events, enhancing community participation skills, and strengthening sense of control and social responsibility. (Luginbuhl et al., 2016, p. 55)

Research in Math and Science

In the area of mathematics, Gutstein (2003) used critical mathematics with his Latino seventh- and eighth-grade students as a tool to facilitate social justice. As a teacher-researcher, he had his students complete real-world projects that used mathematics as the primary analytical tool. His students examined data on real-world scenarios such as wealth distribution and racism in housing, thereby relating to students' lived experiences as urban youth from Latino working-class families. Gutstein found that nearly every student exhibited sound mathematical thinking: "Overall, students not only communicated their findings well, they also developed confidence, represented mathematics in multiple ways, created their own solution methods, applied and extended others, and generally developed mathematical power" (2003, p. 59). Students also developed sociopolitical awareness and began to view mathematics as a valuable tool for making sense of issues that were important to them.

Brantlinger (2014) conducted a discourse analysis of students' participation in critical mathematics lessons. He reported that his students engaged in lively discussions and previously disengaged students participated more actively; furthermore, the examination of social and economic inequalities helped to create a classroom community. Interestingly, he reported that teacher–student relationships improved throughout the course and that several students began coming early to class or staying after school to talk about issues raised in the lessons. At the same time, however, some students voiced resistance and expressed that critical math instruction was a distraction from their academic aspirations.

In the sciences, Morales-Doyle (2017) reported on a study that he conducted in an urban high school chemistry class. Students measured concentrations of lead and mercury in soil samples to assess the impact of a recently closed power plant in their community. By analyzing students' course binders, Morales-Doyle determined that students' academic work met and even exceeded various national standards and College Board expectations. Moreover, he suggested that the curriculum allowed students to position themselves as "transformative intellectuals" in that they were able to demonstrate complex thinking about science and social justice.

Research in the Social Sciences

Cammarota (2007) described a socially relevant project that he implemented with working-class Latina/o students in a Tucson, Arizona, high school. Called the Social Justice Education Project (SJEP), it taught Chicano studies, critical social theory, and participatory action research and fulfilled students' social science requirements for graduation. SJEP students developed their own action research projects that focused on social problems that were important to their lives and presented their findings to school officials and community members. Although many of the students had been labeled "at risk" of dropping out prior to the project, evaluation data revealed that 93% of the students enrolled in the project felt that the curriculum had made them more likely to graduate from high school, and all SJEP students agreed that the project had helped them prepare for college and had encouraged them to think about education beyond high school. In the reported SJEP cohort, 88% completed high school and 58% enrolled in college—figures significantly higher than the national averages for Latina/o students.

Research in Literacy

In Chapter 1, Walker-Dalhouse discusses the importance of using culturally relevant texts to create a welcoming classroom community and to develop respectful and affirming relationships with students. Here, we discuss the importance of literature for addressing issues related to social and environmental justice. In the next section, we provide examples of how literature can be used to challenge societal inequities and to help students develop a critical stance.

Stevenson and Beck (2017) shared how they used literacy to empower students during a summer literacy program for intermediate- and middle-level children of migrant workers. After reading several young adult novels and children's books that represent their lives, the children created their own illustrated narratives about growing up as migrants. The authors reported that students made substantial text-to-self links in their writing, produced longer and more elaborate written responses as the weeks passed, and were empowered to tell their own stories by reading culturally relevant texts. Perhaps most telling was that most students, who generally had a high degree of absenteeism, attended the program every day, and some even asked if it could be extended. The researchers also noted success in developing students' emergent conscientization among these preadolescent migrant students.

Wood and Jocius (2013) shared the results of implementing critical literacy using culturally relevant texts with Black male elementary students. They found that the use of these texts led to rich conversations that gave students the opportunity to challenge and inform one another's ideologies. These critical discussions also allowed students to reflect on their own racialized identities. A positive racial identity has been found to be instrumental in supporting Black student achievement (Butler-Barnes et al., 2018; Carter, 2008; Hurd et al., 2012).

Critical Consciousness: From Research to Practice

Several years ago, near the beginning of the academic year, newspaper headlines reported that there had been a shooting within a block of our elementary school. The next day the fifth-grade teachers were holding their regularly scheduled planning meeting, and after discussing math plans and literacy plans, I (Rebecca) pulled out a copy of the local paper. We all agreed that the shooting would be on students' minds and that it should be addressed. This conversation led to a major student-sponsored community event called Take Action Day. In preparation for the event, students wrote essays on various issues related to violence—gun control, the effects of violent video games, and bullying. Throughout the year, we were fortunate to have police officers volunteer regularly at the school, and some helped the students develop their essays. Officers also helped us procure space and food for the event and set up the stage at the local park. A number of local dignitaries were on the stage, including the chief of police, sheriff, fire department chief, superintendent, and even the city's mayor. Several students read their essays, and others performed raps and introduced the guests, each of whom gave a brief presentation. Prior to the main event, every fifth-grade student signed a pledge of non-violence, and the banner was displayed in the entryway of the school. At the end of the year, several students asked if they could interview their classmates and teachers on what Take Action Day had meant to them. Students talked about the importance of meeting the mayor and police chief, the opportunity to perform in front of a real audience and to present their views, and the positive impact on the community. The resulting video was shown at the fifth-grade graduation ceremony.

That same year, a controversial pipeline was scheduled to be built through our state of Kentucky that would transport oil from Canada down to the Gulf of Mexico. A group of nuns from a convent in a rural part of our state were protesting its construction, arguing that fracking and oil leaks could have a devastating effect on the ecosystem. The fourth graders had been studying the regions of Kentucky in social studies and had been learning about ecosystems in science. Their teachers felt that examining the pipeline issue would be an ideal project to show students the real-world applications of what they had been learning. We arranged to have representatives from a local environmental group to come speak to the students. We also contacted the company, and they sent a representative to present their plans and to discuss how they would assure that the pipeline was safe. Students developed questions to ask before the presentations and were provided with graphic organizers for recording information. They also gathered additional information through articles and videos in preparation for writing letters to the editor, which would be submitted to local newspapers. Prior to writing, students completed a Discussion Web (Alvermann, 1991), which required them to list pros and cons on whether the pipeline should be built, thereby forcing them to consider both perspectives. Using mentor texts as models, students then wrote individual letters, several of which were subsequently published in two regional newspapers. Interestingly, students had differing views on the pipeline project, but all were required to support their position with evidence.

These two projects are illustrative of the Critical Consciousness element of the CRIOP. When we share these units of study with teachers, we are quick to point out that projects do not need to be this grandiose. Indeed, these are the exceptions. So while you may be thinking "I could never do anything like that at my school" (which is the honest reaction of many of the teachers with whom we work), we encourage you to think about your curriculum and find ways to integrate a more critical perspective into your teaching. We have found that teachers learn best from other teachers, so we have intentionally included several teacher-written scenarios in this chapter to provide you with some ideas.

Critical consciousness encourages students to take action on issues that affect them at a local, state, national, or global level. One of the requirements of being a critically consciousness teacher is to look at the world with a critical eye. We have found that teachers who implement this element at high levels have an awareness of their own social and racial identities. That is, they are cognizant of how their particular race, ethnicity, socioeconomic class, and gendered positions affect the ways in which they view the world. They work hard to overcome their own biases/cultural assumptions and are open to learning about diverse ideas and perspectives. In short, they see themselves as perpetual learners who are willing to have their own ideas challenged, and they want to instill these same dispositions in their students.

In this section, we share several examples of teachers at various grade levels who have successfully challenged their students to think and act critically. These scenarios are arranged to illustrate the three indicators of this particular CRIOP element.

Issues Important to the Classroom, School, and Community

Often when teachers strive to implement this CRIOP element, they consider the required state standards and find creative ways for teaching those standards through some type of action project. Language arts standards easily lend themselves to action-based learning, as students are able to research issues and present their knowledge and findings to a wider audience. Yet it is also relatively easy to plan action-based units of study around science and social studies standards and to integrate mathematics standards when relevant. In addition to the projects discussed previously, teachers with whom we have worked have implemented studies that address school bullying, racial/ethnic/class inequities, and environmental issues. Although perhaps not as "critical," even very young children can engage in action projects that can benefit their communities (see Figure 6.1).

Figure 6.1. *Students in Kellie Hasenbalg's second-grade classroom became committed to saving pollinators after studying the topic of pollination in reading and science. They wrote persuasive letters to their parents and the school principal and designed and sold T-shirts to create a pollinator garden for their school.*

Here, we highlight two examples of critical consciousness projects at the primary level. Classroom Scenarios 6.1 and 6.2 illustrate the possibilities for addressing critical national and local problems, even with young children.

Classroom Scenario 6.1.: **Blessing Bags**
Anita Johnson

I teach first grade at a Title I school, in which many of our students are considered "at risk" due to poverty, transiency, and homelessness. Because these children face challenging circumstances daily, the Blessing Bag Project was something they understood well and were eager to help create. Early in the year, I had shared with students that I went downtown each Wednesday night to provide hygiene products to the homeless. They were very inquisitive about and interested in this effort, so it easily became a topic of discussion during our Morning Meetings. After I studied Critical Consciousness through the Culturally Responsive Instruction Observation Protocol, it was an easy and natural decision to expand on ideas and activities that were already in place in our environment—and the Blessing Bag Project was born!

When I introduced students to the idea that they could create a positive and important impact on our community, they were so excited, and it became evident that we would need additional time outside of Morning Meetings to develop the project. Opportunities to integrate our project into the curriculum were numerous and were often initiated by students. Our goal would be to collect hygiene items as a class until we had enough of each to divide so that each student could assemble a blessing bag that I would distribute to the homeless population in our city.

We made a list of items that we wanted to collect and composed a letter during Shared Writing to send home to parents. Students also created posters to hang in the hallway to share information about our project to peers and other teachers. Initially, incoming items were stored in a large tub container, but students wanted to know how many of each item we had collected and still needed. Students worked in small groups to sort items and label bins for each product. After they counted the items, students created a bar graph poster representing the amount of each product. Students were so proud to increase the bars on the graph as they brought in new items. As they took ownership of this project, I recognized a stronger sense of community in our classroom and improved self-confidence in my students. During this time, I also saw students exhibit these attributes and intrinsic motivation when they were tasked to set, track, and reach goals for sight words, guided reading levels, and other classroom and standardized assessments.

The Blessing Bag Project was present in much of our learning. When we solved problems with missing addends in math, we produced word problems based on our Blessing Bag bar graph. (We have 17 tubes of toothpaste. How many more do we need to bring in to reach our goal of 21 tubes?) Products from the project were used during lessons and activities about inequalities. Advanced students worked on multiplication and division by counting an item and determining how many equal groups they could make from the total. Other students used the items to practice counting by ones, skip counting, and writing the digits of the quantities. Students were engaged any time our hygiene items were used as manipulatives. It was evident that students were using critical thinking skills as they began engaging in thoughtful discourse, often revealing unique perspectives from their own experiences. The local newspaper articles and video clips we used to broaden our understanding about homelessness provided additional meaning and further inspired students to actively engage in the project and their learning. This media was effortlessly integrated into literacy lessons, such as asking and answering questions, using text features, and developing vocabulary. Our semantic generative vocabulary matrix wall grew rapidly and became primarily student-initiated.

Students began asking questions not answered in our resources. They wanted to learn about the specific circumstances of the people we were helping. We agreed that students would write down their questions, and I would compile them in a document to interview some of the people I served on Wednesday nights. During this process, students used their interview questions to partner with a peer and practice fluency skills by taking turns reading their peer's questions. Sharing interview responses became a favorite part of Morning Meetings for students. However, the discussions were not always comfortable for me. In the beginning, I was reluctant to include some details, such as mental illness, alcoholism, and drug addiction, into our conversations. I quickly learned, however, that most of my students had the background knowledge from their own experiences to understand these ideas. Students had more questions about respondents who were educated, held jobs, or didn't sleep on benches. They were surprised to learn that some of this population had higher education but had lost their jobs or experienced financial hardships stemming from other issues, such as divorce, failed businesses, or the death of a spouse or a loved one. These revelations prompted questions about economics and social issues from students. They wanted to know what supports were available from our government and community. Students began to understand that homelessness is a complex issue and voiced a deeper understanding of the value of the Blessing Bag Project.

The class was very excited when we collected enough items for each student to assemble a bag. It was an effort of teamwork and cooperation, as they took turns filling their bags from the tubs of products they had been contributing to daily. After their bags were filled, the ownership and genuine pride that had evolved in this project became more apparent. Students individualized the bags and made an effort to demonstrate that they cared for the people who would receive them by creating notes of inspiration and drawings to include in their bags. We used photos taken during the course of the project, along with media, student-created anchor charts, and bar graphs to support narrative writing about the experience.

The Blessing Bag Project helped form stronger connections among my students to their community and each other. It built compassion, tolerance, and respect as they learned more about themselves and each other. I have continued this project in subsequent years as it has proved to be a powerful tool for my students to develop and improve on the problem-solving and critical thinking skills that I hope will empower them to be successful, in spite of their own circumstances.

Classroom Scenario 6.2.: **Plastic in the Ocean**
Margot Schenning

I teach third grade at a school in central Kentucky. Our population has changed over the past few years, and we now pull more kids from lower income neighborhoods. We also have more diversity, with many of our students coming from other countries. In my specific class, I had the special education (SPED) cluster (which provided me with a co-teacher) and the English as a second language (ESL) cluster (students in our ESL program who had been in the United States for the least amount of time in comparison to the rest in the program in third grade). Three of my students had only been in the United States for a month. For this reason, I wanted to see the kids come together to not only do something good for the community that they live in but also connect to their communities from previous life experiences. In doing this, the hope was that all the students would have some kind of background knowledge to bring to the project and would be invested in their learning. This project connected to the Culturally Responsive Instruction Observation Protocol (CRIOP) in many ways, but the CRIOP element that I focused on the most was Critical Conscious-ness. The end goal was that through my scaffolding, modeling, and using multiple strategies to get the kids engaged in a real-life issue, the kids would come up with an action plan to help reduce the use of plastic in our community.

We started this unit by letting the kids discuss what they felt were issues in their com-munities. We created a list and, from there, narrowed it down to our top two: bullying and plastic pollution. We discussed both issues and talked about how we wanted to create change in our community. Because they worked so much on bullying in guidance classes, they wanted to raise awareness of plastic pollution affecting their community and the world. Once the topic was decided, I posed a question to them to generate ideas of what we do with water on a daily basis. The students then watched a video of a diver in water completely polluted with trash. This was a great way to get the kids invested because they could see for themselves how much plastic was in the water. One of my goals was to have the students writing in their notebooks with each step of the project so that they would constantly have notes to refer back to and use in the final writing piece.

I incorporated background knowledge building through my reading lessons, small groups, and writing time. I found many articles about big companies that the students knew, such as LEGO and Adidas, and how they were reducing the use of plastic. The students were able to draw on these examples in their final writing pieces.

The next week, we watched a video clip showing a sea turtle getting a fork dislodged from its nose. This is the point at which the students really got into the project. Talk about it hitting home to their emotions! They couldn't believe that an innocent animal had to suffer because of what we were doing as humans. The kids then watched a short news clip about how places like Seattle, Washington, were going strawless to help reduce the use of plastic. This was the perfect segue into discussing the issue of plastic pollution in the ocean and what people were doing about it. I then asked the class what actions we could take right here in our school community.

The students brainstormed lists of ideas, and we wrote them on the board. Again, they were writing in their notebooks as we talked about emotions, things they saw during the videos, and so on. The ideas that kids were able to think of were amazing. They were "out of the box" and beyond what I expected of them. Further, the fact that they were able to sit and write for 30 minutes without stopping was even more incredible.

To finish off the research and idea development portion of the project, we used the Picture Word Induction Model (PWIM; Calhoun, 1999) for centers to create some simple and compound sentences that they could use in their writing, which was really great for our ESL and SPED kids when they got stuck. I printed off pictures of various animals, diagrams, maps, and the like, and the students wrote simple sentences about them on sticky notes. We then stuck the sticky notes to the board, and I had the kids read them and decide how we could group them together. These categories would turn into our three body paragraphs for an opinion piece and would also organize their thoughts for their action project.

The students decided to make posters to hang around the school to inform others about the issue. These posters included photographs that would grab the audience's attention. The kids were working on using text features effectively, so they used captions, graphs, charts, and maps to show where the issues were happening and why it was important for our school to take action. They also decided to write persuasive letters to the cafeteria manager and principal on actions we could do in the lunchroom and throughout the school to reduce the use of plastic. As the students read their letters to them, the cafeteria manager and principal took notes and provided feedback on possible changes they would make in the school.

The students were able to write two full pieces: one opinion piece as to why people should reduce their use of plastic and one persuasive letter to the principal and cafeteria manager. Their writing had great vocabulary, sentence structure, and organization. I have never seen a group so excited about writing, reading, and science class. After going through this unit with them, I truly realized how important it is to allow kids to have a say in what they learn. Adhering to state standards is important, yet this project shows that it is easy to integrate a critical consciousness project into content instruction. I know that all kids can write an essay if you scaffold it enough and constantly discuss and review the information and academic vocabulary. Teaching about current events/topics that affect the kids directly makes for magic in the classroom!

References

Calhoun, E. F. (1999). *Teaching beginning reading and writing with the Picture Word Inductive Model.* Association for Supervision and Curriculum Development.

Confronting Negative Stereotypes and Biases

Several years ago, I (Rebecca) had the privilege of working with two seventh-grade language arts teachers at a local middle school. Together we designed and implemented a project that helped students recognize biases in popular media. We began by having students visualize their ideas of what a princess looks like: her hair, eyes, features. After some discussion, we shared a Cinderella doll and asked if their visualizations looked something like this doll. Overwhelmingly, students agreed they did. Students typically conceptualized a princess as having White features: light skin, blue eyes, blonde hair, and a small nose. Over the next few weeks, we shared cartoon clips, children's toys, magazine images, and television ads and asked students to deconstruct them, looking for racial and gender stereotypes. At the conclusion of the study, students wrote persuasive essays about the many ways that stereotypes are expressed in popular culture and how these reinforce our preconceived notions about "the Other." Thankfully, more recent representations of women and persons of color in the popular media are more realistic, and toy companies have become more cognizant of how they portray women and villains. Yet biases still exist, and those need to be identified and deconstructed.

Two excellent sites that provide resources for teachers to use with social justice instruction are Teaching Tolerance (www.tolerance.org) and the Anti-Defamation League (ADL; www.adl.org). Teaching Tolerance has created a framework for antibias education and provides lesson plans, student texts at various levels, posters, and videos that can be used to address the justice standards, all of which can be obtained at no charge. The ADL, originally established to counteract anti-Semitism, works to promote a social justice platform and fights against hatred and extremism. Its website includes tools and discussion guides for K–12 teachers along with lesson plans and book suggestions to use in antibias teaching. The ADL site also includes an education blog, free webinars, and podcasts.

One of the suggested teaching tools on ADL's website is the Pyramid of Hate, which is a graphic organizer that can be used to explore prejudicial behaviors with students. The bottom levels of the pyramid represent biased attitudes (e.g., stereotyping and microaggressions) and acts of bias (e.g., bullying and name-calling). When these attitudes and behaviors are normalized, it leads to the three upper levels of the pyramid—discrimination, bias-motivated violence, and genocide. This graphic organizer provides a useful framework for exploring biases and stereotypes with students (see Figure 6.2).

Books written for children and young adults provide excellent opportunities to examine biases and to explore the ways that racism, classism, ethnocentrism, and homophobia have worked throughout history to oppress particular groups (see Figure 6.3). Critical conversations around ideas presented in literature are an integral part of implementing this element of the CRIOP, and even very young children can participate in these conversations. For instance, we are reminded of a lesson in kindergarten in which the teacher, Heidi Hamlyn, challenged her students to think about the racism that was evident in *The Story of Ruby Bridges* (Coles, 2010). After reading this book orally, students were given

Figure 6.2. *Students in Samantha Arnold's fifth-grade classroom completed a Pyramid of Hate as part of a discussion on racism.*

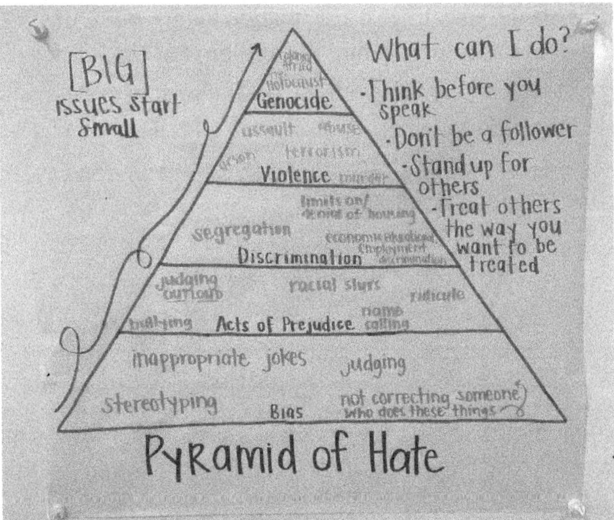

different questions about the story and were asked to express their ideas through drawing. As they shared their drawings with their classmates, their understanding of the story became evident. The teacher asked the students questions such as "How would you feel if this happened in our school?" All the students expressed that they would feel sad as they realized they would not have been able to attend school with some of their friends.

Figure 6.3. *Jennifer Caudill's use of multicultural literature with her fifth-grade students led to critical conversations about racism.*

When combined with accountable talk (see Chapter 5), students often have powerful conversations about themes they encounter in books (see Classroom Scenario 6.3). When reading a book about a controversial issue, we often post a few accountable talk stems for students to use during their discussion. For instance, in reading the book *Baseball Saved Us* (Mochizuki, 1993) about the Japanese internment with first and second graders, we paused the reading of the text periodically to pose a challenging question. Students responded using sentence frames such as "I think ______ because…," "I agree with ______ because…," "I disagree with ______ because…," and "I would like to add on to what ______ said." Using these sentence stems assists emerging bilinguals and helps students learn how to interact respectfully, even when they vehemently disagree with their peers. We have used simple accountable talk frames and books like this one successfully with children as young as kindergarten.

Classroom Scenario 6.3.: **Ghost Boys Reading Enrichment Unit**
Kala Damron

I teach sixth-grade social studies at a middle school in central Kentucky. There are approximately 800 students in the school, of which 86.1% are White (non-Hispanic), 9.9% are Hispanic or Latino, 1.8% are two or more races, and 2.2% are Other. There are 19 English learners in sixth through eighth grades, and all of them speak Spanish as their primary language. Approximately 39% of students are considered economically disadvantaged.

Even though I primarily teach social studies (four class periods a day), I also teach one reading enrichment class. I mostly work with writing and grammar, but this year, I wanted to help encourage students to read young adult literature. I feel that it's important to teach students about diverse historical experiences and perspectives, and I wanted to find a way to do this with my reading enrichment group. I asked our school librarian if she had a book recommendation, and she suggested Ghost Boys *(Rhodes, 2019). This led me to plan my unit around the Black Lives Matter movement and issues with police brutality.*

This unit would challenge me in a couple of ways. First, I come from a family that loves and respects police and other law enforcement because I have family members that are part of those professions. But I had to ask myself, "Do my students feel the same way that I do about law enforcement?" Second, I come from a small eastern Kentucky community that is not very racially or culturally diverse. In fact, the first time I ever spoke to an African American individual was during my freshman year at a regional university. I like to think of myself as culturally minded, but would I really be able to convey the seriousness of these issues to my students if I have never really lived and witnessed these moments?

As I watched, listened, and read from several media outlets, I began to think about how my young students are perceiving the Black Lives Matter movement and the issues of police brutality. I thought about how I would want my child to view racial injustice and police brutality as he grows up. Of course, I want my students and my child to be able to trust law enforcement, but how can they when they see what is currently happening? I looked at my entire classroom of White students and determined that the changes for our future generations will begin with what we as educators teach in our classrooms right now.

I decided to begin the unit with a gallery walk. I displayed various images of young Black men and boys who had been the victims of police brutality. Students walked in groups around the classroom and recorded what they saw and how they felt about each image. This was the first time I had done a gallery walk in my classroom. My students enjoyed the activity and became intrigued as I explained these images would center on some of our discussions throughout the book we were about to read. I also asked students to share the words or phrases that filled their minds as they looked at the images. We generated a list that I displayed on the board. Some examples were protest, racism, Black Lives Matter, race, *and* police brutality. *I explained that we would refer to this list when we did class discussions and writing. Neither my students nor I had read* Ghost Boys. *Despite being sixth graders, I decided to read the book to them instead of everyone taking turns. Even older students enjoy "story time" occasionally!*

I wanted to establish some historical background and make some real-world connections. The story of Emmett Till is central to Ghost Boys. *I handed out an article for the students to read about the events surrounding Emmett's death and the trial of the men who murdered Till, and we did a Think–Pair–Share activity. First, every student read the article. Then students paired up with partners and answered the question, "How are the historical events of Emmett Till's death and the trial that followed relevant to what is happening in our society today?" Once groups were finished answering the question, we had small-group discussions, and each group shared their responses. This activity achieved my goal of having the students make an emotional connection to Emmett Till and the tragedy he endured, and they also realized that similar events are still happening now, 65 years after Till's death.*

As we delved into the book, students quickly noticed various themes. Each day that we read we discussed the main points in the book and how events that happened changed the characters by the end. As we got to the part of the book where Jerome observed how the officer's daughter was dealing with her father's trial, I had my students write down their thoughts. I asked them to express how they felt about the police/law enforcement and to describe any experiences or influences that might have led them to their conclusions. I got such honest and open answers from them. Some students had very positive reactions. A few students grew up with law enforcement family members. Some described how their parents had taught them to respect law enforcement officers, and others shared their experiences in which police officers helped them during a car accident or other emergencies. Some students had negative reactions to police. Several students disliked the police due to family advising them not to trust them, some students were simply scared because police have guns, and one student disliked the police because they witnessed a family member getting arrested.

I took the time to read each student's writing. I also wrote a response on each student's paper. I really wanted my students to know that I took the time to read their responses, and

I cared about what they shared with me. I encouraged students to take their papers home and let family members read them and ask them to write a response too. This was done to keep parents/guardians informed of our classroom activities and as a way for me to seek feedback and input from parents. I received a few responses from parents, and they were positive and supportive of what their children had expressed.

When we completed the book, I arranged for a police officer to visit us. The officer was a parent of one of the students in my class. I informed him of the book we were reading and how we were interested to hear his perspective on police brutality and the measures that officers should be taking to prevent similar events from occurring. Chief Monroe has many years of experience under his belt and is currently the chief of police at the University of Kentucky's main campus. Prior to his visit, I encouraged students to write down questions to ask him. We then categorized the questions and displayed them on the board. Some questions were asked about his personal career as an officer, some questions focused on the duties and responsibilities of a police officer, and others centered on the issue of police brutality.

Chief Monroe was very honest and acknowledged the issues surrounding the use of excessive force. He also assured the class that it should never be the intent to hurt any individual during the arrest process. He expressed that an officer who would wrongfully kill or hurt someone should face consequences for their actions. Chief Monroe took the time to answer every question the students had!

Through this unit of study, my students were able to see the issue of police brutality from both perspectives—those most affected by it, as well as a member of law enforcement. Additionally, the book itself presents a multifaceted portrayal of this issue. By providing opportunities for my students to explore different points of view, I believe they came away with a better understanding of the complexity of issues like this one, which will help them realize that the answers to problems in society are generally not clear-cut and should be examined from multiple perspectives. Certainly, this is essential for participating in a democracy.

In Table 6.1 (*see pages 195–199*), we share a list of books that can be used as catalysts for critical conversations in classrooms. We suggest preparing for a discussion by reading through the text (book or chapter), noting any emerging themes, and developing questions that would lead to higher level thinking. For instance, as a fifth-grade social studies class read the book *Chains* (Anderson, 2010), the teacher posed this question: "Who has the power in this scene?" This question challenged students to think about the ways that oppressed individuals can have power even under severe conditions like slavery.

In our work in classrooms, we have watched teachers grow as critical consciousness educators as they find creative ways to integrate a more critical perspective into their curricula, while also addressing the academic standards they are required to teach. Teacher Scenario 6.4 illustrates how one middle school social studies teacher, Annabeth Edens, challenged her students to explore the many forms of oppression.

Table 6.1. *Books for Inspiring Critical Conversations*

Children's Books	Books for Young Adults
Biography	
• *A Nation's Hope: The Story of Boxing Legend Joe Lewis* (de la Peña)	• *All Boys Aren't Blue* (Johnson)
• *Brave. Black. First.: 50+ African American Women Who Changed the World* (Hudson)	• *Anne Frank: The Diary of a Young Girl* (Frank)
• *Cesar Chavez (Real-Life Reader Biography)* (Zannos)	• *Brown Girl Dreaming* (Woodson)
• *Emmanuel's Dream: The True Story of Emmanuel Ofosu Yeboah* (Thompson)	• *Claudette Colvin: Towards Justice* (Hoose)
• *Hammering for Freedom* (Hubbard)	• *I am Malala* (Yousafzai)
• *Harvesting Hope: The Story of Cesar Chavez* (Krull & Morales)	• *Jeannette Rankin* (Woelfle)
• *If A Bus Could Talk* (Ringgold)	• *Just Mercy – adapted for young adults* (Stevenson)
• *Malcolm Little: The Boy Who Grew Up to Become Malcolm X* (Shabazz)	• *March Trilogy* (Lewis et al.)
• *Martin's Big Words* (Rappaport)	• *Red Scarf Girl: A Memoir of the Cultural Revolution* (Jiang)
• *Mary McLeod Bethune* (Greenfield)	• *Shout* (Anderson)
• *My Name Is Celia: The Life of Celia Cruz* (Brown)	• *The Boy Who Harnessed the Wind* (Lamkwamba)
• *Nelson Mandela* (Nelson)	• *Warriors Don't Cry: A Searing Memoir of the Battle to Integrate Little Rock's Central High* (Beals)
• *Only Passing Through: The Story of Sojourner Truth* (Rockwell)	• *Women in Science: 50 Fearless Pioneers Who Changed the World* (Ignotofsky)
• *Planting Stories: The Life of Librarian and Storyteller Pura Belpré* (Denise)	
• *Queen of Physics: How Wu Chien Shiung Helped Unlock the Secrets of the Atom* (Robeson)	
• *She Stood for Freedom: The Untold Story of a Civil Rights Hero, Joan Trumpauer Mulholland* (Mulholland)	
• *Soldier for Equality: José de la Luz Sáenz and the Great War* (Tonatiuh)	
• *Surfer of the Century: The Life of Duke Kahanamoku* (Crowe)	
• *Vision of Beauty: The Story of Sarah Breedlove Walker* (Lasky)	
• *Wilma Unlimited* (Krull)	

History/Historical	
• *A Sweet Smell of Roses* (Johnson)	• *Accused! The Trials of the Scottsboro Boys* (Brimner)
• *Almost to Freedom* (Nelson)	• *A Few Red Drops* (Hartfield)
• *Barbed Wire Baseball* (Moss)	• *An Indigenous Peoples' History of the United States for Young People* (Dunbar-Ortiz)
• *Brick By Brick* (Smith)	• *Blood Brother: Jonathan Daniels and his Sacrifice for Civil Rights* (Wallace & Wallace)
• *Building a New Land: African Americans in Colonial America* (Haskins and Benson)	• *Burn Baby Burn* (Medina)
• *Dancing Hands* (Engle)	• *Chains* (Anderson)
• *Dinner at Aunt Connie's House* (Ringgold)	• *Codename Verity* (Wein)
• *Encounter* (Yolen)	• *Copper Sun* (Draper)
• *Finding Langston* (Cline-Ransome)	• *Dreamland Burning* (Latham)
• *Freedom on the menu* (Weatherford)	• *Fallen Angels* (Myers)
• *Heart and Soul: The Story of America and African Americans* (Nelson)	• *Fever 1793* (Anderson)
• *Henry's Freedom Box* (Levine)	• *Freedom Walkers: The Story of the Montgomery Bus Boycott* (Freedman)
• *Hidden Figures* (Shetterly)	• *Loving vs. Virginia* (Powell and Strickland)
• *Let the Children March* (Clark-Robinson)	• *Nightjohn* (Paulsen)
• *I Am An American: A True Story of Japanese Internment* (Stanley)	• *Out of the Dust* (Hesse)
• *Many Thousand Gone: African Americans from Slavery to Freedom* (Hamilton)	• *Prisoner B-3087* (Gratz)
• *More Than Anything Else* (Bradby)	• *Refugee* (Gratz)
• *My Heroes, My People: African Americans and Native Americans in the West* (Monceaux and Katcher)	• *Roll of Thunder, Hear My Cry* (Taylor)
• *One More River to Cross: An African American Photograph Album* (Myers)	• *Rose Under Fire* (Wein)
• *Remember: The Journey to School Integration* (Morrison)	• *Saga of the Sioux: An Adaptation from Bury My Heart at Wounded Knee* (Zimmerman)
• *Richard Wright and the Library Card* (Miller)	• *Salt to the Sea* (Sepetys)
• *Separate is Never Equal* (Tonatiuh)	• *The Astonish Tale of Octavian Nothing* (Anderson)
• *Sweet Clara and the Freedom Quilt* (Hopkinson)	• *The Book Thief* (Zusak)
• *Sylvia and Aki* (Conkling)	• *The Girl from the Tar Paper School: Barbara Rose Johns and the Advent of the Civil Rights Movement* (Kanefield)
• *The First Step: How One Girl Put Segregation on Trial* (Goodman)	• *The House of Dies Drear* (Hamilton)
• *The Great Migration* (Lawrence)	• *This Promise of Change: One Girl's Story in the Fight for School Equality* (Boyce)
• *The People Shall Continue* (Ortiz)	• *The True Confessions of Charlotte Doyle* (Avi)
• *The Story of Ruby Bridges* (Coles)	• *The Watsons go to Birmingham* (Curtis)
• *The Undefeated* (Alexander)	• *They Called Us the Enemy* (Takei)
• *The Youngest Marcher: The Story of Audrey Faye Hendricks* (Levinson)	• *Uprising* (Haddix)
• *We March* (Evans)	

Exploring Race/Racism	
• *Black Is a Rainbow Color* (Joy)	• *All American Boys* (Reynolds)
• *Chocolate Me!* (Diggs)	• *Black and White* (Volponi)
• *Freedom Summer* (Wiles)	• *Breaking Through* (Jiménez)
• *Goin' Someplace Special* (McKissack)	• *Dear Martin* (Stone)
• *Grandpa, Is Everything Black Bad?* (Holman)	• *Dreamland Burning* (Latham)
• *Iggie's House* (Blume)	• *How It Went Down* (Magoon)
• *Migrant* (Mateo)	• *I'm Not Dying with You Tonight* (Jones)
• *New Shoes* (Meyer)	• *Loving vs. Virginia* (Powell and Strickland)
• *Nina Bonita* (Machado)	• *Monster* (Myers)
• *Not My Idea: A Book About Whiteness* (Higginbotham)	• *Stamped* (Reynolds and Ekndi)
• *Something Happened In Our Town* (Cellano et al.)	• *The 57 Bus* (Slater)
• *Tar Beach* (Ringgold)	• *The Hate U Give* (Thomas)
• *The Black Snowman* (Mendez)	• *The Poet X* (Acevedo)
• *The Day You Begin* (Woodson)	• *The Skin I'm In* (Flake)
• *The Other Side* (Woodson)	
• *The Parker Inheritance* (Johnson)	
• *The Skin I'm In* (Thomas)	
• *White Socks Only* (Coleman)	
• *You Be Me, I'll Be You* (Mandelbaum)	
Native American Issues	
• *American Indian Rights Movement* (Machajewski)	• *Code Talker* (Bruchac)
• *Full In Line, Holden!* (Vandever)	• *Dreaming in Indian: Contemporary Native American Voices* (Charleyboy and Leatherdale)
• *Only the Names Remain* (Bealer)	• *Give Me Some Truth* (Gansworth)
• *Paiute Princess* (Ray)	• *Hearts Unbroken* (Leitich Smith)
• *The Trail of Tears* (Bruchac)	• *If I Ever Get Out of Here* (Gansworth)
• *This Land Is My Land* (Littlechild)	• *Indian No More* (McManis)
	• *Rain Is Not My Indian Name* (Leitich Smith)
	• *The Absolutely True Diary of a Part-Time Indian* (Alexie)
	• *The Marrow Thieves* (Dimaline)
Socioeconomic Class	
• *Crow Boy* (Yashima)	• *Crenshaw* (Applegate)
• *Each Kindness* (Woodson)	• *Homecoming* (Voight)
• *Last Stop on Market Street* (de la Pena)	• *The Impossible Knife of Memory* (Anderson)
• *Joelito's Big Decision: La Gran Decisión* (Berlak)	• *Money Hungry* (Flake)
• *The Can Man* (Williams)	• *Panic* (Oliver)
• *The Hundred Dresses* (Estes)	• *Tyrell* (Booth)
• *Those Shoes* (Boelts)	

Cultural Identity	
• *Call Me Maria* (Cofer) • *Cilla Lee-Jenkins: Future Author Extraordinaire* (Tan) • *Dear Juno* (Pak) • *Dreamers* (Morales) • *I'm New Here* (O'Brien) • *My Name is Sangoel* (Williams and Mohammed) • *My Name is Yoon* (Recorvits) • *So Far from the Sea* (Bunting) • *The Name Jar* (Choi) • *Two White Rabbits* (Buitrago)	• *American Born Chinese* (Yang) • *American Street* (Zoboi) • *Don't Ask Me Where I'm From* (de Leon) • *Downtown Boy* (Herrera) • *Esperanza Rising* (Munoz Ryan) • *I Am Not Your Perfect Mexican Daughter* (Sanchez) • *I Was Their American Dream* (Gharib) • *Mexican White Boy* (de la Pena) • *Persepolis* (Satrapi) • *The House on Mango Street* (Cisneros) • *Yaqui Delgado Wants to Kick Your Ass* (Medina)
Gender Issues/Women's Rights	
• *A Girl Like Me* (Johnson) • *Elizabeth Leads the Way: Elizabeth Cady Stanton and the Right to Vote* (Stone) • *For the Right to Learn: Malala Yousafzai's Story* (Langston-George) • *I Could Do That!: Esther Morris Gets Women the Vote* (White) • *I Dissent* (Levy) • *If You Lived When Women Won Their Rights* (Kamma) • *Rightfully Ours: How Women Won the Vote* (Hollihan) • *Ruth Bader Ginsburg Makes Her Mark* (Levy and Baddeley) • *She Persisted: 13 American Women Who Changed the World* (Clinton) • *The Day the Women Got the Vote: A Photo History of the Women's Rights Movement* (Sullivan) • *The Paper Bag Princess* (Munsch) • *Wangari Maathai: The Woman Who Planted Millions of Trees* (Prévot) • *Why Couldn't Susan B. Anthony Vote?: And Other Questions About Women's Suffrage* (Carson) • *You Want Women to Vote, Lizzie Stanton?* (Fritz)	• *Blood Water Paint* (McCullough) • *Devoted* (Matheiu) • *Feminists Don't Wear Pink and Other Lies* (Curtis) • *Forever . . .* (Blume) • *Just Listen* (Dessen) • *Modern HERstory: Stories of Women and Nonbinary People Rewriting History* (Imani) • *Not Your Princess: Voices of Native American Women* (Charleyboy & Leatherdale) • *On the Come Up* (Thomas) • *Only Ever Yours* (O'Neill) • *Our Stories, Our Voices: 21 YA Authors Get Real About Injustice, Empowerment, and Growing Up Female in America* (Reed) • *Sold* (McCormick) • *Speak* (Anderson) • *The Disreputable History of Frankie Landau-Banks* (Lockhart) • *The Female of the Species* (McGinnis) • *We Should All Be Feminists* (Adichie) • *What's A Girl Gotta Do?* (Bourne)

Worker's Rights	
• *Annie Shapiro and the Clothing Workers' Strike* (Brill) • *Big Annie of Calumet: A True Story of the Industrial Revolution* (Stanley) • *Brave Girl* (Markel) • *Fannie Never Flinched: One Woman's Courage in the Struggle for American Labor Union Rights* (Farrell) • *Harvesting the Hope: The Story of Cesar Chavez* (Krull) • *Kids on Strike!* (Bartoletti) • *Memphis, Martin and the Mountaintop* (Duncan) • *Si, Se, Puede!* (Delgado) • *Undocumented: A Worker's Fight* (Tonatiuh) • *Which Side Are You On? The Story of a Song* (Lyon)	• *A Coal Miner's Bride* (Bartoletti) • *Breaker* (Perez) • *A Different Mirror for Young People: A History of Multicultural America* (Stefoff & Takaki) • *Fire in the Hole* (Cronk Farrell) • *Haymarket* (Duberman) • *Nickel & Dimed* (Ehrenreich) • *Strike! The Farm Workers Fight for Their Rights* (Brimner) • *Uprising* (Haddix) • *Voices from the Fields: Children of Migrant Farmworkers Tell Their Stories* (Atkin) • *Wobblies!* (Buhle)
LGBTQ Issues	
• *A Family Is a Family Is a Family* (O'Leary) • *A Tale of Two Daddies* (Oelschlager) • *George* (Gino) • *Heather Has Two Mommies* (Newman) • *I Am Jazz* (Herthel) • *In Our Mothers' House* (Polacco) • *King and King* (De Haan and Nijland) • *Love Is Love* (Genhart) • *My Footprints* (Phi) • *My Princess Boy* (Kilodavis) • *Phoenix Goes to School* (Finch) • *Pride: The Story of Harvey Milk and the Rainbow Flag* (Sanders) • *Prince & Knight* (Haack) • *Stella Brings the Family* (Schiffer) • *When Aidan Became a Brother* (Lukoff) • *Worm Loves Worm* (Austrian)	• *Almost Perfect* (Katcher) • *Annie on My Mind* (Gardner) • *Aristotle and Dante Discover the Universe* (Sáenz) • *Boy Meets Boy* (Leviathan) • *Geography Club* (Hartinger) • *The God Box* (Sanchez) • *Jaya and Rasa: A Love Story* (Patel) • *Luna* (Peters) • *More Happy Than Not* (Silvera) • *Openly Straight* (Konigsberg) • *Parrotfish* (Wittlinger) • *Rethinking Normal* (Schrag and Hill) • *Simon vs. the Homo Sapiens Agenda* (Albertalli) • *The Miseducation of Cameron Post* (Danforth) • *The Prince and the Dressmaker* (Wang) • *Two Boys Kissing* (Leviathan) • *Will Grayson, Will Grayson* (Leviathan and Greene)

Classroom Scenario 6.4.: **Critical Consciousness**
Annabeth Edens

As a middle school teacher, I strive to create a relevant and diverse curriculum for a predominantly rural White student body. I had participated in conversations, training, and applications of culturally responsive pedagogy and the Culturally Responsive Instruction Observation Protocol. I thought myself to be very critically conscious, and in some ways, I truly was. After an honest conversation in which my Project PLACE (Partnerships for Learning, Achievement, and Community Engagement) coach, Dr. Cantrell, inquired into the authenticity of assessments and the formative checks that built up to those final products, I recognized that I had many opportunities for growth. Although I preached for diverse perspectives, many of the early lessons I taught focused on the predominant White story line. I would have claimed I wanted students to become informed members of society, but I had not yet given them a chance to authentically speak out. I had asked myself questions like "Whose story is begging to be told?" or "How do historians in the field show their work?" but until I had a coach take the time to see me, be a thought-partner, and provide accountability, I was not maximizing my time with students.

Given the historic and current social climate in the United States, it is imperative that (social studies) teachers are cognizant of the stories of the oppressed, past and present, and empower students to pursue justice. In two separate cases this past school year, I was able to facilitate critically conscious thinking and action in my classroom. In eighth-grade U.S. history, students study the events that led up to the American Revolution. Using these examples of protest, I charged students with identifying an issue they saw as unjust and worked with them to create a plan to advocate. I provided students with examples of historic pictures (social media included) and art that has been used for protest. Students created either a letter or a piece of art to speak out for a cause they believed in. Students selected anything from dress code and school policy to modern social movements like #metoo; lesbian, gay, bisexual, transgender, queer, and others (LGBTQ) rights; and Black Lives Matter. For example, a student who was passionate about mental health awareness created a book of resources and inspirational quotes for the school guidance counselors' offices. Another student used her understanding of graphic design to create a flyer to remember Black men and women who had been killed by police. I was amazed by the ownership and creativity my students showed. It was powerful to see students humanize issues and get to the root of complex social movements and make their own meaning. In addition to making a connection between historical events and modern day, many were able to make contact with or share their work with an authentic audience.

Another way in which I engaged students in critical consciousness was through a large-scale research project: National History Day. The theme that year was "Breaking Barriers." I admitted that I felt in years past I had not sufficiently exposed students to examples, nor had I adequately broken down the meaning of the theme. We decided to dissect each word, both "breaking" and "barriers," and ask students to describe barriers they and/or their families had faced. Students were encouraged to have discussions with their families and bring back any stories to share. We then sourced (minority) figures in history who had broken barriers and asked students to explore and hear their stories through a gallery walk. This activity, along with the reading of a children's book, The Undefeated *by Kwame Alexander (2019), sparked student curiosity, exposed them to figures they would not have otherwise studied, and made a connection between past and present. All were invited to attend an Exhibition Night the evening before the school contest during which students practiced their presentations, engaged in empathy-building activities, and interacted with community members. As a follow-up to student and family conversations about personal barriers, all were invited to write their personal barriers on a mural hung in the school. Some answers recorded included addiction, low self-esteem, mental illness, being a woman, and self-harm. The next day, community members were invited in to serve as judges in the school contest.*

Perhaps the most important subject for preparing students to become productive members of society, I felt convicted as a social studies teacher to pursue an authentic experience for students. Rather than memorize dates and historical figures, I sought to make connections between past and present, to analyze themes and patterns, and to empower students to advocate for change. The shift in morale, participation, and depth of learning was astonishing. As a White female teacher with a rural upbringing, I had to intentionally seek out opinions other than my own, listen to the stories of students, and revisit the traditional canon, which is typically whitewashed. I was not raised in a diverse setting, nor was I exposed to diverse texts before college. As Maya Angelou astutely claims, "do your best until you know better, then when you know better, you do better." Our time with students is precious and finite. If the curriculum is not relevant, diverse, and personal, then we are wasting it.

References

Alexander, K. (2019). *The undefeated.* Versify.

Expressing Diverse Perspectives

An important part of critical consciousness is the ability to consider issues from multiple points of view and to form an argument based on evidence. Also integral to this particular indicator is the ability to express one's views through the "discourse of power." In the Bluegrass Pipeline project discussed earlier, students were able to hear experts on both sides of the issue. Through their notes and additional readings, they formed their own opinion and wrote letters to the editor defending their positions.

Any current issue can be dissected and examined through multiple lenses. Years ago, when an orca killed a worker at Sea World, a teacher downloaded articles on the issue, and students were asked to defend whether orcas should be kept in captivity. In today's world, controversial issues abound: Do police respond more positively to Whites than people of color? Should wearing masks be mandated during the pandemic? Are pesticides responsible for killing pollinators? Is the Earth's warming caused by human activity? Are poor people to blame for their own poverty?

Content area teachers can also pose critical questions at the beginning of a unit of study. For instance, mathematics teachers can post a question like "Is police profiling real?" at the start of a unit, and then students can use emerging math skills to answer this question. Social studies units of study can be focused around a single question; for example, "Should this period of history be called Westward Expansion, or Eastern Invasion?" A broad question like this one can serve as an anchor for the unit, and students should be encouraged to revisit the central question as they acquire more information by writing their ideas under "yes" and "no" columns. Nearly every period in U.S. history can start with a critical question such as "Was the American Revolution justified?" "Could the Civil War have been avoided?" "Should the United States have entered World War II earlier?"

We have found that a useful graphic organizer to use to help students gather evidence from different perspectives is the Discussion Web (Alvermann, 1991). Beginning with a broad question such as those above and working in pairs or small groups, students use their notes and other resources to list reasons in both the "yes" and "no" columns. After they have several reasons listed, they discuss their responses together, and based on the evidence, they reach consensus as a team. Students must take a side, even if they are not sure of the "right" response. The point is that they need to be able to justify their conclusion based on sound reasoning. Finally, they write a consensus statement ("We believe that ______") and then state why they reached this conclusion. For English learners, it is sometimes helpful to provide a sentence frame like this one: "We reached this decision because ______."

Seventh-grade language arts teacher Megan Bechard used a discussion web organizer with her students in preparation for writing editorials on human trafficking. Students were asked to respond to one of three questions: Is human trafficking preventable? Would the chocolate industry suffer if all human trafficking stopped? Is human trafficking necessary? Students used the articles they had read previously to devise at least three responses in each column. Once groups had reached consensus on the particular question they had been assigned, they discussed their reasoning as a class (see Figure 6.4). Ms. Bechard reminded them that the purpose of their editorials would be to try to reduce the problem of human trafficking and that when writing an editorial, it is critical to address opposing views.

Figure 6.4. *Sample Discussion Web used in the study of human trafficking.*

QUESTION: Would the chocolate industry suffer if all human trafficking stopped?	
YES	NO
✓ They couldn't get cocoa beans ✓ Not enough supply for the demand ✓ They couldn't offer a good price ✓ They wouldn't be able to make a profit ✓ They need the work done quickly	✓ They could switch to fair trade ✓ It wouldn't matter if the chocolate industry suffered as long as the children don't ✓ They could do it themselves ✓ They could use adult workers
Consensus: We believe that the chocolate industry would not suffer because they could use other people to pick the cocoa beans and they could switch to fair trade.	

In this chapter, we have provided the knowledge base and several examples for implementing a critical pedagogy with K–8 students. As we discuss this particular CRIOP element with teachers, many tell us that they would find it difficult to implement because of feared backlash from administrators and parents. We acknowledge that in some school districts, this might be an issue. (For example, consider that several states [Alabama, Louisiana, Mississippi, Oklahoma, South Carolina, and Texas] have "No Promo Homo" laws, which "are local or state education laws that expressly forbid teachers of health/sexuality education from discussing lesbian, gay, or bisexual people or topics in a positive light"; GLSEN, 2019, "What Are Laws"). At the same time, however, we would argue that developing students' consciousness about social and environmental issues might be our most important task as educators. If we truly believe that our role is to educate students for civic engagement and transformational change, then we need to be willing to take risks. In our many years of working with teachers and collaborating on hundreds of critical classroom discussions and projects, we have never encountered negative reactions from parents. In fact, it has been our experience that most parents value this type of teaching. Allowing students to consider multiple viewpoints, however, is essential to maintaining positive relationships with parents whose perspectives might differ from our own. If we are to respect different voices, we must allow them to be heard.

References

Anderson, L. H. (2010). *Chains*. Atheneum Books.

Alvermann, D. (1991). The discussion web: A graphic aid for learning across the curriculum. *The Reading Teacher, 45*(2), 92–99.

Apple, M. W. (1993). *Official knowledge: Democratic education in a conservative age*. Routledge.

Barber, B. R. (1992). *Strong democracy: Participatory politics for a new age*. University of California Press.

BBC News. (2020, February 10). *Native burial sites blown up for US border wall*. https://www.bbc.com/news/world-us-canada-51449739

BBC News Daily. (2020, February 28). *Greta Thunberg: What does the teenage climate change activist want?* https://www.bbc.com/news/world-europe-49918719

Brantlinger, A. (2014). Critical mathematics discourse in a high school classroom: Examining patterns of student engagement and resistance. *Educational Studies in Mathematics, 85*(2), 201–220.

Butler-Barnes, S. T., Leath, S., Williams, A., Byrd, C., Carter, R., & Chavous, T. M. (2018). Promoting resilience among African American girls: Racial identity as a protective factor. *Child Development, 89*(6), e552–e571.

Cabrera, N. L., Milem, J. F., Jaquette, O., & Marx, R. W. (2014). Missing the (student achievement) forest for all the (political) trees: Empiricism and the Mexican American Studies controversy in Tucson. *American Educational Research Journal, 51*(6), 1084–1118.

Calhoun, E. F. (1999). *Teaching beginning reading and writing with the Picture Word Inductive Model*. Association for Supervision and Curriculum Development.

Cammarota, J. (2007). A social justice approach to achievement: Guiding Latina/o students toward educational attainment with a challenging, socially relevant curriculum. *Equity & Excellence in Education, 40*(1), 87–96.

Carter, D. J. (2008). Cultivating a critical race consciousness for African-American school success. *Educational Foundations, 22*(1–2), 11–28.

Cantrell, S. C., Powell, R., Malo-juvera, V., & Correll, P. (2017, November 30) *Culturally responsive instruction: An exploration of what matters most for student achievement* [Presentation]. The 67th Annual Conference of the Literacy Research Association, Tampa, FL.

Coles, R. (2010). *The story of Ruby Bridges*. Scholastic.

Crawford, K. (2003). The manufacture of official knowledge: The Texas textbook adoption process. *Internationale Schulbuchforschung, 25*(1/2), 7–25.

Cruz, B. C. (2002). Don Juan and rebels under palm trees: Depictions of Latin Americans in U.S. history textbooks. *Critique of Anthropology, 22*(3), 323–42

Delpit, L. (1995). *Other people's children: Cultural conflict in the classroom*. The New Press.

Dewey, J. (1916). *Democracy and education: An introduction to the philosophy of education*. Macmillan.

Diemer, M. A., Rapa, L. J., Voight, A. M., McWhirter, E. H. (2016). Critical consciousness: A developmental approach to addressing marginalization and oppression. *Child Development Perspectives, 10*(4), 216–221.

Freire, P. (1993). *Pedagogy of the oppressed*. Continuum. (Original work published 1970)

Freire, P., & Macedo, D. (1987). *Literacy: Reading the word and the world*. Bergin and Garvey.

Giroux, H. A. (1988). *Teachers as intellectuals: Toward a critical pedagogy of learning*. Bergin and Garvey.

GLSEN. (2019). *"No promo homo" laws: Policy advocacy, & research*. https://www.glsen.org/activity/no-promo-homo-laws

Gutstein, E. (2003). Teaching and learning mathematics for social justice in an urban, Latino school. *Journal for Research in Mathematics Education, 34*(1), 37–73.

Hurd, N. M., Sánchez, B., Zimmerman, M. A., & Caldwell, C. H. (2012). Natural mentors, racial identity, and educational attainment among African American adolescents: Exploring pathways to success. *Child Development, 83*(4), 1196–1212.

Hsu, S. S. (2020, June 4). *Civil liberties groups sue Trump, Barr for forcefully removing Lafayette Square protesters*. Washington Post. https://www.washingtonpost.com/local/legal-issues/civil-liberties-groups-sue-president-trump-barr-for-forcefully-removing-lafayette-square-protesters/2020/06/04/e32c799a-a676-11ea-b619-3f9133bbb482_story.html

Intergovernmental Panel on Climate Change. (2018). Summary for policymakers. In V. Masson-Delmotte, P. Zhai, H.-O. Pörtner, D. Roberts, J. Skea, P.R. Shukla, A. Pirani, W. Moufouma-Okia, C. Péan, R. Pidcock, S. Connors, J. B. R. Matthews, Y. Chen, X. Zhou, M. I. Gomis, E. Lonnoy, T. Maycock, M. Tignor, and T. Waterfield (Eds.), *Global warming of 1.5°C. An IPCC special report on the impacts of global warming of 1.5°C above pre-industrial levels and related global greenhouse gas emission pathways, in the context of strengthening the global response to the threat of climate change, sustainable development, and efforts to eradicate poverty*. https://www.ipcc.ch/sr15/

Jankéliowitch, A. (2014). *Kids who are changing the world*. Sourcebooks Jabberwocky.

Jordan, J. (1988). Nobody mean more to me than you and the future life of Willie Jordan. *Harvard Educational Review, 58*(3), 363–375.

Knoblauch, C. H., & Brannon, L. (1993). *Critical teaching and the idea of literacy*. Heinemann.

Luginbuhl, P. J., McWhirter, E. H., & McWhirter, B. T. (2016). Sociopolitical development, autonomous motivation, and education outcomes: Implications for low-income Latina/o adolescents. *Journal of Latina/o Psychology, 4*(1), 43–59.

McIntosh, P. (1989, July/August). White privilege: Unpacking the invisible knapsack. *Peace and Freedom Magazine*, pp. 10–12.

Meacham, J. (2018). *The soul of America: The battle for our better angels*. Random House.

Mochizuki, K. (1993). *Baseball saved us*. Lee and Low Books.

Monforti, J. L., & McGlynn, A. (2010). Aquí Estamos? A survey of Latino portrayal in introductory U.S. government and politics textbooks. *Political Science and Politics, 43*(2), 309–316.

Morales-Doyle, D. (2017). Justice-centered science pedagogy: A catalyst for academic achievement and social transformation. *Science Education, 101*(6), 1034–1060.

O'Connor, C. (1997). Dispositions toward (collective) struggle and educational resilience in the inner city: A case analysis of six African-American high school students. *American Educational Research Journal, 34*(4), 593–629.

Paris, D. (2012). Culturally sustaining pedagogy: A needed change in stance, terminology, and practice. *Educational Researcher, 41*(3), 93–97.

Pellegrino, A., Mann, L., & Russell, W. B. III, (2013). To lift as we climb: A textbook analysis of the segregated school experience. *The High School Journal, 96*(3), 209–231.

Phippen, J. W. (2020, May 17). *Like 'building a 30-foot wall through Arlington Cemetery': Tribal leaders in Arizona are worried Trump's border wall will decimate sacred sites and leave smugglers no choice but to cut through native land.* Business Insider. https://www.businessinsider.com/trump-border-wall-through-organ-pipe-sacred-tohono-oodham-land-2020-5

Popovich, N., Albeck-Ripka, L., & Pierre-Louis, K. (2020, May 20). *The Trump administration is reversing 100 environmental rules. Here's the full list.* New York Times. https://www.nytimes.com/interactive/2020/climate/trump-environment-rollbacks.html

Rhodes, J. P. (2019). *Ghost boys*. Little, Brown.

Samuelson, R. (2018, May 23). *Meet the student activists fighting against gun violence.* Education Post. https://educationpost.org/meet-the-student-activists-fighting-against-gun-violence/

Singleton, G. E., & Linton, C. (2006). *Courageous conversations about race: A field guide for achieving equity in schools*. Corwin.

Stevens Jr., E., & Wood, G. H. (1992). *Justice, ideology, and education: An introduction to the social foundations of education*. McGraw-Hill.

Stevenson, A., & Beck, S. (2017). Migrant students' emergent conscientization through critical, socioculturally responsive literacy pedagogy. *Journal of Literacy Research, 49*(2), 240–272.

Sundem, G. (2010). *Real kids, real stories, real change: Courageous actions around the world*. Free Sprit Publishing.

Wallace, S. L., & Allen, M. D. (2008). Survey of African American portrayal in introductory textbooks in American government/politics: A report of the APSA Standing Committee on the Status of Blacks in the Profession. *Political Science and Politics, 41*(1), 153–160. http://www.apsanet.org/portals/54/Files/Articles%20From%20APSA%20Journals/PSJan08WallaceAllen.pdf

Wood, G. H. (1984). Schooling in a democracy: Transformation or reproduction? *Educational Theory, 34*(3), 219–239.

Wood, S., & Jocius, R. (2013). Combating 'I hate this stupid book!': Black males and critical literacy. *The Reading Teacher, 66*(8), 661–669.

Yee, V., & Blinder, A. (2018, March 14). *National school walkout: Thousands protest against gun violence across the U.S.* New York Times. https://www.nytimes.com/2018/03/14/us/school-walkout.html

About the Authors

DR. SUSAN CHAMBERS CANTRELL is a professor of literacy in the Department of Curriculum and Instruction at the University of Kentucky, where she teaches courses in literacy education. Her research is focused on teachers' professional learning, efficacy development, and instructional change, particularly for underserved students.

DR. PAMELA KNUCKLES CORRELL is an assistant professor in the Department of Reading, Foundations, and Technology at Missouri State University, where she teaches literacy courses for elementary, middle-level, and secondary preservice and graduate candidates. Her research focuses on the language development of English learners, culturally responsive instruction, and preservice teacher preparation.

DR. VICTOR MALO-JUVERA is an associate professor of English Education at the University of North Carolina Wilmington. He has coedited three books addressing young adult and canonical high school literature, has published numerous research articles, and is on the board of the directors of the Assembly on Literature for Adolescents of the National Council of Teachers of English as well the editorial board of *English Journal*.

CAROLYN OLDHAM is a doctoral candidate and Research Coordinator for the Southern Farmer Rancher Stress Assistance Network at the University of Kentucky. With a combined 20 years in English learner education and postsecondary quality improvement, her current research and evaluative efforts focus on cultural responsiveness in the educational and health care sectors.

DR. KRISTEN H. PERRY is a professor of literacy education and director of graduate studies in the Department of Curriculum and Instruction at the University of Kentucky, where she teaches courses on language and literacy development, family and community literacy, and literacy in English as a second language contexts. Her research focuses on real-world literacy practices in family and community contexts, particularly among refugee and immigrant communities, as well as adult literacy.

DR. REBECCA POWELL is professor emerita and former director of the Center for Culturally Relevant Pedagogy at Georgetown College, where she held the Marjorie Bauer Stafford Endowed Chair. She has written/coedited four other books and numerous articles and currently serves as an independent consultant in culturally and linguistically responsive instruction.

DR. SHANNON O. SAMPSON is a professor of educational policy studies and evaluation and director of the College of Education Evaluation Center at the University of Kentucky. Her background includes second-language pedagogy and educational measurement, and her research includes work with the assessment of language learners.

DR. DORIS WALKER-DALHOUSE is a professor of literacy in the College of Education at Marquette University, Milwaukee, Wisconsin, and professor emerita of literacy, Minnesota State University Moorhead. Her research conducted with preservice teachers and in after-school and community reading programs focuses on sociocultural factors impacting the literacy development and instruction of struggling readers and teachers' attitudes and beliefs in instructing underserved and marginalized students across multiple forms of diversity.

DR. TIFFANY R. WHEELER is an associate professor of education at Transylvania University in Lexington, Kentucky, and teaches courses related to literacy and social studies education, children's literature, and race and ethnicity issues in education. Her research interests include culturally responsive pedagogy, historical perspectives of African American education, and critical race theory.

Name Index